Blue Shirts; Red Sox

Blue Shirts; Red Sox

Philip Keating

Copyright © 2013, Philip Keating

All rights reserved. No part of this book may be reproduced, stored, or transmitted by any means — whether auditory, graphic, mechanical, or electronic — without written permission of both publisher and author, except in the case of brief excerpts used in critical articles and reviews. Unauthorized reproduction of any part of this work is illegal and is punishable by law.

ISBN
Hardcover 978-1-300-28264-8
Paperback 978-1-300-88114-8

To Connie, till death do us part.

"Life is fraught with this and that."

Joseph Keating, philosopher
1905 - 1986

Table of Contents

Chapter 1	Liverpool, 1914	1
Chapter 2	Liverpool, 1916	9
Chapter 3	Liverpool, 1926	21
Chapter 4	Liverpool, 1926	29
Chapter 5	Liverpool, 1926	43
Chapter 6	Liverpool, Winter and Spring, 1927	55
Chapter 7	London, 1926	67
Chapter 8	Brockton, Massachusetts, 1923-1926	71
Chapter 9	Liverpool, 1926	77
Chapter 10	Liverpool, 1927	91
Chapter 11	The North Atlantic, May, 1928	99
Chapter 12	Boston, Massachusetts, 1928	109
Chapter 13	Boston, Massachusetts, Fall, 1927	117
Chapter 14	Boston, Fall, 1927	129
Chapter 15	Boston, January, 1928	151
Chapter 16	Boston, May, 1928	171
Chapter 17	Boston, Summer, 1928	179
Chapter 18	Boston, July, 1928	191
Chapter 19	Boston and Liverpool, July, 1928	203
Chapter 20	Liverpool, late July, 1928	209

Chapter 21	Liverpool, July, 1928	221
Chapter 22	Boston, September, 1928	245
Chapter 23	Boston and Cape Cod, September, 1928	257
Chapter 24	Boston and Cape Cod, 1928	269
Chapter 25	Liverpool, December, 1928	281
Chapter 26	Boston, July, 1928	297
Chapter 27	Boston, March, 1929	309
Chapter 28	Liverpool, April, 1929	319

CHAPTER ONE

Liverpool, 1914

With the German invasion of Belgium in August 1914 and the subsequent outbreak of war, the 17-year-old Frank Kelly left his job at Higson's Brewery in the South End of Liverpool and joined the tens of thousands of his fellow Liverpudlians in line at the recruiting offices. As volunteers, they had their choice of several famous regiments. The most popular were the locally based King's Regiment (Liverpool) and the Lancashire Fusiliers but Frank opted for the Irish Guards and found himself in the 19th Battalion (Reserve) of that illustrious regiment.

Liverpool was a fertile recruiting ground for the Irish Guards. There had been daily ferry service between Liverpool and both Dublin and Belfast for over a hundred years and Liverpool had served as the first leg of the journey for Irish emigrants en route to North America during the desperate years of the Potato Famine. The massive and tragic exodus of Irish families during the second half of the 19th Century left many Irish families along the way. By 1914, one third of the citizens of Liverpool could claim Irish ancestry. The names Flanagan, O'Toole, Murphy and Donahue were as common in Liverpool as Brown, Johnson, Smith or Jones.

On his eighteenth birthday, Pvt. Kelly found himself in the trenches of Flanders shortly after the First Battle of Ypres. He survived, almost miraculously, without serious injury until the summer of 1917 despite having been involved in dozens of skirmishes, patrols and bombardments. He had gone *over the top* at Paschendale and had been concussed within twenty yards of his own lines: an injury that probably saved his life given the carnage that occurred that day. In the spring of 1916, he had been promoted to Corporal and shortly thereafter, was awarded the Military Medal (M.M.) for his role in leading his squad in a counterattack during a desperate hand-to-hand trench battle. Frank's luck ran out in August of 1917 in the random manner that typifies modern warfare when an errant German shell overshot its target and landed behind the trench lines and found Corporal Kelly's working party engaged in transporting supplies to the front. The explosion killed three of his squad and wounded four more including Frank. At the Clearing Station, the unconscious Kelly was noted to have severe lacerations of the left side of his face. These were patched up. Of more ominous import was an injury to his left eye that was far beyond the competence of the overworked front line doctors of the R.A.M.C. He was stretchered out, still unconscious and then evacuated further by field ambulance to the Base Hospitals where more sophisticated skills and facilities were available.

By the summer of 1917, the medical services of the Allied Armies were stretched out almost to the breaking point. America had declared war on Germany at about that time but it would be 1918 before a sizable American fighting force would be in the field. However, the Surgeon General of the U.S. Army, Major General Gorgas, had anticipated the declaration of war and had realised in 1916 that there was not a single Field Hospital in the U.S. Army inventory. He had taken a bold and imaginative step by requesting six of America's finest teaching hospitals to prepare themselves for military operations in the field. This they did. Thus, when America joined the conflict, the U.S. Army had six General Hospitals ready to deploy in the summer of 1917 each staffed by the finest talents that American medicine had to offer. The Massachusetts General Hospital of Boston was the home base for the Harvard Medical School. It had become the 5th U.S. Army General Hospital. Its staff were among the first American troops to deploy and had, in fact been the first American unit to suffer a fatality. They had been loaned to the B.E.F. for a year as there would be no U.S. troops on the ground until 1918. At the time of Frank's evacuation, the hospital was located in what had been the Casino in Boulogne. It was in this unlikely setting that Corporal Kelly regained consciousness. It was forty-eight hours after his injury. He realized that he was in hospital and that his face was heavily bandaged. He was relieved to find, on checking, that he seemed to have four functioning limbs but was surprised and a little bit intrigued to note that all the staff appeared to have North American accents.

"What happened to me?" he asked of the nurse who came to take note of his conscious state.

"I'm glad to see you awake, Corporal. You've been unconscious for two days."

"Where am I?' he asked. The nurse who was wearing a uniform decorated with a large red cross was a formidable lady of ample girth and a cheerful manner.

"Welcome to the 5th General Hospital. You were too close to an exploding shell and your face is cut up pretty badly and you've had a concussion."

"How bad is it? I've got a bandage over my left eye. Will I be able to see?" He was sick with fear. He had seen the damage that modern warfare could wreak on the human body.

"I'm not the one to ask but the doctors will be around first thing in the morning to change your dressing. I'll tell you this much. Everything that can be done to put you back together will be done. I've seen our surgeons do miraculous things since we arrived. Our Chief of Staff, Major Harvey Cushing, is the most famous surgeon in America."

"What's he doing here? Are you all Americans? I thought maybe I was in a Canadian hospital."

"Hush your mouth, Sugar!" Lucinda Mae Calhoun was aghast. She had been raised in Charleston, South Carolina and had travelled north for her nurses training. "You, Corporal Kelly, are a patient of Boston's finest hospital."

Frank was taken aback. It was a lot to absorb. His last conscious thought had been how best to organize the transportation of 200 lbs. of bully beef to Company Headquarters. Now here he was lying in a clean bed in what had recently been a casino with his head bandaged and his left eye a question mark. He had also apparently offended a formidable American nurse by suggesting that she might be Canadian. She certainly wasn't English. Of that he was sure. In a British Army hospital, he would have been addressed as Corporal until the day they carried him out for burial.

"No offense intended, Nurse. Believe me. I'm very grateful for everything you're doing for me. I just didn't know that there were any Americans here yet."

****

Morning brought three surgeons to his bedside and the dressings were removed from his face. His eye patch was retained in place at first.

"What do you think, Mack?" said one, obviously the most senior.

"Those front line guys did a darn good job when you consider the conditions they're working in but I think we can do a neater one with plenty of time and good OR facilities."

A younger one, presumably Mack, responded, "Don't worry Corporal. Your wife will still recognize you."

"How about my eye, doctor? I don't have a wife but a soldier with one eye isn't much use."

"That's a question that's still to be resolved. The cornea was lacerated in the explosion. We have repaired the laceration but with a contaminated wound the chances are that your vision will be severely impaired even if the cornea heals. We also have to be aware of the risk to your other eye."

"Was my right eye damaged too? I can see just fine out of it now". He was terrified. One lost eye was a severe injury; two meant blindness.

"Don't be upset. There's no damage to the right eye but we have to be on the lookout for a condition called *Sympathetic Ophthalmia*."

"What's that?" he asked, now thoroughly scared.

"Sometimes when one eye is inflamed or infected, the undamaged eye becomes inflamed. We don't know why. Never fear. We will be watching like a hawk to make sure that that does not happen or, if it does, we will treat it right away. Dr. Kearney here will be examining you twice every day and, if there is any sign of inflammation in your right eye we will remove the damaged eye immediately and fit you with a prosthesis."

"You mean a glass eye, sir?"

"Yes, Corporal," the older man chipped in. "They're really lifelike these days and we can attach the eye muscles so that the glass one moves with the real one. You won't be able to see with it, of course, but in all truth, there's not much hope for useful vision with such a scar on your cornea. I commend your desire to return to your unit. You're a brave man but I'm afraid your war is over."

True to his word, Major Cushing, which was the name of the senior man, had Dr. Kearney keep a close watch on both eyes and meanwhile two of America's leading plastic surgeons worked on minimizing the deformities caused by the facial lacerations. Four days after his admission there was evidence of Sympathetic Ophthalmia; the right eye became painful and red. Frank's scarred left eye was removed and replaced by a prosthesis and the inflammation in the right eye subsided. A week later, Sgt. Kelly was transferred to a British hospital. He had been promoted during his hospitalization on the recommendation of his erstwhile Company Commander. One month later, in the autumn of 1917, he was mustered out and returned to Liverpool as a civilian and a wounded veteran.

****

The management of Higson's brewery was happy to give Frank his old job back. Able-bodied young men capable of tossing barrels of beer around were in short supply in Britain in 1918 and Frank was welcomed back. He was glad to be gainfully employed and able to contribute to the family's finances but he was no longer an innocent and naive seventeen year old. He had been tested under fire and had earned the three stripes of a sergeant; no mean feat for a twenty-one year old. He wasn't ready to accept that his lot was to remain an unskilled labourer at a local brewery. His brief stay in an American hospital had stirred his imagination. Perhaps there might be openings for him that would give him opportunity for advancement. He had been intrigued by the democratic attitudes of the American staff. He still smiled to himself at the unlikelihood of a British Nursing Sister referring to him as 'Sugar.' It occurred to him that he had returned to one of the few cities in Britain with deep-rooted commercial and maritime connections with North America.

Before the war Liverpool had been the busiest player in the North Atlantic Passenger business serving, as it had, as homeport of both the Cunard and the White Star Lines. The war had put a stop to that but the end of the war was finally in sight. Frank's monocular status had rendered him unfit for active service but he was otherwise able-bodied and his war record and Military Medal must surely count for something. The American surgeons at Base Hospital No. 5 had repaired his wounds expertly and his face now, though scarred, was interesting rather than terrifying. Women would now find his face vaguely piratical rather than repulsive. He talked it over with his father.

"What do you think, Da? Should I have a shot at getting on with Cunard or White Star?" His father, Frank Sr., had worked on the docks as a stevedore since his late teens.

"I think you should give it a try, son. You've earned the right to a chance of something better than carting beer barrels around all day. I wish I'd got on with Cunard when I was your age. Besides, what have you got to lose by applying for a job with them?"

"It would mean I'd be away from home for most of the time."

"You've been gone almost four years. We all survived. Get your bid in now, lad. This war is going to be over soon and there'll be millions of lads looking for work."

RMS Carmania, a Cunarder of 20,000 tons, had been built in 1905 for the North Atlantic as a passenger liner. It had been converted into an Armed Merchantman at the outbreak of hostilities and had been involved in one of the first naval battles of the war: the Battle of Trindade, off the coast of South America. This had taken place in September 1914 and had resulted in the sinking of the German Armed Merchantman *SMS Cap Trafalgar*. The battle was remarkable in that both ships arrived at the engagement disguised as its opposite number. At the conclusion of the war, *Carmania* was refitted and returned to her original function, that of a transatlantic liner plying the seas between Liverpool and North America. Frank Kelly had been in the right place at the right time and was taken on as a trainee steward and so began his slow advancement up the ladder of the strictly hierarchical structure of the Cunard staff. *Carmania's* larger and more famous sister ships, *Mauretania* and *Aquitania*, had also sailed out of Liverpool before the war but had been re-based out of Southampton in 1919, much to the chagrin of thousands of Liverpudlians who considered employment by the Cunard or White Star Lines to be a birthright.

Frank's advancement was slow but sure. His innate friendliness and carefully retained hint of brogue intrigued the American passengers and his industry and honesty endeared him to his bosses. When ashore and between voyages he shared a room with his brother, Brendan, in his parents' home in St. John's Parish, Kirkdale. His three sisters, Mary, Bridget and Kathleen, shared the second bedroom and his parents the third. It was tight quarters in the narrow row house with its three small bedrooms. Brendan, the baby of the family was considered to be the lucky one having to share his room for only a few days every month. Truth to tell, he hero-worshipped his older brother and would have gladly forgone the extra space afforded by Frank's absences to have had him home all the time. On the whole they were a family content with their lot of genteel poverty. Mam--Margaret Mary--was commonly known as Meg and worked at a poultry stall in St. John's Market in the city centre. The younger girls were in elementary school: St. John's Parochial and Kate, the oldest, was a pupil at Everton Valley Convent School. The home in Garnet Avenue faced a small park. The Kellys were acknowledged upstanding members of the parish and the parish was itself one of the largest and most cohesive enclaves of Catholicism in the city.

Chapter Two

Liverpool, 1916

Kate Kelly and Isabel Iskandar had both entered Everton Valley Convent School at age twelve and became fast friends from the first day of their acquaintance. Kate had taken the shy olive-complected girl under her wing and they had become inseparable. Kate, who had never traveled more than five miles from her North Liverpool home, was fascinated by the diffident and mysterious foreigner.

Isabel's father had been an officer in the Merchant Marine and had been torpedoed in the North Atlantic in the winter of 1915. He had been rescued after 48 hours in an open lifeboat and transported to Liverpool where he gradually recovered from the after effects of exposure but never regained his enthusiasm for the maritime life. By name Adlai Iskandar, he was a man of genial disposition and a Levantine instinct for commerce. Finding himself in a thriving port in the heart of Imperial Britain, he studied the market and decided that there was a niche to be filled in supplying Britain with tobacco from the Middle East that Turkey's involvement in the war on the 'wrong side' had curtailed. Adlai resolved to fill that niche. In addition to the financial possibilities that he could envision, the enterprise would greatly reduce the chance that he would have to spend any more time in a lifeboat, or worse, *in* the North Atlantic. This was a definite plus. One such experience was already one too many. Also on the plus side, he reasoned that he had, in addition to an intrepid entrepreneurial spirit, a formidable array of family connections in the Eastern Mediterranean and a small reserve of capital. This latter resided with and was under the control of his wife, Marie.

Marie was Lebanese by birth, proud of her country's reputation as the Paris of the Mediterranean littoral. Educated by the Sisters of Notre Dame de Namur, she was fluent in both French and Arabic and was, by the mediaeval standards of the Arab world of the early 20th century, an emancipated woman. All these attributes were no defense against the charms of the dashing young first officer of the coastal freighter, *SS Osiris*, who had laid siege to her over a period of two years during its periodic stopovers in Lebanon.

They had been introduced some months before by a mutual friend. At first, when they would meet for a decorous afternoon coffee in La Place de St. Denis, she was alarmed by the intensity of his obvious infatuation. However, she gradually found herself looking forward to his next port call and would scan the shipping news for the time of his arrival, the better to prepare to be surprised by his subsequent invitation to coffee or even, as their liaison progressed, to a *thé dansant* at the Lido. It was not entirely unexpected therefore when, upon obtaining his Masters Ticket in the spring of 1905 and the subsequent promise of his own ship, Captain-to-be Iskandar proposed and was accepted. But the acceptance was not without a certain apprehension.

Certainly the young Egyptian sailor appeared to be an almost perfect mate. He was charming, polite and well educated. He made her laugh. She was the envy of all her friends and, most of all, he was obviously smitten by her. But marriage! That would mean a sundering of all her ties to family and her beloved Lebanon. She would have to establish a new family home in Egypt and raise her children as Egyptians; live, in short, as an Arab family living in an Arab world. The saving grace was that Adlai, although an

Arab, was also a Copt. Not even the prospect of becoming Mme. Iskandar could have reconciled her to becoming a Muslim. *Quelle horreur!* she thought to herself at that possibility and, but for her strict upbringing, might have added *Zut-Alors!*

The Copts were an ancient branch of Christianity that traced its lineage back to the arrival of Mark the Evangelist in Egypt in A.D. 42. St. Mark was now considered to be the first Bishop of Alexandria. The Coptic Church had flourished in Egypt, particularly around Alexandria and, by the 20th Century, having survived suppression during the spread of Islam, was to be found in significant strength throughout the Near East. The split from the Catholic Church (at that point simply the Christian Church) occurred during the Council of Chalcedon in A.D. 451, over issues of different interpretations of the deity of Christ. The deliberations had been long and occasionally acrimonious involving subtleties and shades of meaning that only the most erudite and monomaniacal of theologians could have considered important; something akin to the debates over 'the number of angels that could dance on the head of a pin' which had so exercised the minds of mediaeval clerics. Still, the Coptic Church had clung to its autonomy and even had its own pope, albeit its beliefs and practices were, for all intents and purposes, identical with those of the Roman Catholic Church.

Marie, she realized, would have to convert and raise her family as Coptic Christians if she were to become Mme. Iskandar. She was, at heart, pragmatic. There was a historical precedent for such a conversion she remembered from Sister Jeanne D'Arc's history classes. If Henry of Navarre had been willing to convert to Catholicism to become the King of France in the Middle Ages reputedly saying "Paris is well worth a Mass," then she, too, could accept 'that Christ was *from* not *in* two natures' if accepting it brought with it such a worthy husband. It seemed a small price to pay. She had never given much thought to either definition if it came to that. She became a Copt and married Adlai in the church of Saint Athanasius in the spring of 1905 supported by her rather bemused family and a cohort of officers from the good ship *Osiris*.

The couple spent the first month of their marriage on board ship as *Osiris* meandered from port to port amid the islands of the Greek Peninsula and the smaller ports of the Adriatic and Aegean and the crew noted, with approval and some amusement, the sunniness of the skipper's disposition. Eventually, however, the honeymoon ended as they berthed at Port Said and a tanned Marie was introduced to her new family and her new hometown, Alexandria.

The ensuing decade proved to be very rewarding. At the outbreak of the war, the Iskandars were well established and highly regarded members of the large and vibrant Coptic community in Alexandria. Only one element cast a faint pall over her content. Only her first born, the ten-year-old Isabel, conceived during those first idyllic weeks cruising the Eastern Mediterranean, had survived infancy. A harrowing series of first trimester miscarriages had followed Isabel's birth but she, at least, was a source of great joy: sweet natured, with her father's quirky sense of humor and the promise of her mother's spectacular looks.

In 1915, the *Osiris* was torpedoed and sunk. Marie received word of her husband's loss but due to the vagaries of international communication in the wartime era she had already heard of his rescue before she received word of his loss and thus was spared considerable anxiety. She was also not excessively bothered. As the wife of a sea captain, she was accustomed to his lengthy absences and he, in turn, downplayed the extent of his medical injuries and lengthy convalescence. Consequently when, in late 1916, she received a lengthy letter from her husband and learned of the proposed tectonic shift in the family's geographic and mercantile orientation that it contained-- he proposed to liquidate all their assets, sell their home and re-locate the family to war-time Britain--she was not entirely or immediately delighted. Had she been a Muslim she might have consoled herself with the thought that this was the will of Allah. This was not the will of Allah but, irritatingly, the will of Adlai Iskandar. She would do as he requested. As an obedient Egyptian wife, therefore, but with considerable apprehension, she undertook the complex negotiations and financial transactions required to transport the family to Britain. She complied with his directions but with reflections on her husband that were not entirely filled with Christian Charity, Coptic or otherwise.

****

The journey from Alexandria to Liverpool was arduous but not particularly dangerous; crossing the Mediterranean to Marseilles and then traveling overland to St. Malo minimized the threat from German submarines, as they were almost completely limited to the North Atlantic. Marie, a native of French-speaking Lebanon, took a certain amount of guilty pleasure in eaves- dropping on her fellow passengers who, reassured by her Arabic garb and appearance, opined uninhibitedly as the SNCF, the French National Railway, chugged its way north to Paris and thence to the Channel. *The wife of Corporal Leboeuf of Fontaine-de-Vaucluse had been 'no better than she should have been during the corporal's heroic deployment to Verdun'* was the widely held opinion. Interesting revelations like this helped *passer le temps* but it was still a tedious trip. The journey skirted the North Eastern corner of France and thus, the most ravaged parts of the nation, but there was no escaping the pervasive ambience of a nation at war.

Soldiers filled the trains with representation from all departments: *poilus* in their blue grey greatcoats and some, in uniforms more exotic in appearance, from Colonial

France. The last legs of the trip involved the crossing from St. Malo to Southampton; the nadir of the entire odyssey it turned out thanks to a bout of *mal de mer* that affected Isabel piteously. They attempted to bear their burden stoically and tried to stifle, unsuccessfully, homicidal thoughts in re: *Cher Papa*.

The final stretches, after a hot meal on dry land had restored their spirits, were first to London and thence to the northwest, courtesy of the London Midland and Scottish Railway. Understandably, there was no great animation or *joie de vivre* evident among the crowds but rather it was with a dogged, 'lets see it through' resignation that the people seemed to handle the inconveniences and hardships that the war had brought on.

Two young Scottish soldiers--Seaforth Highlanders she deduced from their shoulder flashes--even yielded their seats on the journey from London to Liverpool. Grateful for this unexpected courtesy, mother and daughter shared the sandwiches and sausages rolls that they had picked up at Euston Station with the two privates who were, by now, seated on their kit bags in the corridor. Communication was rather constrained by the ladies' modest familiarity with the English language and by the young Scots well nigh impenetrable accents. Sausage rolls, delicacies previously unfamiliar to them, were a fairly alarming introduction to *cuisine Anglaise* but the two soldiers polished them off with enthusiasm and no apparent ill effects. At Crewe, they parted company with the Scots changing for their Glasgow connection. Finally–Liverpool!

Lime Street Station was notably dismal on their arrival. Men in uniform were everywhere; khaki the prevailing colour. Despite the bustle, an air of suppressed sadness was evident. Two years exposure to the realities of trench warfare had sobered the population. Long past was the excitement and patriotic fervour that had set young Britons flocking to the recruiting stations in 1914. Casualty lists were scanned daily in every town, village and hamlet. 'Lord Derby's Pals' four battalions of the King's Liverpool Regiment which had paraded so bravely not a quarter of a mile from this very railway station a scant two years before, had been decimated. They had suffered appalling carnage: 500 casualties on the first day of the recent Somme Offensive alone. The B.E.F. had taken 100,000 casualties before noon on the first day of the Paschendale offensive and this ill-conceived adventure was ongoing with little gain to be shown for the loss of life and no end in sight.

Marie experienced a momentary panic as they passed the turnstiles and emerged onto the crowded concourse, recognizing no one. Where was the dapper mariner who had left Alexandria eighteen months ago in all the splendid regalia of a ship's captain? He had promised, by telegram and through the good graces of Thos. Cook and Co., Ltd., to meet them at the barriers without fail. Surely this anxious looking middle-aged businessman couldn't be her Adlai. Recognition however was swift and the relief and obvious delight on his face on seeing them reassured her that this was, indeed, her 'lord and master.' A year of austere living in Britain following 48 hours in an open boat in the North Atlantic had taken its toll on his appearance and a dark winter overcoat and a bowler hat had completed the transformation.

"Adlai! What on earth is that growing on your upper lip," was her first utterance. It was not what she had planned to say but she had not entirely forgiven him for wresting her from her comfortable family home. Furthermore, she and her daughter had not had a good night's sleep in two weeks. She relented however when she saw how crestfallen he looked. He was secretly quite proud of his new mustache; thought that it made him look like Lord Kitchener.

"Cheri," she cried and threw her arms around him. "What have they been feeding you?"

"Papa! Papa! Don't forget me!" his daughter said tugging in his coat.

"As if I could, *mon ange*," he said transferring his attentions to his daughter and enfolding her in a bear-like embrace.

The Iskandars were trilingual; equally fluent, roughly, in Arabic and French but significantly less so in English. After nearly two years in Britain, Adlai's English was almost fluent though rather heavily accented. Typically, the family had spoken French when chatting informally or affectionately. Arabic was the language for formality: for business, for religious matters and for those infrequent occasions when Adlai felt the need to function in *Paterfamilias* mode. A discrete cough from their porter, who was standing guard over their trunks, brought them back to reality and they trundled off to the nearby taxi rank.

"Moorfields please," Adlai instructed the cabby as they emerged from the station and skirted the soot-blackened Saint George's Hall, a massive public building that flanked the western side of Lime Street for over a hundred yards. The cab then turned towards the river. The girls could sense Adlai's eagerness to show them the progress that he had made in his grand scheme.

"I've found the perfect spot for our first shop," he said. "It's just tiny, mind, but its such a great location, just a stone's throw from Exchange. That's the station facing to the north and for people coming into town on the electric commuter trains--and I've got such a bargain. The lady who ran it lost her husband at Ypres and she has found it too much to keep up. So she decided to sell up and move back to St. Helens to be with her family. I was able to finance the down payment with the funds that Uncle Avram sent me from Aleppo. There are some tiny rooms over and behind the shop where we can live until we get ourselves going. Don't worry. We won't have to live there long. I definitely want you involved in finding a more permanent home for us when you know one end of Liverpool from the other."

"Steady, Darling," she smiled. "Let me catch my breath and gather my wits. There's a lot to see."

Indeed there was. The main streets were lined by steel rails that bore the clanking double-decker tramcars. The trams received their power from overhead electric cables suspended from wooden poles and accessed by trolleys which emerged from the middle of the tram roof and which could be reversed in orientation when the tram was required to travel in the opposite direction. The driver simply moved to the identical controls situated at the opposite end of the car. The main streets were lined with a full panoply of buildings: shops, offices, restaurants and pubs. The elegant Royal Court Theatre and the Playhouse, home to the famed Liverpool Repertory Company passed on the left and ahead loomed the red brick facade of the Daily Post and the Echo--the morning and evening city newspapers. On to Dale Street where the character of the city changed, becoming more oriented to business on a wholesale rather than on a retail scale--past the main police station and the Town Hall, the portico of which protruded into the street and from the overhanging balcony of which Queen Victoria had greeted the dignitaries of the city on a State Visit.

The original Town Hall had been built in 1515 and had been thatch-roofed. It had been re-built several times after fire and the depredations of weather had taken their toll. At about the time of the American Revolution, it had been hit by cannon fire from striking sailors on the river irked by a proposal to cut their pay by fifty percent. It had even survived an attempt by the Fenians to blow it up in 1881. The trams clanked noisily by, lurching alarmingly at the momentary detour caused by the protruding portico. They were not the most nimble of conveyances but the taxi bearing the Iskandars negotiated the bends handily and pulled up minutes later outside a tiny tobacconist's shop in Moorfields.

The shop in front of which the taxi had deposited them was indeed small and partially below street level; not more than twenty feet across the front and requiring a descent of two steps to reach the front door that was recessed, creating a small overhang.

'Chas. Lamb Tobacconist and Newsagent' read the sign across the windows which were mullioned except for a small central area of plate glass. Wrought iron containers, one each side of the door, contained a pile of the evening's Echo on the left and, on the right, a few unsold copies of the morning editions of the national dailies.

"What do you think, Darling?" He was bubbling over with enthusiasm that she was not yet ready to share. "It's a perfect spot. We will get all the traffic passing to and fro from the business district through Exchange. They'll pick up their papers and stop in for their cigarettes and, you'll see, we'll have an array of sweets, even stationery and Oh! Who knows? We'll gradually build a wider clientele when we establish a regular supply of Turkish and other Oriental tobaccos."

Moorfields was not part of an arcade of retail shops. Offices lined both sides of the street and tramlines went right down the middle but it was wide and excellent street lighting ameliorated the developing evening darkness. It was mid-December and evening came early in the north of England.

"Let's go inside. We're blocking the pavement," Marie said hoping to sound appropriately enthusiastic. The ancient cabbie, uncharacteristically, helped them to move their luggage down the steps into the overhang. He was tipped handsomely by Adlai and, reflecting to himself that his customer was *not too bad a sort of gent for a bloody foreigner*, departed to join the taxi stand at Exchange Station.

When they got their trunks inside the shop they almost filled the customer area and were greeted by a pleasant, middle-aged lady of diminutive stature who was wearing a white apron over an ankle length dress of floral print. This was the redoubtable Penny Lamb, widow of the former owner. She had agreed to stay on for a few weeks during the transition to the new ownership. Seeing them entering the shop she bustled out from behind the counters that lined the small shop on two sides: on the back wall and on the side furthest from the door.

"Oh my dears!" she exclaimed wearing a welcoming smile. "You must be Missus Iskandar and you must be Isabel. Aren't you the prettiest thing? You must be worn out. Let me help you with those bags, Captain. It'll be dark in half an hour and I'll be able to shut up the shop. I've made us a little supper and you can come inside and I'll put the kettle on. You'll be glad of a nice cup of tea and then, while you're settling in, I'll put up the shutters."

Pausing finally to draw breath, she then folded the two somewhat startled but gratified ladies into a hearty embrace and ushered them behind the counters and through the door into the living quarters.

"Aren't you the lucky one," she said to Isabel, once she had regained her breath, "living in a sweet shop. All the 'Licorice Allsorts' you can eat. They're my favorites, you know."

****

For most of the winter the family survived on the residual income generated by their small retail tobacco shop. All three members shared the workload. The shop was open at 6:00 a.m. to collect the daily papers delivered in small bales to their front door. Isabel helped her father to sort the Daily Mails, the Daily Expresses and Liverpool Daily Posts into appropriate piles. There was little demand for the Times of London or the Manchester Guardian. Marie served behind the counter and contrived to keep her family fed between customers. Isabel had not yet enrolled in school. She was intimidated by the cockiness and self-confidence of the urchins who 'patronized' their shop.

"Three penn'orth of Mint Imperials and ten Woodies please, Missus." These would, presumably, be her schoolmates if she enrolled in the local school. She was a stranger in a strange land. She even had trouble in interpreting their language. *Was this really English that they were speaking?* She was making her first acquaintance with 'scouse', the local *patois*. Scousers were to Liverpool what Cockneys were to London or Cajuns to New Orleans, if it comes to that. It was very different from what she heard on the BBC.

The Iskandars simply had not enrolled her in school and were hoping that the authorities would not detect the failure before they got their business off the ground and found a more permanent home.

CHAPTER THREE
Liverpool, 1926.

That the Iskandars had become long-standing members of the Catholic parish of St. John's by 1926 was a reflection on their pragmatic approach to religion and to life. They were traditional Coptic Christians. Marie had accepted conversion from Roman Catholicism on her marriage and had been willing to live up to her end of the bargain. Adlai's family had been Copts since the dawn of time, it seemed to him. But Copts were thin on the ground, to say the least, in the Liverpool of 1916, whereas, in the area where they had settled at the time of their arrival and in the streets around Everton Brow to which they had moved six months later, they were surrounded by hoards of Christians who barely knew what the term 'Copt' meant. If asked, they might have ventured 'apprehended by the local constabulary.' Marie had pointed out to her husband that she definitely expected an active religious life for herself and for her family.

"Let's at least see whether or not we would be comfortable attending an English church. What's more, if were going to attend I'd want to join that church. After all, Adlai, I was raised a Catholic and I converted for the sake of our marriage."

It was an astonishing proposition for Adlai whose ancestors had been Copts since the first century of the Christian era. He had eventually come round to the logic of his wife's revolutionary proposal. She had given up her Catholic identity for him. Besides, there was no Coptic presence in Britain. They would be alone in a non-Coptic world. They decided to attend Mass at St. John's, a large Catholic church a few miles out from the city centre. This they did shortly thereafter. Adlai felt fairly comfortable throughout the service. There was incense, the vestments were similar and the sequence of the prayers was familiar; though the Latin was incomprehensible and the organ music and choral singing were very unlike the *a cappella* chanting that was typical of the church in Alexandria. For Marie, it felt like coming home. Adlai could sense her pleasure and knew that his agreement in the compromise would only make a wonderful marriage even more wonderful.

After the service they had introduced themselves to Monseigneur Kieran who, by happy chance, was an above-average theologian and student of church history and who had studied for the priesthood at the English College in Rome. Consequently, he was familiar with the history of the Coptic Church and the almost identical beliefs and practices to those of the Roman Catholic Church. He was considerate and charming. The Iskandars would be very welcome as members of St. John's parish in 'full communion' with the born Catholics who comprised most of his flock. Only some, largely bureaucratic, approval from the Chancery Office would be necessary. This proved to be shortly forthcoming.

After a few years the Iskandars felt that they were right at home at St. John's and Isabel's transition was facilitated when she enrolled in Everton Valley Convent School. The fortunes of the family had fluctuated over the decade following their purchase of 'Chas. Lamb Tobacconist and Newsagent' in 1916. The establishment of a reliable source of tobacco from the Balkans, Turkey and Syria during a war was a complex and even dangerous process. The Iskandar family was extensive and far-flung throughout the region and possessed a reputation for honest commercial dealings that dated back to the Phoenicians. Aleppo, his Uncle Avram's hometown, became the nexus of a web of cousins, uncles and business associates that was spread out throughout the Eastern Mediterranean. They had entered the business of acquisition, distribution and transportation of the distinctive highly aromatic and sweet tobaccos known, generically, as Balkan or Oriental. Turkey had opted for the 'wrong side' at the outbreak of the war and Turkish tobacco was, by now, essentially unobtainable except for small quantities that could be filtered over the Syrian border. Uncle Avram managed to acquire a little of that. Most highly prized was the *yenidje* leaf that had been grown in Western Thrace in Macedonia since the 1600's. The Yenidje Company Ltd. had been founded by Louis Rothman in Britain just before the outbreak of the war but production had been hampered by the vicissitudes of the global conflict. It was precisely because of that disruption that the former Capt. Iskandar hoped to find his niche.

By the spring of 1917, several developments occurred on the Western Front that brought a ray of hope to the embattled Allies. America, finally provoked into action by the sinking of the *RMS Lusitania*--a grim day for Merseysiders--had declared war on the Central Powers. The anthem *The Yanks are Coming* soon threatened to replace *Keep the Home Fires Burning* as the most popular song on the wireless but the impact of the news was, for a long time, psychological rather than military. Significant numbers of doughboys did not arrive in Europe until 1918 except for several invaluable Field Hospitals. One of these, to be known as the 5th U.S. General Hospital, was staffed entirely from the ranks of the Massachusetts General; America's premier hospital. They were desperately needed by the overstretched British medical services and initially served with the British troops. This unit took the first American fatality of the war. A half dozen of these Field Hospitals arrived in the spring of 1917. They represented the cream of America's teaching hospitals and proved to be invaluable over the ensuing months. Corporal Frank Kelly had been one of thousands of British troops who benefitted from their presence.

The delayed arrival of the fighting men was inevitable. It takes a significant time to recruit, equip and train a modern army. Right now, the hard-pressed Allies were struggling to deal with the massive German reinforcements that had been transferred from the Eastern to the Western Front after the collapse of the Tsar's Army in 1916. The lines held--bent but not breached--and the announcement of a declaration of war by the United States meant that ultimately the Allies would prevail.

Of more immediate consequence to the Iskandars was the arrival of their first shipment of Oriental tobacco from Syria. It was only a small quantity--one hundred cases--but the quality was excellent and it was a harbinger of things to come, or so they hoped. Uncle Avram had, literally, delivered the goods. Now it was Adlai's responsibility to exploit his good fortune.

The firm of W.H. Ogden, now an important subordinate of the British Tobacco Company and an important part of the local economy, had sprung from small beginnings, Thomas Ogden had opened a small retail tobacco shop in Park Lane in 1860. In 1870, he had branched out specializing in the manufacture of pipe tobacco. His St. Bruno and St. Julien brands, now the market leaders in Britain, were originally produced in a tiny factory in St. James Street but, by the turn of the century, the enterprise had grown to include six satellite factories and a snuff mill. The tobacco that was to become St. Bruno was exclusively of Virginian origin and so its availability had not been significantly hampered by the war. By now the manufacture had been consolidated into one large facility on Boundary Street, some three miles from the city centre. Now a huge billboard was to be seen featuring a large Saint Bernard carrying a pack of St. Bruno Flake under its chin in place of the traditional keg of brandy. The dog's mouth emitted a large puff of smoke at regular intervals. This was cutting edge advertising in 1917 and the hoarding had become a Liverpool landmark.

On the strength of his minute foothold in the tobacco trade Adlai finagled a meeting with a 'mid level executive' of his acquaintance: a Mr. Walters. Thomas Ogden had long since passed away and Ogden's was now part of the British Imperial Tobacco Company. For the meeting, he had brought with him a carefully wrapped sample of his prime Latakia leaves and he informed Mr. Walters that he had one hundred cases of it available. One hundred cases of tobacco was only a minute, token amount to a company as massive as the Imperial Tobacco Company and indeed the St. Bruno brand did not contain Oriental tobacco. Mr. Walters was, however, well versed in the tobacco trade and was a man who had worked in several of the subordinate firms that constituted the company. He was well aware that prime tobacco from the Balkans was at a premium and that Imperial Tobacco could use all it could get its hands on for one or other of its corporate offspring.

The Rothman brand alone could utilize everything that this earnest Egyptian could deliver; particularly if this included the *Queen of Tobacco,* the Yenidje leaf. Could Mr. Iskandar guarantee the delivery of one hundred tons of Oriental tobacco within six weeks with, at least half of it being Yenidje? Adlai swallowed deeply and imperceptibly, he hoped. Indeed, "a cold perspiration bespangled his brow." This is how he might have expressed his reaction had he been familiar with 'The Mikado'. He was not and was therefore limited to breaking out into a mundane 'cold sweat'. He was faced with a decision that would make or break him. If he failed to deliver on a contracted delivery, the penalties would undoubtedly bankrupt him. He had not, to this point, seen more than his token cases of the prized commodity but his most recent correspondence from Aleppo had promised a large shipment due to arrive at the Albert dock in ten days.

"Certainly," he said, "and I will sign a contract to that effect right now if you so choose." *In for a penny in for a pound,* he reckoned.

They agreed to settle on the details in three days. Mr. Walters was duly impressed and was equally certain that he had made a deal with little or no risk to Imperial Tobacco when three days later they signed the contract for the delivery of 100 tons of specialty tobacco leaf, (as specified in Annex 1), for a price that made Adlai's head spin. The sum was negligible to Imperial Tobacco but it was mind boggling to a *titan of industry* whose only hard assets currently on hand were 100 cases of Latakia and the mortgage on a small tobacco shop near Exchange Station. Still, of such gambles are great fortunes made. Today the gods chose to smile. The first critical shipments arrived at dockside in the nick of time and were inspected, accepted by a representative of Imperial Tobacco and dispatched to the Rothman's factory. The reputation of 'Adlai Iskandar, Importer of Fine Tobacco' was established and for the next four years flourished. He was able to pay off the mortgage on his first shop for which he had developed a sentimental fondness.

Marie had spent many happy days acquainting herself with her new hometown; poring over street maps, and walking the streets in areas that seemed to be promising as the new home for her family. With their newfound modest affluence they bid on a small-but-handsome mansion overlooking Stanley Park--some miles north of the smoking St. Bernard advert and within earshot of both of the city's football stadiums. Mrs. Iskandar handled the negotiations. She was not Lebanese for nothing and drove a good bargain. They had concluded that the tobacco trade was obviously destined to be the major factor in the their lives and so, in addition to their import business, they bought up a series of four small retail tobacco/newsagent shops located within a square mile and close to their new home.

When Napoleon described the English as a "nation of shopkeepers" he probably didn't have families of immigrant Egyptians in mind but this is what he would have found in suburban Liverpool if he had survived until 1926; admittedly an unlikely eventuality. The restoration of international trade that occurred after the end of the war gradually ate into the market edge that it had provided to the Iskandars. The pre-war suppliers from Turkey and the Balkans rose, phoenix-like, from the ashes and fought to reclaim their old customers. Adlai was, by now, a sufficiently astute insider in the trade and recognized that he was facing insuperable odds if he decided to remain as an independent agency. He therefore once again approached his old friend, Walters, who by now had risen to the senior ranks of Imperial Tobacco. He offered to sell out his business. As before in 1917, his proposal was accepted. The family retained ownership of their small chain of retail tobacconists' shops. Five in-house managers were recruited and installed, all delighted with the living quarters that came with the job. Money, jobs and housing were still very tight four years after the war.

Marie had involved herself intimately in the process of recruiting for the positions. Time was to prove her to be an excellent judge of human nature. In the ensuing years only once was there an occasion of dishonest behavior involving their employees: Mrs. Edna Purvis, who ran the shop in Spellow Lane. She was a widow with three children. Indeed, this fact had partly influenced her selection. An occasional temporary drop off in receipts was to be expected periodically in a small business like hers but when it persisted over several months Marie had no alternative but to look more rigorously into the books and inevitably it was found that Mrs. Purvis was not reporting all her receipts and was submitting altered 'weeklies.' It was not a very sophisticated swindle. Mrs. Purvis was not a sophisticated thief. When confronted with the evidence of her crime, she immediately broke down and pleaded for forgiveness and begged for a second chance. Jamie, her second, was a sickly child. He had been labeled with the dreaded diagnosis of tuberculosis, the bane of the inner city poor. The only treatment was good food and rest in the fresh air, preferably in a sunny climate. None of these were readily available. Marie could not bear to throw the family out into the street and talked her husband into allowing them to make amends. In time they became the most loyal of employees even when Jamie succumbed to the dread disease the following year. T.B., as it was generally known, was at that time rampant throughout the slums of most industrial cities of Britain where crowding, indifferent hygiene and poor food were the rule. The stigma of 'weak Irish chests' was a canard. Tuberculosis affected chests and indeed, eventually, most of the organs of the body, with complete indifference to the national origin of said chests.

Chapter Four
Liverpool, 1926

From her dormitory window Isabel Iskandar could look down into Hope Street and, by peering to the left, glimpse the intersection where Mount Pleasant started its descent into the heart of the city. It was early evening on a gloomy late November day and she was faced with another three hours of study. Pages of French and Arabic translation loomed ahead along with the preparation of lesson plans for her student-teaching chores. French was not an unheard of field of study at Mt. Pleasant Teachers Training College but Arabic was and, on enrolling at that institution, she had caused a great deal of consternation among the good sisters of Notre Dame who ran the college and the adjoining high school. The nuns had been startled but rather intrigued by the prospect of one of their young ladies studying Arabic. After all, the young Miss Iskandar had arrived at the college with an impeccable record. She had attended Everton Valley Convent, Mt. Pleasant's crosstown sister school where the Sisters of Notre Dame de Nemours, the self-same nuns who had taught her mother in Lebanon and who operated both institutions, had nothing but praise for their star pupil.

She had obtained her Higher School Certificate with distinction and had even received a small bursary. She could have chosen to enter the University but had opted, instead, for the more sheltered environment of an all girls training school for teachers. Mother Celestine, the principal of the College had conferred with her senior advisers and had negotiated an arrangement with the University, only a few hundred yards distant, to permit their would-be-polyglot to enroll as an external student in the Faculty of Arts and the Department of Arabic. She could take the London University External Exams and earn her degree that way. Teacher's training colleges, at that time, were not degree-granting institutions.

Isabel was, generally speaking, content with her lot but, occasionally, she felt that much of life was passing her by. The girls in her language studies at the university appeared to have a much more exciting life. Their behavior was much less inhibited; their clothing much more daring with hemlines approaching the knee. They smoked, laughed a lot and talked about their romantic encounters in a manner she found shocking but intriguing. She had thought that, on her escaping the limited social life permitted by her straight-laced father, a vastly more liberal and fulfilling world would be open to her. She had soon discovered that the restraints placed on her life as a Mt. Pleasant student teacher were almost as formidable as those she had left at home. The Sisters were not about to let their girls stray from the straight and narrow; not on their watch. The doors were locked at ten o'clock during the week with an eleven o'clock curfew on Saturdays. Gentlemen callers were expected to greet their young ladies in the austerity of the formal parlor under the disapproving gaze of St. Elizabeth of Hungary whose statue was the room's only ornament.

Isabel was, by now, well into her third year of study and she was feeling a little depressed. English Novembers will do that to even the sunniest of Northern Europeans and she was, after all, an Arab, genetically speaking. French was, of course, a breeze for her. She had been fluent since childhood and was as familiar with the classics and poetry of Baudelaire and Victor Hugo as she was with Dickens, Jane Austen and the Romantic poets. She had no doubt that she could graduate and look forward to employment as a French teacher. Her mastery of Arabic was an issue of greater uncertainty.

Conversation between the Iskandars, since their arrival in Britain, had always been held in an amalgam of the three tongues to which they could lay claim; switching seamlessly from one to the next as the mood took the current speaker. Classical Arabic and the use of Arabic script was an entirely different matter. Neither of her parents had thought it necessary and Isabel was as little familiar with it as she would have been with Cyrillic or Chinese. The Arabic language classes at the university were very much oriented towards classical Arabic and Isabel discovered that this imposed a greater burden on her stamina than all her other classes put together. She was also put out of patience by the oppressively paternalistic orientation of much of the Arabic literature, so much of which reflected the misogynistic aspects of Islam. In that Isabel was her mother's daughter.

The traffic passing beneath her window was intermittent and humdrum but a nightly occurrence produced a predictable flurry of activity around 10:30 p.m. as the nearby Apostleship of the Sea disgorged its patrons onto Hope Street and shortly thereafter, the young ladies who had been entertaining them. The hostesses were representatives of proper Catholic womanhood who, after careful vetting by their parish priests, served tea and sandwiches and danced sedately with the assorted seafarers who, in turn, made overtures, illicit and otherwise, to them; all this under the scrutiny of gimlet-eyed chaperones. Extramural contact with the sailors was, of course, forbidden and the chaplain, Father O'Brien, patrolled Hope Street and its environs after closing time for half an hour in an attempt to enforce this rule. He was not always successful.

One of these nights I'm going to take Kate up on her offer, Isabel thought. *I feel like I'm in a monastery here, not a college. I'm 20 years old and I haven't been out with a boy since last summer. Perhaps a monastery wouldn't be so bad in fact.* That antic thought flashed through her brain but was blushingly put aside. The Kate in question was Kathleen Kelly, her classmate at Everton

Valley. For a year they had been inseparable until Kate had left school at sixteen to practice her secretarial skills in the world of commerce and Isabel had progressed into the sixth form, destined, it seemed, for a career in Academia. They had made an unlikely pair; Kate, a tall, outgoing hoyden, pretty rather than beautiful, with a freckled mischievous face and a head crowned with an unruly mop of auburn hair. Isabel, in contrast was the introverted one, blessed with a slim figure and lustrous blue-black hair. She had a slightly aquiline nose, almond shaped eyes of the darkest brown and olive skin. She was emerging from childhood with a promise of striking beauty in later life. They had drifted apart after Kate left school and they had shared only chance encounters on the street or at church events since then. They still considered themselves friends but Kate had become a young adult while Isabel was still considered to be a schoolgirl and indeed thought of herself in those terms. Now, however, five years had gone by and so it was on level terms that she met her old friend late one afternoon and suggested that they stop in at a nearby restaurant for a cup of coffee.

"It's so great to see you Izzy. What are you up to these days?" Kate said as they settled down in the local Kardomah Cafe for a chat over a cup of appalling English coffee and a delicious Eccles cake. "I bet you've got those university boys falling for you in droves," she teased; a running joke given Isabel's notorious shyness.

"Oh! You know," she protested, "I'm up to my ears in work and these nuns watch us like hawks. I might as well be one of their novices for all the fellows I meet. Besides, I've too much I want to do before I start looking for a mate," she grinned slyly.

"Who's talking about looking for a mate? This is 1926, not the Dark Ages. I'm not looking to settle down either but I don't mind looking over the field. Tell you what. Why don't you ask the old battle-axes to let you come and be a hostess at the Apostleship of the Sea?"

The Apostleship of the Sea was an establishment housed in an old hotel now known as Atlantic House. It was sponsored by the Archdiocese of Liverpool and provided seafarers with more wholesome food, lodging and female company than was available in the seamier fleshpots that abounded between the docks and Scotland Road.

"Atlantic House is just down the street from here. I've been going there for two years now. We could go together. It would be a lot of fun without having to get too involved with anybody in particular. It will be just the two of us Valley Girls out on the rampage. I'm sure your parish priest will give you the old *imprimatur*," she added somewhat irreverently. '*Imprimatur*' was the designation inscribed on books that had been approved by the Catholic hierarchy for their theological content. Isabel had to admit to herself that she was intrigued by the idea but the leap from sheltered convent dweller to sophisticated woman of the world was too much to take in one bite.

"Give me a while to think it over and I'll give you a call," she temporized. With that the two friends parted with Isabel certain in her mind that she would never follow up on the invitation. The next two weeks, however, had reinforced Liverpool's reputation for awful weather and this, plus a series of practice teaching sessions with a particularly thick group of juvenile delinquents had put her in a rebellious mood.

Let's see what Kate's hangout has to offer, she found herself thinking. Monsignor Kieran proved to be no obstacle. The Iskandars were well regarded in the parish and the good man had had no qualms in recommending Isabel as a hostess in an organization that had the longstanding support of the Archbishop. Her father proved to be rather more of a problem. He had, by now, been a committed landsman for over ten years but he had not entirely forgotten his days as a sailor. He himself might not have had a girl in every port--he had probably missed one or two before he met Marie--but he had no illusions but that the reputation of sailors *vis-à-vis* girls was well earned. As far as he was concerned the status quo was just fine: his precious Isabel under the watchful eye and protection of the good Sisters. He was undermined in his opposition by the acquiescence of Mother Celestine, who had approved a trial period of attendance: once a week, on Saturday evenings for three months with the caveat that the quality of her academic work must remain high and that the eleven o'clock curfew must be observed.

Adlai was eventually reconciled to the decision by the complacence of his wife. Marie had met him when she was only twenty and she had been a married woman by twenty-two. Her support for her daughter rather surprised him. The fact that Isabel would be accompanied during her hostess duties by Miss Kathleen Kelly served to quell his concerns. He had known Kate since she and Isabel had been classmates at the 'Valley'. He had always had a soft spot in his heart for the pretty redhead. Kate, he was assured, had worked at the Apostleship of the Sea for two years without incident and she assured Captain Iskandar (as she always referred to him) that she would look after his pride and joy with a vigilance worthy of a mother hen guarding her brood. Neither Miss Kelly nor the former captain had any personal knowledge of the protective propensities of poultry but he was impressed by her eloquence and agreed to the trial run that Mother Celestine had ordained.

A date was chosen for their first foray into the 'wicked world' and at 6:30 p.m. on the last Friday before Christmas they rendezvous-ed at the Hope Street entrance of the College and made the short walk to their destination. Kate introduced Isabel to the Chaplain and the supervising chaperone. They were shown around and given a brief description of their duties and responsibilities. It was a friendly reception. Hostesses were expected to help with the preparation and serving of the food in the restaurant and to operate the little shop that sold assorted toiletries, newspapers and magazines and a limited selection of clothing. The duty roster was posted on a notice board in the hostesses lounge.

"Food preparation is the least popular assignment," Kate whispered.

The lounge, which gave access to the Ladies bathrooms and a small cloakroom lined with lockers, provided the girls a place to rest their feet and to act as a refuge in case any of the visitors became unruly or importunate. This happened very infrequently. The main attraction of the hostelry was the ballroom: a surprisingly elegant affair which boasted an eight-piece band that performed six nights a week and was situated on a small recessed and raised stage. The music was a fairly decorous mixture of foxtrots, quicksteps and waltzes. In the event that the customers indicated an above average enthusiasm for Latin rhythms, the band would break out its repertoire of tangoes, sambas and rhumbas. The Charleston had only lately arrived from America and was generally disapproved of by the more hide-bound members of the supervisory staff but once in a while the band let loose to general approval.

The dancing that evening got underway at 7:30. There was a brief period during which the sailors and hostesses tried to survey the field without looking too obvious about it. Eventually, one intrepid tar took a chance and crossed the dance floor to ask one of the girls to dance. She accepted and this, it seemed, was taken to be a signal that had been anticipated and soon the floor was filled. Over the next hour, Izzy and Kate had their hands full and their toes frequently trodden on. There was no shortage of partners. Conversation was frequently quite limited if their current partner spoke little English. Izzy smiled a lot and they seemed to be to be content to be dancing with a pretty girl, even if her Spanish or Greek or even Hindi was minimal. On one occasion she was able to have a livelier conversation when she was asked to partner by a *matelot* in a French Naval uniform. When the word was passed to his shipmates that there was a hostess who was not only a knockout–*"sensationelle"*--but was a French speaker, she soon had a small coterie of admirers vying for the next dance. By nine, she had danced almost non-stop and she needed a breather. Kate, who had been similarly occupied, suggested that they pay a visit to the lounge to give their feet a rest. She agreed and the two made their way across the room with eyes averted to preclude invitations for further terpsichore.

"Izzy," Kate said when they had reached their sanctuary. "I've got somebody who you must meet. It's my brother Frank. I've told him all about you and he's dying to meet you."

"Your brother! What's he doing here?" Isabel asked.

"He isn't here yet but he promised me he'd be here before half past nine."

"But how does he fit in here? Isn't this place meant just for sailors?"

"He goes to sea: has done for seven years ever since the war. He's a steward on the *Carmania*. He doesn't come here very often. Most Liverpool lads spend their time at home when they get back to the 'Pool' but they're quite welcome here. You'll really like him. When I told him that you'd be here tonight he couldn't wait to meet you. Of course I gave you a big build up--didn't mention your cross eyes or wooden leg."

She gave her friend a big stage wink and a nudge in the ribs. In the description of her brother's response, Kate had not been strictly truthful. When invited by his sister to come dancing and meet her friend Izzy, Frank had said, "Isn't she that skinny Egyptian girl who you used to chum around with in school?" He was now twenty-seven and thought of himself as belonging to a different generation to the shy teenager he vaguely remembered.

"I think that you'll find that she has aged nicely," she answered wryly.

"Okay, pretty sister of mine," he had teased, "I'll give her a shot."

"Give her a shot indeed and who do you think you are Francis Xavier Kelly, God's gift to women?" she shot back.

Truth to tell, Frank was a little sensitive about his scarred face and black eye patch. He was not particularly glib and was a little awkward in strange female company. He had never mastered the arts of flirtation, of lighthearted badinage or even of airy persiflage. He had begun to think of himself as a confirmed old bachelor.

"Come on, Lothario," his sister relented. "Maybe Izzy will discover your hidden charms. You do have some hidden charms don't you?" she couldn't resist adding. After all what were big brothers for if not for needling? They finally called a truce and agreed that he would get there at half nine.

Hope springs eternal. *Perhaps*, he thought to himself, as he entered the ballroom--*perhaps tonight won't be too bad. At least I'll have Kate to introduce me and help to keep the conversation going if I can't think of anything to say.* As he looked around the crowded room to find his sister he was trying to think of something pithy to say to get the conversational ball rolling. He was failing and could feel perspiration breaking out on his forehead. Pithy was not his long suit. Suddenly, a half a head taller than most of the girls there, was his sister with her unmistakable red mop waving to him across the room and arm in arm with her was the most beautiful girl he'd ever seen in his life.

"Izzy, this is my brother Frank," Kate said after giving him a sisterly buss. "Frank, this is Miss Isabel Iskandar."

Momentarily, Frank stood mute as though spellbound and then uttered the words that were to change his life forever: "My God, you're gorgeous," he blurted out.

In the clutch, his pith had returned at just the right time. Even his sister was taken aback by the unexpected utterance. She had, of course, hoped that her brother and her best friend would hit it off. She was a matchmaker at heart. Frank was notoriously slow off the mark where women were concerned. Not a few young ladies in New York, Boston and Halifax, as well as those closer to home had given up in despair after their subtle, and sometimes not-too-subtle, hints as to their availability were met with his apparent lack of interest. It wasn't really lack of interest. He just didn't know what to say. Even now, after his burst of unwonted eloquence, he seemed to be at a loss for words as he blushed to the roots of his hair.

"Aren't you the saucy one?" Izzy improvised somewhat startled by the unexpectedness of his opening gambit; not but that she was unaware of the impact she had on young men, nor was it first time that she had been told that she was beautiful by an aspiring Romeo--but in the past she had been unmoved by such protestations. It was part of the *modus operandi* for aspiring mashers. (Her attitudes to the conventions of courtship were still rather Victorian and she brushed off importunate admirers with a hauteur worthy of one of Jane Austen's heroines). Frank Kelly however, was obviously not your run of the mill smooth operator. *Au contraire*, she thought to herself. No one would ever confuse him for a smooth operator.

Even now he could hardly look her in the eye and after an embarrassed long minute's silence murmured that he was pleased to meet her. She immediately regretted her 'aren't-you-the-saucy-one?' retort. By no stretch of the imagination could he be considered that. She must have sounded like a shop girl at an Open Dance night at the Rialto. He was obviously a nice, unremarkable young man and, to boot, her friend's brother. So why did she notice a quickening of the pulse and a catch in her breath? Perhaps it was the scarred cheek that gave a somewhat piratical cast to his other wise unremarkable Hibernian features. Appeal to her he did. Some primordial female instinct told her that here was a young man worthy of serious consideration. It also told her how to further proceed if this encounter were to lead to bigger and better things. Frank, although shy and unpracticed in the arts of courtship, was, obviously, much more at ease dealing with his sister. Even now the Kellys were exchanging good-natured insults. Izzy would have to become his new honorary sister. She admitted to herself that the fact that he thought her gorgeous wouldn't hurt in helping the masquerade along.

"I'm so pleased that you're not much taller than your Amazon sister." The two were about equally tall with Kate's high heels giving her perhaps a one-inch advantage. "I hate to dance with chaps who tower over me. I feel like I'm talking to their belly buttons. You are going to ask me to dance aren't you, Frank? I should about come up to your chin."

Kate was relieved that her matchmaking appeared to be going well after a rocky start. Izzy had obviously taken a liking to her stodgy brother and, she noted approvingly, was taking exactly the right conversational tack not to scare him off.

"Let's get a cup of tea and then you can dance with both of us all night--but don't think you can have us all to yourself, Fred Astaire. We are supposed to share our charms with anyone who asks. I think you might have some competition from the French Navy."

"The Cunard line can handle the French Navy any day of the week," he replied, getting into the spirit of the give and take. "Just save the last dance for me, Izzy."

"Aren't you the saucy one?" she repeated, but this time the remark was accompanied by a dig in the ribs and big grin.

As promised, they did manage to dance the last dance together. It was 'See You In My Dreams'. This sentiment was very appropriate because the house rules precluded any further social contact. Besides, Izzy had the eleven o'clock deadline to meet at the Convent and the Kellys had a tram to catch. They were all anxious that their hurried departure didn't signal the end of their friendship. Everything had gone so swimmingly. Frank and Izzy were obviously all agog about each other and Kate felt the satisfaction of the successful matchmaker off to a promising start. She had also, along the way, had a pretty good evening in her own right with no shortage of partners eager to dance with her.

Frank suddenly remembered that he only had four more days before he was due to sail again. It was a round trip to Halifax, Nova Scotia and would take him away from home for nearly three weeks. In normal circumstances he loved the Canada voyages. Thousands of Irishmen had made the trip before him in rather less comfortable circumstances and Quebec was a glorious place to visit at any time. He looked forward to the summer season when Halifax would only be a stopover with a further cruise up the St. Lawrence to Quebec. This next trip, however, would coincide with the Christmas holidays. How perfect!

Now his only thoughts were that it would be nearly a month before he could see Isabel again. Happily he then realized that the Christmas break would mean that she would not, for a few precious days, be under the watchful eyes of the redoubtable Sisters of Notre Dame. He knew that at least one sister--Kate--would be on his side. Undoubtedly, he would have a stern and suspicious father to contend with but he felt that he could convince any reasonable parent that his intentions were honorable. Kate would be a great help; she could be a veritable Trojan horse in the parental defenses. Frank's formal education had ended at age fifteen but he liked to read and had come across a collection tales from Greek Mythology during a lay over in Boston. Kate, he felt, had Captain Iskandar wrapped around her little finger.

"I'd love for us all to get together again," he said, somewhat disingenuously. What he really has in mind was a party of two but he didn't want to rush his fences. "Izzy, won't you be home from school soon? Perhaps we could all go out to the theatre. I don't suppose a football match would be your cup of tea," he reflected ruefully. Like most Liverpool Irish Catholics he was an Everton man: a supporter of one of the two professional teams in the city. This idea was treated with the disdain that it deserved.

"You said the theatre. The pantomime season is just getting under way. I hear that Jessie Matthews is playing the principal boy at the Empire. We could get tickets up in the 'gods'. It won't be too expensive. Why, we could even bring Mary and Bridget along and make it a real family outing," was Kate's contribution.

"If I'm to be outnumbered by four females, I'm bringing Brendan along," he replied. If he couldn't have an outing *a deux* with Isabella, and it was certainly too soon for that, then at least he could use the occasion to give his brother a treat. It did occur to him that his brother would have been a keen advocate of the Everton proposal. Brendan was a great fan of the young phenomenon Dixie Dean, the Everton centre forward. But women were notoriously obtuse when presented with making a choice between a seat in a warm theatre and being jostled on the wind swept terraces of Goodison Park. So, *Aladdin* it was to be.

For those members of the reading public who are not acquainted with the English pantomime it should be explained that it was the traditional Christmas fare in theatres throughout the land. The plots were based on children's stories. The hero, known as the Principal Boy, was played by the female star of the show and for whom long shapely legs were the *sine qua non*. These were shown off by her short shorts and high-heeled shoes. Comic relief was provided by the male star; his character known as the Dame, and was typically dressed in a burlesque version of a working woman's clothes. In Sleeping Beauty, for example, the principal boy would be Prince Charming and in Aladdin, the dame was, traditionally, Widow Twankey, Aladdin's mother. For some reason Aladdin was never referred to as

Aladdin Twankey. The music consisted of the popular songs of the day and the humour was very broad with audience participation in abundance and many of the comedy routines were as familiar to the audience as to the performers.

It was the antithesis of the works of Noel Coward, the young sophisticate whose repertoire was just beginning to spread to the 'provinces;' this latter being the condescending term used by the denizens of London about anywhere not in London.

Still condescension on the part of the nation's capital was little on the minds of the three as they hurried to beat their curfew deadlines. Plans were speedily agreed to and it was decided that Kate would act as the go-between. A date for the following Tuesday was agreed to and a rendezvous was established: the lobby of the Empire at seven-thirty. Frank would see to the tickets and Kate would convince the senior Iskandars of the respectability of the outing. With deviousness worthy of Machiavelli, the two girls recommended that Frank should attend the eleven o'clock Mass next day at St. John's and chance to run into the Iskandars. Eleven o'clock High Mass was, by then, their customary ritual. This could not help but enhance his standing as a suitable companion for the young Miss Iskandar.

CHAPTER FIVE
Liverpool, 1926

The *paterfamilias* of the family Iskandar, leaving the eleven o'clock Mass in the Year of the Lord 1926, stood on the steps of St. John's and gazed about with some complacency. The family were now established citizens of their adopted country and members in good standing of the local parish. They lived in modest affluence and were financially secure. His only child was beautiful, docile and intelligent and was within months of completing her degree. He was, therefore, quite unsuspecting when his daughter greeted a young couple that was emerging with the rest of the congregation. In fact, he was delighted to note that half of the couple was his daughter's tall and vivacious former school friend, Kate Kelly. Kate had charmed him even as a teenager with her innocently flirtatious manner which amused him and which he enjoyed immensely. Like most men in their early fifties, he enjoyed being teased by a pretty girl. Quite a few in other age groups too, he might have noted. They gathered on the church steps.

"Hello, Kate," said Marie as the two girls proclaimed delighted surprise at the chance encounter. "We haven't seen anything like enough of you in these past few years. How are your parents and who is this young man?"

"Oh! Excuse me. Meet my brother. This is Frank Kelly. He is a senior steward on the *Carmania*. He's off to Canada on Thursday."

Introductions were made all round and general chit chat ensued, life histories were brought up to date and Kate resumed her innocent flirtation with Captain Iskandar while Mrs. Iskandar gazed on benignly with the complacency of a happily married wife with some twenty-five years tenure.

"Why don't you come over for tea this afternoon. I'd love to hear all about North America," Mrs. Iskandar said. She loved entertaining.

The two girls exchanged conspiratorial smiles. This was going over better than they had hoped.

"Well I don't claim to be an expert on America. I haven't got too far beyond the quays in Boston and New York but I'm sure that we'd love to come to tea. We've walked past your house often and its one of the prettiest on the park," Frank replied.

He couldn't have chosen a better remark to ingratiate himself. The senior Iskandars were very proud of their elegant home; the visible affirmation of their status in their adopted country. Marie Iskandar was every bit as shrewd an observer of human behavior as her daughter and her friend. She had not been as ready as her husband to believe that the meeting on the church steps was entirely fortuitous. Isabel and her mischievous friend were up to something but she reasoned that their machinations could fit in very well with her own plans. The young Kelly boy--(not really a boy any longer at twenty-seven)--would do very nicely in helping her daughter to shed her shyness. She was in no hurry to see Isabel married, but, unlike her husband who would have been content to keep his daughter under lock and key until he could arrange a suitable marriage, Marie would like to see Isabel begin to emerge a little from her self-imposed chrysalis. Frank Kelly appeared to be a proper young man; not perhaps the up and coming professional whom she would eventually marry but one with whom she could be introduced into the social world.

The Twenties were Roaring, even in Liverpool, and Marie wanted Isabel to roar, a little, along with them; *mezzo piano* perhaps. She still considered herself to be an emancipated woman and sometimes regretted that she hadn't cut a rug a little more herself before settling down so soon into marital bliss. She therefore suggested that they reconvene at five o'clock and, as it now was twelve-thirty, the two families parted with each quite content that the encounter had gone off splendidly.

Sunday high tea, as presented *chez Iskandar*, was quite an impressive affair. It took place in the large front parlour that overlooked the Stanley Park. The food was arrayed on an elaborately carved buffet. There were sandwiches of cheese, salmon, ham and cucumber, salads with tomatoes, lettuce and spring onions, fruit tarts and a delicious orange rum cake. These were served by a manservant in morning suit and a uniformed maid who dispensed the tea along with biscuits and *petit fours*. The hosts were genial and welcoming. Adlai and Frank were soon engaged in lively reminiscences about life at sea. Of the two, the erstwhile Captain had had the less happy memories of the North Atlantic. He did not linger over his most harrowing experiences but spoke of happier times on the *Osiris* in the Mediterranean. Frank was a little overawed at first. The Iskandars lived in a style that was several large steps above that of the Kellys and Frank had the sense that Capt. Iskandar would not readily accept him as an escort for his daughter. But he was very affable and Frank had the impression that Mrs. Iskandar looked on him favorably. Furthermore he was not intimidated by the elegance of the furniture or the formality of the service. He was, after all, a senior steward on a Cunard liner and well used to grandeur and sophisticated service, albeit he had previously been on the delivery end of the service rather than the recipient thereof.

He ate his crustless triangular sandwiches, balanced his plate on his knee and managed to avoid dropping the silverware while making polite conversation with the older couple. His sister, meanwhile, made animated girl talk with Isabel and Mrs. Iskandar but surreptitiously watched, with admiration, the ease with which Frank kept his conversational end up. Was this the same inarticulate brother, tongue-tied in the company of young women or even the brother of a thousand teasing sibling jousts? No matter! He was obviously doing well in presenting himself as a suitable escort for the daughter of the house for an innocent evening at the theatre.

"Papa," Izzy asked when the time for departure approached. "Kate has just been telling me that Frank is taking his brothers and sisters to the pantomime at the Empire on Tuesday. She wants me to come too."

"Do let her come with us Captain Iskandar. It'll be so much fun. Jessie Matthews is playing the Principal Boy and Frank only has a few more days at home before his next voyage."

"Jessie Matthews eh! I wouldn't mind seeing her myself."

"Now Adlai, you know that they don't want old codgers like us along," said his wife rightly interpreting the look of horror on her daughter's face.

"Old Codgers, indeed!" he harrumphed but then relented. "You outshine Jessie Matthews any day of the week, *ma chérie*," he added; ever the gallant.

It was agreed. The expedition was given parental approval. Frank would pick up the tickets and ensure that the Kellys would be present *en masse* in the Empire lobby at the appointed time. The Iskandars undertook to have Isabel delivered in the family sedan. The car was an elegant Hispano-Suiza and Hutton, the chauffeur, also doubled as the manservant. In the early 20th century, live theatre was entertainment for every man. It catered to all spectrums of the population. Its only competition was music in the pubs. Size, quality and cost, similarly, varied greatly but there was something for every taste and purse. At the turn of the century, Liverpool had boasted twenty-eight theatres and thirty-eight music halls. By 1926, the popularity of music halls was in decline and cinema was just beginning to be a factor in public entertainment but there were still a dozen or so live theaters: the Prince of Wales, the Shakespeare and the Royal Court in the heart of the city. But the biggest and most famous was the Empire on Lime Street. There had been great anticipation during the winter of 1924 when the Moss company, the owners of the Empire, decided to replace the old building with a new one which was to be the biggest and most up-to-date in Europe. It seated nearly twenty-four hundred customers when it opened in March 1925; an event that was the talk of the town for months.

Frank was being generous but not spendthrift in offering to take his brother and his three sisters as well as his would-be sweetheart to the pantomime. Seats in the 'gods' were only sixpence and he could even afford to splurge and lay out for the Upper Balcony without breaking the bank. The Dress Circle was just a little rich for his blood or his purse. Isabel's family would, undoubtedly, choose the Dress Circle or the Stalls for a theatrical outing but Izzy was not the girl for him if she didn't realize that the wages of a steward on an ocean liner, even a 'senior' steward on a Cunarder wouldn't run to six tickets in the Dress Circle. He was certain on that score. Isabel had struck him as a sensible girl who would not be afflicted with delusions of grandeur.

The Kellys made the trip downtown from Kirkdale by tram comfortably under half an hour. The youngsters were a twitter with barely suppressed excitement. Mary and Bridget had been to the theatre before but this was Brendan's first visit. They were eager to show off their superior knowledge and sophistication but Brendan did not care or even notice. He was too enthralled by the excitement of the prospects to notice his older sisters' condescension.

"I can hardly wait to see Jessie Matthews. She's only eighteen but she's already a star," Mary enthused.

"She's only two years older than you, Bridie. Did you see that photo of her in the Echo? She's so pretty."

Brendan could not bring himself to acknowledge such female enthusiasms.

"Its George Robey I'm dying to see. I saw him at the pictures a couple of weeks ago. He was a real scream."

"I hear that he was offered a knighthood for his work during the war and turned it down but accepted a CBE," Kate chimed in. "I wonder what that was all about."

George Robey, 'the Prime Minister of Comedy', was now fifty-six and was, perhaps, past his prime but he was still enormously popular and a big box-office draw. It said much for the publicity generated by the opening of the grand new Empire that stars of this magnitude could be lured from the capital but Liverpool pantomimes were considered the *ne plus ultra* of the genre though very few Liverpudlians would have put it quite like that.

They arrived at the theatre comfortably in time and Frank hurried to purchase the tickets. They were available. He had correctly assumed that they would be. It was, after all, a Tuesday evening and the theatre seated twenty-four hundred. Isabel arrived in style; "like a proper toff," muttered Brendan as the chauffeured Hispano-Suiza pulled to the curb.

"Come on Brendan. Best behavior tonight," Frank pleaded. He wasn't too worried. Brendan may have recently showed signs of an incipient social conscience but Frank knew that his younger brother idolized him and wouldn't say anything to spoil the evening. Kate, a Victorian at heart, reinforced this aspiration with a swift rap of the knuckles to his head.

There is nothing quite like the atmosphere of a theatre in the minutes before a big musical production. It was a Tuesday evening but there were still over two thousand in the house. Most of the audience was dressed to the nines. In the Stalls and Dress Circle most were in formal attire and even in the Upper Balcony everyone, it seemed, was in his or her Sunday best. There was a loud buzz of conversation and a corresponding beehive of activity as seats were located, settled into and programs studied. Then the orchestra filtered in and made their customary contribution to the general cacophony. Down went the lights--a smattering of applause for the conductor as he popped up from the depths of the pit. Then a crash of chords; up went the curtain and the 1926 performance of *Aladdin and his Wonderful Lamp* was underway.

Live theatre has always required a willingness on the part of the audience to suspend disbelief. The audience at the Globe theatre in Shakespeare's day knew, at some level of consciousness, that it was not the field of Agincourt that they were looking at when enjoying Henry the Fifth. Nor did they expect that the stage direction 're-enter Macduff bearing Macbeth's head' to have been literally taken to heart. As it was true for the Elizabethans, even more so was it true for the pantomime goers of the twentieth century. Jessie Matthews and her celebrated legs made their entrance as Aladdin, buyer and seller of old lamps. She and they were duly appreciated and the unlikeliness of her attire and high-heeled shoes was ignored. Her singing of the opening love ballad was rapturously applauded. A few in the audience might have opined that her distinctive warbling and cherubic round cheeks were perhaps more suited to the role of the Principal Girl but they would have been in the distinct minority and their carping derided. Aladdin's mother was the washerwoman, the redoubtable Widow Twankey. The role was to be played by George Robey. She was down on her luck; down but not out, as was soon made clear...

Act I, Scene III   **"Dear Me"**   Widow Twankey

Now listen girls I'll tell you all a secret.
I know that you won't breathe it to a soul.
I've got a little plan.
I really think I can.
I'm going to get--'ere closer yet.
You'll never guess--a Man.

Dear Me!

I'm so excited about it.
I'm going on the warpath once again.
I'm going to buy a frock.
Put powder on my clock.
A nice old gent I'm going to find with plenty in his sock.
Dear Me!

Just take a look at my glamour
A dab or two of lipstick on me gob.
When I'm dolled up in me doodads
You can mind your "p's" and "q's" lads
For Arabella Twankey's on the job (Lord help the sailors)
For Arabella Twankey's on the job.
Dear Me!

I'm Fair, I'm fat and I'm forty and don't intend to linger on the shelf.
What's Gertie Lawrence got
That little 'Bella's not?
Except of course that I had mine when she was in her cot.
Dear Me!

Just take a look at me figure. I really think me curves have come to stay.
Neither Clara Bow nor Maisy can out bump MY bumpsy daisy.
For Arabella means to win the day. (Oh Chase me Charley)
For Arabella means to win the day.

The bump that accompanied the bumpsy daisy was of the bustle, it should be pointed out, but Robey was an old hand of the music halls and knew how to get the most out of the most innocent sounding material. The applause was rapturous and when, with the timing of the veteran, he sensed its apogee, he rebuked the audience with his trademark "Desist" and "Kindly temper your hilarity with a modicum of reserve," which, of course, had the opposite effect.

From that moment on the pace never flagged. The players 'owned' the audience. They could do no wrong. From the Stalls to the Gods the audience had well and truly set aside its disbelief and was delighted to be living vicariously in a fairyland Arabia. Genies appeared in a puff of smoke and villainous wazzirs lurked menacingly behind the stubbornly dim-witted hero.

"Look behind you," the audience implored but somehow he never looked in time. The high point of the second act was the duet between the King and Queen, (where did they come from?), which led up to the finale.

Act II Scene V   ***"You Look Good to Me"***   King Hubert and Queen Utopia

Here we are alone together.
All the rest have slipped away.
And my dear I'm wondering whether
You'd be sorry if I say…

Tonight I've a wonderful feeling
I'm right at the top of the tree.
The chances are strong that I may be wrong
But you look good to me.

I've been to the old Jolly Miller
So heigh ho and fiddle-dee-dee.
My specs now I find that I've left behind
But you look good to me.

You are the leading attraction
You're like an old violin.
You drive me clear to distraction
You look so good through a bottle of gin.

You look, if I choose the right angle,
No older than, say, fifty-three.
The fact must be faced that I've got no taste
But you look good to me.

Tonight I've a wonderful feeling
I'm right at the top of the tree
The chances are strong that I may be wrong
But you look good to me.

My judgment may be a bit faulty
Just now when were out on the spree.
And although the light is just not quite right
Still you look good to me.

You're like an Epstein creation;
Rugged and ruthless and quaint.
You have a queer fascination
Only a chap like Picasso could paint.

I may be the slightest bit pickled.
I've certainly had two or three.
Oh Gosh! But its sad, but we must be mad
'Cos you look good to me.

There followed another chorus during which the royal couple did a rather elephantine time step before collapsing into each others arms with

I must be cuckoo and you're loopy too
'Cos YOU----LOOK-------GOOD----TO--ME!

There remained only the audience sing-along led by Widow Twankey now happily united to the miraculously reformed Wazzir to send the audience into the December evening singing to the smiling passers by...

Act II Finale   **"All Swish Your Cares Away"**   Company

What is the good of a gloomy face?
Why must you wear a frown?
I've got a remedy for your case.
Don't let it get you down--just listen.

All swish your cares away--cares away--cares away
All swish your cares away. Every morning get out your broom and just
All swish your cares away. Party spirit's the thing
And when you have done all the dirty work just
Sing---Sing---Sing

Their high spirits persisted as the Empire disgorged its happy patrons onto Lime Street. They looked about for the nearest tram stop with the girls giving an *a cappella* reprise of 'All Swish' to the amused smiles of the passers-by. Frank was so overcome by the apparent success of the outing that he hailed a taxi. *Surely*, he thought, *an evening that had started with Izzy in a chauffeured Hispano-Suiza shouldn't end with a ride on a clanking No. 49 tram.* The cabby looked a little askance at the proposed load. Six passengers were a bit much for a Liverpool taxicab even with its two jump seats. Frank resolved the impasse with the promise of an extra half crown over the meter fare and off they went with Brendan and Frank perched chivalrously on the fold-down jump seats and the four girls wedged in across the back seat. If there had been any reserve left in the manner in which the Kelly girls regarded Izzy with her elegant clothes and chauffeured arrival, then they were well and truly shattered by the trip home. It is difficult to be overawed by a young lady when you are sitting on her knee or wedged in between her and your older sister while all "swished" from side to side in time with the music.

Frank was delighted at the way the evening had turned out. Izzy was obviously a big hit with his family and she appeared to have had a great time. He might have wished for a smaller audience when they arrived at *chez Iskandar* but

Izzy slipped her arm into his as he walked her up to her front door and when he took her hand to say good night she kissed him modestly on the cheek and said, "Thank you, Frank. I've had a lovely time. I love your brother and sisters." Then, with a theatrical pause worthy of Jessie Matthews herself, she added, "You're not so bad yourself," and gave him a light kiss on the mouth.

"I hope I can see you when I get back from Canada," he croaked.

"I'd like that." She smiled and topped it off with a slightly more emphatic kiss. Not even the merciless teasing of his siblings could bring him down to earth when he climbed into the waiting taxi, claimed a spot in the back seat and ejected two of his tormentors to sit in the jump seats for the short trip to the Kelly menage.

CHAPTER SIX

Liverpool, Winter and Spring, 1927

It seemed a shame to be leaving home so soon before Christmas but 'time and tide wait for no man' and the Cunard line felt the same way about its ships. Cunard was in highly competitive business, not only with the White Star line (also Liverpool based) but North German, French and even U.S. lines. Many passengers liked to cross the Atlantic over the holidays, enjoying the festivities on board and blending them with the seasonal celebrations. By the time that they had negotiated the intricacies of the Mersey Ship Channel and were off the coast of North Wales, the staff were furiously preparing for the Welcome-Aboard Gala and for the first of the lavish meals and top notch entertainment that would start on Christmas Morning. By that time they would be 100 miles off the South Coast of Ireland and would continue right across the Atlantic to Halifax.

There was no time for Frank to brood over the harsh reality of having to earn a living. He was, in fact, delighted with life when he stopped to think. He had a steady job. There was even the prospect of promotion. His superiors--his job came under the Pursers administrative control--had given hints that he might be considered for elevation into the supervisory ranks. And then there was Izzy! Could such a beautiful and educated girl consider him as a serious boyfriend? He'd certainly hoped so and that final kiss had given him some reason to think that he might not be hoping in vain. In the meantime, a transatlantic voyage would keep him fully occupied.

Isabel, too, was not given too much time to pine for a lost love. In truth, the impact of her first tryst with young Mr. Kelly had not had quite the overwhelming effect on her that it had had on Frank. She had thoroughly enjoyed the evening with the Kellys and Frank was a nice young man: generous, funny and attractive in a curiously inexplicable way. He was certainly not handsome by any normal standards. She had enjoyed their first exploratory kiss and had been amazed and rather gratified at the effect it had apparently produced in him. She would certainly like to see him again but he would be gone for almost a month and, by then, the Sisters of Notre Dame de Nemours would be putting their customary crimp in her social life.

"Roll on June," she sighed to herself.

The long winter months seemed interminable to Isabel. The weather was, predictably, awful and the student teaching assignments equally depressing. The training colleges, of which Mount Pleasant was one, produced the teachers who would preside at the Elementary schools; that is with pupils from five and up to the school-leaving age of fifteen. From five to age eleven they were, therefore, roughly representative of the general population. But at ages beyond eleven, a selective process occurred whereby the brightest, the most motivated and those with the wealthier parents were transferred to schools which were variously called college, high school, grammar school or, even more confusingly to the non-English observer, public schools--the last named being the exact opposite of what that term appeared to suggest. The result of this winnowing out was that the teachers in the elementary schools dealt with an 11-15 year old population that had come from homes with no academic tradition, where poverty and hunger were commonplace and where many of the kids were just not too bright. It was dispiriting work. The Elementary schools run by the Catholic nuns were perhaps a little less depressing because the intimidating presence of the parochial Sisters helped maintain some semblance of discipline. The teachers who functioned best in this environment were those who had developed a carapace of indifference and/or a repertoire of painful, if marginally legal, disciplinary techniques. Isabel was increasingly daunted by the prospect of teaching in an Elementary school, parochial or other.

There was, of course, no place for a French teacher in the Elementary School System. For that she would need to teach in a Grammar School and for that she'd need a degree. She just had to complete her degree. The degree would be a B.A. in Arabic, of course, but she would also be a fully qualified teacher of French. She believed that this paradoxical situation could be finessed to enable her to find employment in a Grammar School; more specifically a Catholic Grammar School. That edge might be called the sisterhood of the Sisters. A discrete word in the ear of the principals of Belle Rive, Seafield, La Sagesse, Everton Valley or Mount Pleasant Convent High Schools would be golden if there was a post to be filled for a French teacher. If such a post was available and she remained in Sister Clementine's good graces then she would have a fighting chance to get the job. Of paramount importance was the degree.

This conclusion was reinforced when, at the end of the Easter term, all the prospective certified teachers submitted their applications for jobs for the upcoming school year. Most were applying for jobs in the city with a handful seeking employment in the surrounding towns and villages of South Lancashire and others aspiring to the somewhat more upscale Wirral Peninsula across the river. Sister Clementine counseled each individually. She took pains to do this. She was eager to see 'her girls' well and appropriately situated.

"I don't want to seem stuck up Sister but I don't think that I'm cut out to teach in a parochial school. I've always had my heart set on teaching French," said Isabel when her session came up. To her pleasant surprise the Principal agreed.

"I think you're wise. You're one of the brightest girls we've had here and you have a definite ear for languages. I know that you will surely complete your teaching certification and, so far, your reports from the University have been excellent. But your degree is a must and for that you need to take the Orals in London to complete the requirements for the London University External B.A. A wave of apprehension swept over Izzy as she returned to her room and digested the words of the principal. She had learned Arabic in her parents' home and had spoken it fluently until her parents had transplanted the family to Britain when she was nine. Inevitably, however, it was spoken less in the home over the years and, of course, not at all outside it. Even at University the emphasis had been on Classical Arabic and on the written rather than the spoken word. In short, she was terrified at the thought of Oral Exams.

Whether the terror was justified or not, it was real to her. She slept very poorly that night. After thirteen years in Britain she had absorbed, willy-nilly, some of the prevailing misperceptions of life in the Arab world. In the cold clear light of day she knew that her gentle loving parents were fairly representative of life in the Middle East but this night her dreams were filled with turban clad ogres straight out of Decameron Nights demanding that she recite the entire Koran or be beheaded. The next morning inspiration struck her and she promptly requested another interview with Sister Clementine.

"Sister," she implored after explaining her apprehension over the upcoming Oral exams in London, "I know that this is a little unusual but do you think that I could be given permission to live at home for this last term. We've almost finished classwork and I know that it would really help me if I could live in an environment where

Arabic completely engulfed me. My mother and father would go along with me. They're both Arabic speakers. They would agree to speak nothing but Arabic in the house. By June I should be really fluent again."

Sr. Clementine was not so hide-bound as she pretended and she had a soft spot for her prize student.

"Well, if it's all right with your parents and you complete you other classroom assignments, I don't see why it couldn't be arranged. Talk it over with them and let me know how they feel."

Needless to say Marie and Adlai were delighted with the plan and flattered and excited that they should be part of her Arabic *renaissance.*

Frank meanwhile, during the months of winter and early spring, had made seven round trip voyages to North America; one more to Canada and the rest to Boston or New York. True to her word, Izzy always made a point of being available for them to see each other. When his turnarounds in Liverpool included the weekend she could generally get permission to overnight at her parents' home. They would go to the pictures, now becoming all the rage, or they might go dancing; there the choice seemed to be between a *ceilidh* in a nearby parish with music provided by fiddle, piano and accordion or the elegant and recently-opened Grafton rooms, where a twelve-piece orchestra provided more sophisticated fare. One advantage of the Grafton was that they would be unlikely to run into his younger sisters who had started to spread their wings. Irish dances under the aegis of the church were considered by most Catholic parents to be an appropriate and prudent channeling of pubertal energies and Bridget and Mary were frequent and enthusiastic participants.

The time together was quite limited and the time spent together in private even more so. Frank would sedulously deliver Isabel to her front door no later than 11:30. He was now recognized by her parents as a 'boyfriend' and they seemed content with the arrangement. They now kissed goodnight as a matter of course when they arrived at her home. Izzy rather enjoyed that. She was not thrilled to the very marrow of her being as the lady's magazines seemed to indicate was par for the course but it was pleasant. Frank was a good kisser and getting better. She could not know just how much he looked forward to their goodnight ritual or how often he relived those moments between his visits but she could scarcely be unaware that he had fallen for her in a big way. It was gratifying but a little unnerving. She was just on the brink of entering the wider world beyond the classroom and she was not certain that she wanted to limit her options. It occurred to her that her upcoming retreat from the Anglophone world would give her the opportunity to put a brake on their relationship; to slow down the pace of their affair. He was becoming too urgent in his embraces for her comfort and she was not yet ready, she thought, to reciprocate his passion. The unease in the pit of her stomach during their goodnights irritated rather than pleased her.

During the weeks before their next get together the Easter holidays had come and gone and Izzy was safely domiciled in her family home. Frank, meanwhile, had been back and forth to New York. He had brought a present which he claimed was for her parents; a brand new recording by King Oliver's Creole Jazz Band which was all the rage over there and which featured an up and coming trumpeter named Louis Armstrong. He knew that the Iskandars owned a brand new Victor Orthophonic Victrola, the cost of which, it was rumored, was about that of a new Ford automobile. The Iskandars were enjoying their prosperity. When he gave it to Izzy she had to bring it in to present it to her father and what was probably the first performance in Liverpool of the soon-to-be-legendary trumpeter took place. Recorded music was so new then that they actually broke into applause when the recording ran out. After this promising start the evening took a decided turn for the worse as Izzy dropped the bombshell of her proposed retreat from the English-speaking world.

"Do you mean to say that I won't get to see you till you graduate? You can't mean it," he said when the implications of the proposal gradually registered.

"It's only for a little while and you'll be gone for most of that," she protested.

"But you don't know how much I look forward to seeing you. I can't bear the thought of not seeing you for so long."

He was not normally as forthright in his protestations of affection but the seemingly arbitrary disregard for his feelings had upset him badly. She could not care for him as much as he had hoped or as much as he yearned for her if she could face the prospect of a three-month hiatus in their relationship with such equanimity.

"Frank, I really need to do this. It's so important that I do well in my Orals. My degree depends on it and right now that's the most important thing in my life."

Frank was devastated but there was little more that he could say. He put on as brave a face as he could manage and agreed to honour her request that they remain *incommunicado* till June. The evening, for which he had had such high hopes, had ended at eight-thirty. He couldn't face the thought of going home at that hour and so he adjourned to the nearby Gregson's Well, where he spent the next two hours downing rather-too-many pints of mild and bitter and brooding over the heartlessness of women. Isabel had not exactly given him the 'old heave ho' but she had certainly shown him where he stood in the list of her priorities. At twenty-seven he had lost his heart late in life but he had lost it unreservedly. It would take a while to come to terms with the fact that love given is not always returned in equal measure.

Still the Kellys were a resilient breed. Next morning, after his headache had subsided, he felt more cheerful. Izzy had not actually broken off their relationship and what was three months after all? You don't survive four years in the trenches if you can't take a punch and come back for more. *'The slings and arrows of outrageous fortune'* would not get him down: no Hamlet, he! At least he still had his dignity. He hadn't pleaded--or at least not much--and he hadn't slammed the door when he left. He had even come up with a plan as to how to help to fill the gap in his social calendar. He would take Brendan and go to 'the match'. The Blues were at home to Aston Villa and he hadn't been to Goodison since he took up with Isabel. It just shows, he thought to himself, how women could mess up your priorities.

So she thinks that she can put me on hold for three months does she? I'll show her, he almost convinced himself, and sought out his brother to suggest the outing. Brendan's reaction to the proposal cheered him up too.

"Wait till you see Dixie Dean, Frank," he enthused. " He's the best centre forward in the league. He's already scored thirty goals this season."

It was indicative of the extent to which Miss Iskandar had dominated Frank's thoughts that, since Christmas, he had scarcely given a thought to the fate of his beloved Everton F.C. or for the young footballing phenomenon William Ralph Dean, whom they had acquired from Tranmere Rovers only last year for the sum of 3000 pounds.

"Tell you what, Bren. Let's get Da to come with us. He used to be a regular fan when he was a bit younger. We'll get tickets for the stands and neither of you will be shoved around standing in the terraces."

The outing was a resounding success. They were able to get seats in the stands; (a verbal paradox that crossed none of their minds). The crowd was a robust 48,000 and the Toffees delivered a convincing 3-1 victory over the Birmingham team with Dixie notching two goals. That evening Frank was entitled to a small glow of self-satisfaction. He had given his brother and his dad a day to remember. It had been almost a re-affirmation of tribal loyalty. Affiliation with Everton (the Toffees or the Blues, as they were sometimes hailed) was part of the genetic makeup of half the male citizenry of Liverpool. Of the other half, the less said the better. They simply didn't know any better: poor souls.

It wasn't until he again sailed, this time for New York, that he thought about his banishment from Izzy's company and he counseled himself with the thought that *he'd shown her, that he could get along just fine without her,* and *perhaps I'll even go out on the town in New York. There's plenty of fish in the sea.*

****

The subject of these ruminations was, by now, fully absorbed in the process of re-learning to speak and think in Arabic. Her parents entered into the spirit of the endeavour and treated it almost like a game. They were a little taken aback by the realization of how rusty their own Arabic had become. Their over ten years in England had inevitably seen a drop off in the frequency of usage of their native tongue. They would find themselves occasionally stopping to recall the exact Arabic word or phrase for even commonplace items. However, this was of minor significance and they, after a few days, were back up to speed. Isabel's progress was rather more gradual. Eleven years of living in Britain had had a much bigger influence on her fluency coming as it had been on a pre-adolescent mind than it had had on her parents.

She had never stopped speaking Arabic at home on occasion and had been studying the language in the rather more stilted environment of the University Language Department but she had long since stopped thinking in Arabic.

After the restrained exchange that had marked her last meeting with Frank Kelly, she was troubled for only a brief few minutes. She was not too unhappy that their relationship would have a cooling off period. She was not yet ready to decide that he would be the only man in her life. Anyway, it wasn't as if he was out of her life forever. She just needed the next two months to prepare for finals. *If Frank didn't like it he could lump it,* she thought with uncharacteristic vehemence. Besides he didn't seem to take it too hard. She had been a little surprised and maybe a little disappointed at the apparent nonchalance with which Frank had taken his exile. The British *penchant* for the stiff upper lip was a little overrated she thought.

Too much of a good thing eventually palls. For the first week or two the Iskandar family reveled in their new project. In a shorter time than she had feared, Isabel found that she was conversing effortlessly with her parents. They too made a conscious effort to have conversations with her. Therein lay the problem. When the purported object of her stay was to make conversation in Arabic, all the Iskandars felt an obligation to converse all the time. When silence broke out each of the three felt that he or she was letting the side down. They found themselves looking forward to the various expeditions into the outside world that life still required of them; Isabel in completing her assignments at school, Marie running errands and attending the social obligations that were part of her upper middle class life and Adlai making his daily trips to the small office he maintained in Walton from which he supervised the affairs of his retail business 'empire' and other investments. These outings, though normally of no great general interest, at least gave some fodder for conversation. By early May, Mr. and Mrs. Iskandar were desperate for a change of plan. They didn't want to let their daughter down but they were all getting on each other's nerves. It was up to Adlai, his wife insisted, to break this news to Isabel. After supper the next evening was agreed to as a suitable time and he had all day to prepare.

"Dear heart," he said after the dishes had been cleared away, "We need to talk." The fact that he said this in English was, of itself, enough to get her attention.

"You know that we love you and want nothing more than your success--in school and in life. But your mother and I think that we need a change of plan. You already are speaking Arabic as though you had never left Egypt. We don't need to have longwinded formal conversations with each other. We are getting on each other's nerves. Why don't we just live together as though you were just home for the weekend. We can still talk in Arabic but if we lapse into English we needn't apologize. If those idiots down in London think there's anything wrong with the way you speak they'll have me to deal with," he added with a comic grimace.

"Oh Papa! Maman! You've no idea how happy you've made me," she sobbed with tears of relief. "I never thought that I'd actually look forward to dealing with a class of thirteen-year-old horrors but I just had to get out of the house occasionally and not be talking all the time. Now we can simply live together and let the chips fall where they may."

She wasn't sure how to say 'let the chips fall' in idiomatic Arabic but they were able to come up with a reasonable alternative. A lively etymological discussion ensued in both English and Arabic and the new regimen of assimilation rather than total immersion was instituted with great relief all round. In truth, Isabel's apprehensions concerning the Oral Exams were ill founded. She had an enormous advantage over the vast majority of British born would-be Arabists. It was only the thought of the awful consequences of failure that had caused her to panic. In the event, the experience was even enjoyable if only in retrospect. Her parents decided to make a family outing out of the ordeal. They would travel down together by train and book in at the Hotel Russell on Russell Square. It was very convenient to the Examination Hall and not too far from the West End. They proposed to take a few days afterwards to stay in London, see the sights and take in a few plays. The setting for the actual exam was fairly intimidating: the building austere and the exam room more suited for sixty participants than for one candidate and four examiners. Oddly enough her first inquisitor closely resembled one who had appeared in her earlier nightmares.

"Recite the fifteenth Sura of the Holy Koran," demanded a rather ferocious looking, middle aged, dark complected man with a prominently aquiline nose. She was struck by his remarkable resemblance to the *Wazzir* in Aladdin and this comic image served to allay her jitters.

"I am, of course, familiar with the Holy Koran, sir, but I cannot claim to know it by heart," she answered in flawless Arabic. "I would be glad to read it for you." She noted the relaxation on the faces of the two other male examiners and a ghost of a smile on the lips of the sole female.

"And are you Sunni or Shiite, Miss Iskandar."

"I am not of the Islamic faith, Sir. I am a Catholic," she said, "but," she added, "I don't see what my religion has to do with my proficiency as a speaker of Arabic."

"Quite right, Miss Iskandar," jumped in another examiner--the chairman as it turned out. He had had some trouble with his colleague before and didn't want any complaints forwarded to the Board of Regents. Even judges have to be accountable to some one. From that point on the exam became a formality: more of a conversation than an interrogation. The lady examiner had obviously enjoyed the comeuppance of her male colleague and was openly friendly.

"Your accent intrigues me, Miss Iskandar. I think that I'm hearing an Egyptian but then a touch of Lebanon creeps in. Where did you acquire that?"

"Well Madam, my father is from Alexandria and my mother was born in Lebanon but the final gloss was put on it in Liverpool."

CHAPTER SEVEN

London, 1926

A nice feature of Oral Exams is that there is a very short time to wait for the outcome. The examiners have to make their minds up as soon as each interview is over. Delay would only make their impressions hazier. Evaluation of a candidate's proficiency in language is inevitably a highly subjective one. It was only five o'clock on the evening of the same day that the results were posted on the notice board of the Examination Hall. Isabel was not particularly anxious. She knew that the examination had gone well. The female examiner had virtually told her so; by her manner if not by her words. Isabel was content to wait until the crowd milling around the notice board had subsided. It was not difficult to tell how the other examinees had fared. Their faces told the story as they turned away. Most had obviously done well. Typically, students who survived the rigors of obtaining a degree through the non-traditional paths of the London University External Curriculum were highly motivated. Only two of the two dozen had obviously received bad news. With averted gaze they hurried from the building. In contrast the successful candidates lingered to congratulate each other. Smiling faces abounded and relieved laughter rang out throughout the hallowed halls. Isabel had recorded an outstanding mark of 95; by a margin of eight points the highest on the list. A mark higher than 95 would have been unprecedented. It was theoretically possible to achieve a perfect score in the Mathematical Sciences but not in the

Arts. Shakespeare could not have achieved it in English Lit, or Gibbon in Roman History.

She was now, in all but for the presentation of the diploma, Miss Isabel Iskandar, B.A. London. She hurried to the Hotel Russell where her parents were waiting for her in the lobby.

"Oh! Ma chère, I am so happy," said Marie relapsing into French as she so often did in times of high emotion.

"This calls for a celebration," said the proud papa giving his daughter a huge hug. "Let's all go into the bar. I just knew that you'd pass. I've got a bottle of *Veuve Cliquot* chilling."

Both Marie and Isabel promptly burst in to tears. Who can explain women? After they had done justice to the champagne they adjourned to their suite upstairs. Adlai had proposed a big night on the town. This was Isabel's first visit to the capital but the Iskandars had made annual trips since his business successes and they were quite familiar with the West End, its restaurants and its theatres.

"How about we take in *No! No! Nanette* at the Palace and then we can have a late supper at the Café de Paris?" He and Marie had dined at the Café de Paris on their first trip to London and it was their favorite. For Isabel the occasion not only marked her academic success but the recognition of her status as an adult. It was a very happy young woman who finally fell asleep that night with the rumblings of the city traffic four stories below.

On her return home she made an appointment with Sister Celestine at the Mount to discuss her prospects for employment and to get her counsel. Sister C. was well known to have a comprehensive knowledge of the Liverpool job market, at least where Catholic schools were concerned.

"First let me congratulate you, Isabel. You've been a great credit to Mount Pleasant. You are only the third one of our girls to have earned the London degree in the last decade," said the nun after first offering her tea and a plate of biscuits; the first time that this courtesy had been proffered during Isabel's student years.

"Thank you, Sister. What do you think of my prospects for getting a post as a French teacher?"

"Right now, I'm afraid that I know of no openings in the local high schools. But don't be downhearted," she added as Isabel's face fell. "You have at least three options and then, if you don't like them, I know of one other possibility that just might suit you. First, you could consider one of the non-Catholic high schools. I believe that there'll be an opening at Holly Lodge. That's out on Queens Drive."

"Yes, I know Holly Lodge. Its right behind the Jolly Miller." The good nun ignored this piece of incidental intelligence and moved on. "Secondly, you might widen your search to include schools further out from the city. Most of our Catholic schools are in the north of England or even Scotland but perhaps you will not want to live so far away from your parents. Finally, you could try teaching in the Elementary schools till an opening for a French teacher turns up. You are qualified, you know. I know you're not enthusiastic about that idea," she added as Isabel's face fell, "but maybe you might find the youngsters more to your taste--perhaps the seven or eight-year-olds.

"This last suggestion, in fact, is what I'm going to recommend to you. You are probably not aware but the Sisters of Mercy have acquired a beautiful property out in West Derby and are planning to build a convent school. It's to be called Broughton Hall and it's due to open next year. There will certainly be openings on the staff for a French teacher. Indeed, they'll be recruiting an entire staff. I think its safe to say that, with the recommendation that I will give you, and your academic record, you could count on a post in the fall of 1927."

"Thank you, Sister," Isabel replied and tried to hide her disappointment. It wasn't what she had hoped for. She wasn't enthusiastic about any of the options that Sr.

Celestine had laid out. She had spent the last dozen years of her life in an almost exclusively Catholic environment and was reluctant to leave its comfortable familiarity. She liked the thought of familiar Merseyside landmarks and the proximity of her parents. Finally the thought of trying to cope with the little horrors in the parochial schools--even the seven and eight-year-olds--gave her a cold chill. Isabel was not an adventurous girl. She was conventional in her outlooks. She was modern enough to wish to pursue a career but she envisaged that in the context of marriage and family presumably within the Catholic faith. She lacked her mother's courage: to follow her heart and to leave behind the comforts of the known and familiar.

"Let me have a week to mull over my options and I will let you know my decision on Friday," she said. This was too big a decision to make on the spot.

"Don't take too long. I know that at least three Elementary Schools haven't yet filled out their staffs; St. Sylvester's, Sacred Heart and Our Lady's, Wavertree. Let me know your decision and God bless you, my child," the Sister Superior said bringing the interview to a close and gently propelling her from her office.

Chapter Eight
Brockton, Massachusetts, 1923-1926

At about the time when the Iskandars were bidding a tearful goodbye to their daughter as she started the crosstown trip to Mount Pleasant, the parents of another seventeen year old, one Josefina Lucca, were breathing a sigh of relief. They had just delivered their daughter into the trusted hands of the Dominican Sisters of the Presentation who operated St. Anne's Hospital in Fall River, Mass. in the U.S.A. and, more specifically, its highly regarded School of Nursing. The teenage years of young Josie had provided them with many anxious moments and they were glad to shift the responsibility to the Sisters.

Miss Lucca had reached puberty early. By age thirty she would probably be matronly and *deo volente*, safely married. At seventeen she was a disaster waiting to happen. Blessed (or cursed, depending on your point of view) with long shapely legs and a figure that could, and often did, stop traffic, she also possessed a Madonna-like tranquility of countenance which made a provocative contrast and an irresistible challenge to the young males at Brockton High School. Only the Lucca family name gave the aspiring *Don Juans* pause. Gaetano Lucca, Josefina's father was the owner and operator of the Club Genovese and he was known to be connected to the Mafia.

That Mafia activity was a factor in Brockton was widely accepted but its presence was not too onerous. Brockton was a smallish town with small town values and, except for a little gambling and loan sharking, there was little scope for Mafia activity. Most of the numerous shoe factories that dominated the local economy were even non-union. This was the situation until 1920 when the 19th amendment to the U.S. Constitution was passed and prohibition became the law of the land. Nationally, the country went on a drinking binge. It hadn't been exactly abstemious before. 'Crime' became 'Organized Crime'. In Brockton, little changed on the surface. Prohibition was a movement largely driven by the Protestant churches and Boston, with its large Irish population that included most of the police force and was governed by Mayor James Michael Curley, was careless to a fault in enforcing the law. The Taverna Genovese became the Club Genovese; a fraternal organization complete with a trap door window in a heavily reinforced front door and blacked out windows.

The town of Brockton is roughly half way between Boston and Providence, Rhode Island and it had been formally agreed by Filippo "Phil" Buocola and Rosanno "Red Ball" Testarosa, the respective dons of the two towns, that Brockton would be considered a neutral zone. The Club Genovese would serve as a meeting place for the resolutions of inter-familial differences. Still even this minimal association with *la Cosa Nostra* was sufficient to keep randy teenagers from taking too many liberties with the daughter of Gaetano Lucca. This did not entirely please Josefina for she was a lusty girl. She had no doubt that she could handle teenage boys and would have liked the opportunity to practice her technique.

Somewhat to her surprise Jo found that she enjoyed Nursing School. She was intelligent and found the study of Anatomy and Physiology stimulating: the relationship of form to function. Pharmacology and Chemistry were a bit of a drag but Pathology, the study of disease, was fascinating in a macabre sort of way. As with most of the schools of nursing of the time, St. Anne's students were launched into the clinical practice of Nursing at a very early stage in their training and indeed provided a major part of the care rendered on the wards. By the end of their first term they were doing much of the routine work; making beds, emptying bedpans, serving food and taking vital signs. Administration of medications came later but in her second year of training, she was taking serious responsibility, particularly in the nighttime hours. She was frequently in sole charge of a thirty bed ward with only one senior staff nurse, 'the ramp tramp,' as back up for the whole hospital. She liked taking care of the women and children but she *loved* working on the men's ward. The convalescent men clamored to help her distribute the meals and she was well aware of the enthusiastic scrutiny that she underwent when she walked the length of the ward. She had a quick wit and developed a talent for *repartee* that she indulged when the supervisory nurses were not within earshot. She was becoming a good nurse and a great morale booster.

The student nurses lived and took their classes in the Nurses Home adjoining the hospital. There was a great sense of camaraderie. Previous weekends were discussed. Gossip was exchanged and lies told but conversing with the same girls for three years was not enough to meet the needs of a healthy and highly sexed twenty-year-old young woman. Of course there was time off on weekends and an occasional event that involved the Medical as well as the Nursing Staffs, but St. Anne's was not a teaching hospital. There was no resident medical staff to provide romantic possibilities and the visiting staff were, overwhelmingly, she discovered, middle-aged, married, or both. When the third year finally came to an end-- the state exams passed and she was awarded the prized R.N.-- she decided that a drastic change was in order. She didn't fancy going back to Brockton where she would again be under the loving but watchful eye of her parents. The siren song of Boston was calling her and she listened.

****

Boston General Hospital was an enormous institution with over 640 beds. It was situated in South Boston on Harrison Avenue and was still generally considered as a 'charity' hospital as it had, indeed, been originally intended. It provided the entire spectrum of medical and surgical specialties and provided low cost or free medical care for much of the population of Greater Boston. If it lacked the prestige of the hospitals associated with the Harvard Medical School--Mass. General, Peter Bent Brigham, and Boston Children's--it made up for it, in Jo's estimation, by being affiliated with both of the city's other two medical schools. Both Tufts and B.U. had a major presence at the General and, in fact, essentially divided the patients up between them. This meant that the place would be teeming with young doctors and medical students. She wasn't particularly mercenary; she simply wanted to be surrounded by young men who were eager to get her into bed. If they were also good-looking and potentially well off, even in the distant future, she could live with that. After three years in Fall River she could not wait to spread her wings in the big city.

The first necessity was to find a place to live. She thought that she could probably afford to rent a small apartment if she could find a compatible flat-mate. That shouldn't be too difficult. Boston was a city with an enormous annual turnover in the 18-30 year old population. No city in the country could match its percentage of students within the city limits. Well, perhaps Ann Arbor, Michigan where the entire population attended the University of Michigan, she had been told. The most obvious and cheapest plan was to pin a series of hand written adverts on the various student notice boards in the hospitals and nearby colleges. This she did.

> Recent R.N. graduate seeks young woman to share apartment within walking distance of Boston General Hospital. Please contact me at the YWCA, Commonwealth Ave, Boston. Jo Lucca

She wanted to avoid the need for a car and she particularly wanted to steer well clear of the North End, which was the Italian section of town and where her older married sister, Theresa, was living with her family. She loved her sister but wanted as complete a break as possible from the surveillance of disapproving eyes. She hadn't exactly decided on earning that disapproval but she hadn't ruled out the possibility. The next step was to survey the adverts that other seekers of flat-mates had posted and to survey the listings of apartments for rent. The problem appeared daunting but the reality proved to be surprisingly easy. On a break for coffee during her first duty shift; noon to 10pm, on Womens Surgical/BU Service, she was approached by a short attractive blonde staff nurse whose name plate proclaimed that she was Jennifer Hudson, R.N., a young Yankee presumably and a prototypical WASP (white Anglo-Saxon protestant).

"I was hoping to catch you tonight," she said as they sipped the much-needed coffee. "I'm Jenny Hudson. I'm from over on the Tufts side--Mens Med. I saw you putting up your notice and I thought I'd try to catch you during your break. I've just broken up with my boyfriend and I need someone to share the expenses. Do you think you might be interested?"

Jo was a little taken aback by the forthrightness of this statement. She was planning herself on becoming a free spirit but this girl had obviously taken to the Bohemian life with a vengeance. Still, she was intrigued. Jennifer Hudson looked like she might be the perfect flat-mate for her. She obviously knew the ropes. She would know the local haunts and (an important 'and') she was cute; cute enough to be a roommate but not so beautiful that she would be serious competition.

"I'm really happy that you stopped by, Jenny. By the way, I'm Josefina Lucca but I go by Jo. I'm certainly eager to be settled in somewhere. The YWCA gets old in a hurry. Where's your place?"

"It's just off Commonwealth Ave; not more than ten minutes from the hospital," Jenny replied.

"Maybe we could get together and see it tomorrow morning. I'm not back on duty till noon. I could meet you in the lobby if you're free--say nine o'clock and you can show me your place. Give me all the sordid details--like the cost," she added with a grin.

"It's a deal. I'm sure that we'll hit it off just fine even though I can see that I'd better put blinkers on any boyfriends I may have from now on."

"Oh! I'm sure that you can hold your own," Jo lied, and on this mutually satisfactory note they parted leaving Jo to finish her coffee and her shift.

CHAPTER NINE
Liverpool, 1926

Isabel left Mount Pleasant Teachers Training College for the last time as a student with mixed emotions. The possibility of teaching at a brand new Convent High school in what she knew was one of the more pleasant suburbs of Liverpool was exciting; exactly what she had been hoping for. How to make her living while waiting for the job to become available was what was putting a damper on her happiness. Finding herself on Hope Street she decided to stop in for a final farewell to her friends at the University. She had travelled between the two institutions so frequently during the past three years that she was scarcely aware of the massive construction project that was proceeding to her left; the crypt of the Metropolitan Cathedral. With the hubris generated by presiding over a population of over a quarter of a million Catholics in the city, the Archbishop of Liverpool had commissioned a magnificent and enormous edifice that would, when completed, be second in size only to St. Peter's in Rome.

The impracticality of that was far from her mind when she reached the University and sought out her former teachers and colleagues to say goodbye. On the way out she stopped to read the notice board, more by force of habit than with deliberate intent. Under the impressive letterhead of *La République Francaise* was a job notice.

Fluent French Speaker needed for Secretarial and Administrative duties
Hours 9-5:30 Mon-Fri, Sat 9-12 noon
Consulate of the French Republic
Suite 27. Royal Liver Building
Liverpool

The thought hit her like a bolt from the blue. This could be the solution to her dilemma. Granted, it was not exactly how she had envisaged her first job out of school but she only needed it for a year and how many opportunities to work in a French-speaking environment could there be in Liverpool. She resolved to act at once. *Audace! Toujours L'Audace!* This had been the motto of a French general who had sent tens of thousands of brave French soldiers to their deaths in the First World War. Isabel, who had never heard of the gentleman, was obviously cut from the same cloth. Audacity had not characterized her decision-making in her life to this point but today it showed itself. Climbing aboard a passing No. 81 tram, she trundled down Brownlow Hill and onto the Pier Head. There sat the Royal Liver Building that dominated the Liverpool skyline and perched atop, the mythic Liver bird. She entered the building and sought out the French Consulate.

"*Je veux faire une application a travailler dans le Consulat,*" she announced to the receptionist in flawless, if faintly Lebanese-accented French.

"*Yer wha',*" the young lady replied in Scouse, complete with glottal stop. The consulate had been having staffing problems and the receptionist was a temporary and not very satisfactory placeholder manning the front desk. Fortunately for all the parties concerned, no lesser personage than the Consul General himself happened to be walking by and overheard the exchange. He did not, as a practical matter, involve himself in the routine hiring and firing decisions made in the consulate. It was only a small operation with a half a dozen employees and he did have a deputy who supervised most of the routine affairs that justified its existence. He was a courtly elderly gentleman and a minor member of the French aristocracy--one whose career was now on the wane. Consul General to the City of Liverpool was certainly going to be the pinnacle of his diplomatic career. He was neither particularly intelligent nor ambitious and would happily retire in another three years to his ancestral home in Gascony. He had not, however, lost his eye for a *jolie fille* or his penchant for nineteenth century gallantry.

"Permit me to help you *Mademoiselle*. I am Etienne, Comte de St. Brioche, Les Trois Cloches, Consul General. I gather that you seek employment. How did you know we had a vacancy? Come into my office and we can discuss your qualifications. I can hear that your French accent is as flawless as your *visage*. Mademoiselle Longbottom, bring me three cups of coffee and ask Monsieur Martin to come to my office in a few minutes."

When they were seated, the Count behind an impressive desk with a panoramic view across the river to Birkenhead, Isabel gave a brief *précis* of her curriculum vitae and added that she had caught sight of the advertisement at the University Faculty office.

"I've asked Jacques Martin, my deputy, to step in in a little while. The hiring of staff is part of his er -er *Bailliage*," he stammered, "*Qu'est ce que c'est le mot juste en anglais?*"

"Bailiwick," Isabel supplied.

"I don't like to pre-empt his authority but I will be amazed if he doesn't think that you're the perfect choice. A girl who can pull 'bailiwick' out of the air must impress even him and his English is very good. The fact that you also speak Arabic will certainly intrigue him. His family owns vineyards in Algeria as well as in the Rhone valley near Avignon. I believe that he was born in Algeria and spent several years there in his teens. He speaks Arabic himself as you might expect. He is a regular *pied noir*. You are probably aware, Isabel, that *Algérie* is an integral part of France, and has its own representation in the General Assembly; just like Guadeloupe in the Caribbean.

At that point in the conversation the coffee was delivered by Miss Longbottom who proved that her coffee making was, fortunately, better than her French. She was followed, almost immediately, by the deputy consul, who proved to be a strikingly good-looking man in his early thirties. He was almost painfully thin and stood well above six feet tall. He had jet-black hair; combed straight back from his forehead and dark deeply seated eyes. He cast a frankly appraising gaze over her and Isabel felt an almost visceral jolt in her abdomen.

"Come in and meet Mademoiselle Iskandar, Jacques. She is applying for our open position. I think that you will find her exceptionally well qualified. Not that I wish to influence your decision," he lied flagrantly. "I think that you, in particular, will find interesting is that she is fluent in Arabic as well as French and, in fact, just completed her degree in London."

"Well congratulations, Mademoiselle," he said with a smile which transformed his rather severe features and again made her stomach lurch uncomfortably. *Look out for this one,* a voice in her subconscious said but she was all too conscious of the blood rushing to her face and the blush spreading down into her neck. If M. Martin was annoyed that his superior had invaded his province in recommending Isabel so blatantly, he gave no evidence of it.

"I think that we should waste no time in snapping her up, M. le Comte," he said. "Mademoiselle Iskandar, the job is yours. As of next Monday, if it is convenient to you, you will be an employee of *La République Francaise.* "Vive La France," he added with a disarming grin.

Isabel left the consulate walking on air. Her mind was a complete whirlwind of conflicting thoughts; elation at acquiring a new and exciting job; anxiety that she might have made a decision too rashly and without adequate consideration of the possible consequences. She needed time to reflect and also the counsel of a trusted confidante who could give her impartial advice. *But I do have such a friend,* she suddenly remembered, *and not only that, I believe she works in this very building.*

Her best friend, Kate Kelly, had worked for nearly six years in the London and NorthWest Assurance Company that was, if she remembered correctly, located in the Liver Building. A rapid scanning of the floor listings next to the lifts proved this to be correct and she promptly rode up to the eleventh floor and looked up her friend. Kate turned out to be off in half an hour and they agreed to travel home on the tram together. Kate was almost as anxious to learn what it was that was causing her normally placid friend to sound so excited, as Isabel was to discuss all the amazing upheavals in her life.

Between the Liver Building and the Pier Head where the ferries docked was an open area of about 100 yards depth that stretched from the Albert Dock to the south and the Huskisson Dock to the north. It was the only spot on the Liverpool side of the Mersey where the public had ready access to the river. The area served also as the terminus for many of the tram routes that converged on the city centre. Thus it was very convenient for the workers in the Liver and the Cunard offices and so it was, shortly after 5:30, that the old friends were safely installed on the upper deck of the No. 74 tram heading home.

"So, tell me what you're up to?" prompted Kate. "What are you doing in my part of town?"

"I've just got myself a new job," replied Isabel, "and I don't know whether to be glad or sorry."

"What sort of a job? There aren't any schools within a mile of here," her friend asked.

"It's not a teaching job. I'm going to be working at the French Consulate."

"Lord! You're a deep one. You're the last person in the world that I would have taken for such a leap in the dark."

"It's not quite such a bold step and anyway, that's why I wanted a chance to talk it over with an old friend;

somebody older and wiser," she added with a dig in the ribs. The two were born six weeks apart.

"I'm always willing to give the benefit of my worldly wisdom to youngsters. Come on! Spill the beans."

Isabel gave her friend a brief account of the circumstances that had led up to her decision and pointed out that it would only be for a year; a fact that she had omitted to mention to her prospective employers. But then, they hadn't asked.

"Izzy! That's fantastic news," gushed Kate. "We'll be working in the same building. If our working hours coincide we could even travel back and forth together." A sudden thought struck her. "You know what? I've been thinking about this for quite some time. We're both twenty-two years old and still living at home. It's not so bad for you living with your folks in your posh mansion but I share a room with two teenage sisters. They're decent kids but they can be a pain at times. How about if we move out and get a flat together?"

Isabel was more than a little taken aback by this idea. She knew that her father would be horrified at the thought of his little girl out by herself in the wicked world.

"Daddy would have a fit," she temporized.

"Come on Izzy; you're a big girl now. You're over twenty-one. You'll be earning your own living. Besides, you've been living away at school for the past three years. He can hardly object. Especially if he knows that you'll be living with a model citizen like me," she countered. "I'll admit. I have the most to gain from the deal. In fact I simply couldn't afford a flat by myself but think of all the fun we can have together. My brother Frank isn't the only fellow I could introduce you to," she added with a cynical lack of sisterly loyalty.

This last proposition, though intended largely in jest, did spark a flicker of interest in Izzy. She liked Frank and liked the convenience of having a steady beau. In fact she half expected that at some time, probably in the dim and distant future, they would marry and raise a family but the thought of a little innocent dalliance along the way held a certain illicit attraction. This thought quickly triggered another.

"Tell me Kate; you've been working in the Liver Building for nearly six years. What can you tell me about that Rudolph Valentino character who works in the Consulate?"

"Izzy, my old friend! You've got a side to you I didn't suspect. Pick on somebody your own size. There aren't enough fellas around here tall enough to want to be seen with an Amazon like me. Besides, he's married--got a wife back in France--so the rumor goes."

"Ah well! *C'est la Vie,* as we say at the consulate," Izzy countered with a rueful grin. "I've never noticed that you had any shortages of boyfriends," she added.

"Shortage! Shortage! That's the problem. I'm looking for a white knight whose about six foot six, who'll sweep me off my feet and we can raise a family of giants."

"Well, don't hold your breath. I bet you end up falling in love with Jimmy Murphy," Isabel teased referring to one of Kate's shortest and most inarticulate admirers. They bantered back and forth as the tram clanked up the low hills that led to Everton Brow.

"Here comes your stop. I'll think over your idea. I must say it sounds appealing if we could pull it off. I'll lay the groundwork with Daddy. I'm sure he won't be too happy but *Maman* will stick up for me. She was a bit of a free spirit when she was my age or so she tells me."

Surprisingly, as it turned out, it was in the Kelly household that the prospect of the departure of their eldest daughter from the family hearth and home produced the greatest resistance. For the Kelly family the reasons were mainly financial. Frank Senior had been unwell for some time. He had been a heavy smoker since age fourteen and was addicted to his two packets of Woodbines a day. His smoker's cough and wheezing had become almost an accepted part of the ambient background noise of the Kelly household. A stevedore's job calls for hard physical labour in all kinds of weather. Of late he had been unable to handle it and recently had been bedridden for two weeks with a bout of flu that had ended in pneumonia.

Kate's contribution to the family budget would be vital if Dad couldn't work regularly. On the positive side, Bridget was now fully employed at a local ladies hairdressers shop and Mary had just started working at Hartley's Jam Factory in Aintree. The girls were supportive of the move and looked forward to gaining a little more space in the bedroom. With Kate gone, each could have her own bed. The family, finally, agreed that they could forgo Kate's salary as long as Dad was able to continue working. Frank had also been contributing a little more each year as he'd assumed greater responsibility with Cunard. Kate could, of course, have left home without the family blessing but her conscience wouldn't have permitted this. Family loyalty is often stronger among the poor than among the better off.

Isabel, meanwhile, had a double shock to deliver to her parents; not only was she proposing to defect from the family home but also to make a drastic change in her career path. The impact of the latter was such that the former-- moving out--was approved almost without objection.

"But Isabel, darling," her mother cried when Isabel explained her plans. She had waited till dinner was over and had requested a meeting with both parents. "You have been preparing to teach since you were fifteen years old. How can you throw that away?"

Her father chimed in, "You'll be giving up a respected profession to be a glorified secretary. You're not even qualified to be a proper secretary. I know you can type but you can't even take shorthand."

"But *Papa! Maman!* Don't you see? I'm not giving up on becoming a teacher. This is just a temporary job before this perfect position becomes available." She told them about the 1928 opening of the new convent school one year hence and described how Sr. Clementine had given her a virtual assurance of obtaining the post there as French teacher.

"At the French Consulate I will at least be able to keep up my language skills. I would otherwise have to spend a year teaching grubby urchins how to read in the parochial school or else to find a job miles away."

She knew that this prospect would be the telling factor that would reconcile her parents to her decision. At least the French Consulate was located in the city. They would be able to stay in close touch. With much hemming and hawing, they acquiesced. Adlai, in fact, proved to be a huge help in the move once he had come to terms with the idea. If Isabel wasn't to live at home, at least he could assure himself that she wasn't living in squalor. The girls had found a very promising flat which occupied the first floor of a large Victorian house that had been divided into three apartments. It was on Shiel Road in Kensington. It had two bedrooms and a decent kitchen as well as a large living room, which had been the master bedroom in the original house. The furnishings were sparse and rather battered in appearance; the previous tenants had been university students and the entire flat had a hangdog appearance.

The girls had not realized how formidable would be the expense of furnishing and refurbishing of a large flat; nor had they realized the work involved. Here Adlai stepped into the breach with an enthusiasm that even Henry the Fifth would have admired. In less than a week, moving men and painters had been hired, new mattresses, bed linens, cutlery and kitchenware had been purchased, the expenses being assumed by Izzy's doting father. Furniture, deemed disposable in the Iskandar house, was transported and installed. Fresh paint made a definite improvement in covering up the depredations of the years of student occupancy. Exactly one week after signing the lease they moved in. They were very excited. The main living room had a magnificent bay window that overlooked the park. They settled down that evening after dinner in their two serviceable armchairs to discuss further plans for the beautification, starting with new curtains. They had even purchased a bottle of celebratory wine from the off-licence to mark the occasion and they toasted each other and congratulated themselves on their good fortune and good judgment.

"We're only five minutes walk from London Road. We'll be able to catch the tram from there. We'll only be twenty minutes from work," rejoiced Kate.

Izzy added, "We can reach our folks home in under fifteen and there's plenty to do within striking distance."

"Wait till Frank sees our new place," Kate said. "Won't he be amazed to see us living together? His favorite sister and ONE of his favorite girlfriends," she teased. Frank's constancy was a well-established fact. Julius Caesar, who had pronounced himself 'constant as the Northern Star,' had nothing on him.

"He's due home on Thursday. Why don't we plan on having a welcome dinner for him." Isabel had almost forgotten about Frank. The two months of self-imposed solitary confinement had been followed by the excitement of all that had happened since graduation; a new job and a new flat. Remembering Frank produced mixed feelings. She was ambivalent. On the one hand, she found him weirdly attractive: the scarred face and the black eye patch. She enjoyed his company. He had become a pleasant, if predictable, feature of her life. On the other hand, her life was now abrim with new possibilities: a new job and new domestic circumstances, new people in her life. *Who could tell, maybe even a new lover.* Even as that term popped into her brain, it gave her a *frisson* of guilty pleasure. The word 'lover' was certainly not the way she thought of Frank. The physical aspects of their friendship had scarcely progressed beyond the modest goodnight embrace at the front door of her parents' home. When she thought of him, and she thought of him only occasionally of late, it was with imaginings of a vague future domesticity rather than with passion or excitement. *Still, she thought, there's much to be said for domestic bliss. Too much is happening in my life for me to want to ditch Frank as well. I do like having him around.*

"I'll tell you what, Kate," she said. "Why don't we have a real party and invite your folks and mine? It'll give us the chance to say thank you for all the help that they have given us." They agreed that this was a great idea and resolved to purchase formal invitations next day to mark the importance of the event. They then spent a thoroughly enjoyable evening planning the menu, dividing up the shopping duties and, finally, fell contentedly into their new beds at 11:00 p.m.

The *S.S. Carmania* docked on the morning tide two days later and by mid-afternoon the passengers had all been landed, their luggage sorted out and they had passed through H.M. Customs and were on their way; many on the boat-train to London and most of the rest by taxi to one of the city's three main railway stations. The housekeeping duties that occupied the staff had been completed and they were all looking forward to five days at home. Frank arrived home in Garnet Avenue to find the household in a tizzy. His return from Canada--this time it had been a round trip to Quebec--produced a predictable excitement but the invitation from Kate and Izzy had put his parents into a veritable dither. They were respectable working class folk, and in normal circumstances had little or no social contact with their 'betters' and the Iskandars with their elegant home and live-in servants were definitely 'toffs.'

"What shall I wear?" Mrs. Kelly agonized.

"I won't know what to talk about," Frank Sr. muttered aloud pacing back and forth in the two steps that were all that the tiny kitchen permitted.

"Don't worry, Da," his son reassured him. "I listen to the toffs rattling on at the dinner table on board ship and they talk about exactly the same things that we do. Try the Captain on football or the price of beer. Better keep off trade unions though," he added.

Frank Sr. was an avid trades unionist and had participated in the abortive General Strike of 1926. In this he was actually misjudging Adlai who had been firmly on the side of the strikers during their recent confrontation that had witnessed the middle class, students and bank managers operating the tramcars and policing the streets to help break the strike.

"You'll be union too if Cunard ever threatens to cut your wages and your job benefits," added Frank Sr. It was a long-standing difference between them and they had agreed to let sleeping dogs lie. The party was going to provide enough conversation and excitement without getting into politics.

****

The party proved to be a great success. Through her mother's connections at the market, Kate had obtained, at a great price, a spectacular goose that they had served with stuffing, roast potatoes, carrots and Brussels sprouts. Izzy had consulted with her mother's cook and had tried her hand at an apple pie. Adlai had even provided two bottles of his prized Sancerre from his cellar; a generous contribution. It had cost him five guineas a bottle. For two babes-in-the-kitchen it had been an ambitious meal but 'fortune favors the brave', it is said, and all had gone off well. An 'epicure' may have carped that the stuffing had absorbed rather too much of the grease with which geese are so abundantly blessed but this was family, not some self indulgent Greek philosopher. Everything was found pleasing and the cooks were showered with compliments. The older Iskandars, sensing the apprehension of the Kelly parents, went out of their way to be friendly. Adlai paid Mrs. Kelly some courtly compliments and soon coaxed Mr. Kelly into conversation with comic reminiscences of his days in seaports around the Mediterranean. Dockland humor was, apparently, the same all around the globe.

Marie was soon sharing an animated chat with Mrs. Kelly. She knew that she could do no wrong if the conversation leaned heavily on the virtues of her elder son. Mrs. Kelly was soon convinced of the soundness of Marie's judgment and was equally eloquent in singing the praises of the young Isabel; her beauty and her accomplishments. The party broke up at eleven o'clock with the Iskandars offering to transport the Kellys home in their elegant car. This may well have been the high point of the evening for the senior Kellys, neither of whom had even ridden in a Morris, never mind a Hispano-Suiza. The only member of the party with joy somewhat alloyed was Frank Jr. who had not been able to have more than a couple of minutes alone with Isabel. He was, however, mollified by her agreeing to see him again. This time, he resolved, it would be just the two of them.

The remaining three days of his stay ashore set the pattern for their relationship. They went to the cinema and stopped off for fish and chips on the way home. They went to a dance at the Grafton and on the eve of his departure they rode the tram to the Pier Head and took the ferry to Birkenhead and back. If you started on the Liverpool side and didn't get off in Birkenhead, the round trip didn't cost anything. This only saved a couple of pence but it is always nice to get something for nothing and the ferry ride back provided the best possible view of the Liverpool waterfront.

When the couple arrived back at the front door of her new apartment Isabel was faced with a new decision: how to end the evening. She hesitated momentarily but realized that a modest peck on the lips, which had been the extent of their intimacy at her parents' front door, would not satisfy an ardent suitor anymore. It would seem odd not to invite him in if only on the pretext of saying goodnight to his sister. Kate, ever the loyal sister, had gone to bed, it transpired, and Frank took advantage of his first opportunity to pull Isabel onto his lap and to subside into the depths of the larger of the two armchairs. For Isabel this was the most intimate experience of her life. She had participated in a few games of Postman's Knock at birthday parties and had experienced some teenage gropings. She had also been on the receiving end of Frank's chaste embraces at her front door but this was intimacy on an entirely new plane. His right arm was around her waist and the other, on her shoulder, with which he pulled their upper bodies together. Her immediate response was a stiffening of her muscles. This was a new experience for her but then she found it pleasant and allowed her body to relax and conform itself to Frank's. She felt her lips soften for the kissing that she knew would follow. It did and Isabel found it very enjoyable. Ten minutes later, her sense of propriety and her lover's increasing ardour made her decide to call it a night. She thanked Frank for a lovely evening and cited her flatmate's presence on the other side of the bedroom door as a reason for bringing the evening to a close.

Frank made his way home in an exhilarated if somewhat confused state. The evening had gone better than he had ever dreamed possible. By her responses to his lovemaking Isabel had shown that she returned his feelings. He was not upset that she had brought the evening to a close after their embraces in the armchair. He, at some level, expected it and would have been alarmed if the brakes had not been applied. He was not, technically, a virgin. On one occasion during his army years in France, he had joined his comrades in a visit to a French brothel situated in a village near a rest area. He had found the experience sordid and depressing. Only a sense of pity rather than passion had allowed him to consummate the encounter that left him feeling thoroughly ashamed of himself. He had had very little sexual experience since that time. While it was true that his brain was relieved that the evening's lovemaking was concluded, his body had a different reaction. His dreams that night were very graphic.

CHAPTER TEN
Liverpool, 1927

The situation that now faced the pair was not at all unusual for couples of their generation and social class. Christian teaching, Protestant and Catholic alike, forbade extra-marital sex and most Christians made some effort to live by the rules. Contraception was very unreliable and to many, abhorrent. The threat and consequences of giving illegitimate birth were very inhibiting, not only to women but also to any man with a conscience. For many couples, particularly those of modest means, engagements were lengthy. Saving up to afford the establishment of a household frequently took several years. All these factors contributed to a culture of restraint and self-control within the middle classes and for much of the poor. There were, of course, innumerable violations of these rules and taboos. Nature has implanted in the human race potent urges, both psychological and hormonal that are difficult to resist. Men, in particular, are quicker and more urgently aroused and, in terms of pregnancy, have far less to lose. Polite society, in particular, scorned the unmarried mother but turned a blind eye on its 'gilded youth' when they sowed their wild oats. By convention it had become the perceived responsibility of young women to set and enforce the limits in the dealings with their admirers.

The pattern of behaviour that evolved in the relationship of Frank Kelly and Isabel Iskandar was, therefore, not too atypical in its day and age. It was perhaps a little easier for them than for other couples as Frank was away from home for so much of the time. Over the course of her employment at the consulate, they had gradually become more comfortable with each other and with the fact that they were, in fact, a couple. They had drifted, almost without making a conscious decision, into the acceptance that they were destined for each other. In this regard Frank was the happier. Isabel was more than he could possibly have hoped for. He did not deserve such a beautiful and gifted girl. She was so much smarter and better educated. She should, by rights, be escorted by some handsome young professional man; an architect or lawyer or banker; not a working class lad with a glass eye.

In that matter, his views mirrored those of Isabel's father. He liked Frank but thought that Isabel should set her sights higher on the social scale when choosing her beaus. Isabel was troubled, to a degree, by the same considerations as her father. Frank was the first man with whom she had ever been involved romantically. She enjoyed his company and their modest intimacies but she was not completely happy to be drifting into a permanent liaison before she had had a chance to play the field. She knew that men found her attractive. Perhaps there was someone out there who would not only be a more fitting partner for her in the eyes of the world (and incidentally her father's) but who would sweep her off her feet; a man of education, sophistication and dashing good looks. *I am not ready to close the door on that possibility*, she thought.

In the meantime, she was content to have Frank as a predictable and compliant suitor. She could rely on his devotion and enjoy their intimacy without worry that it would get out of hand. They both accepted, without putting it into words, that Isabel was the final arbiter as to the limits of their sexual intercourse. Their kissing became quite comprehensive and pushed the limits of physiological possibility. Isabel came to discover that her nipples, when stimulated by Frank's fingers or, in time, by his tongue, gave her almost as much satisfaction as it appeared to give him.

As the months passed by even her bra and blouse were occasionally discarded in the course of their lovemaking when they were reasonably certain of Kate's continued absence. The belt line and the bedroom door marked the unspoken limits of their tentative sexual explorations. They did not venture into the bedroom and Frank limited his explorations to the regions above the waist. They would wait a year. Then, if all their plans fell into place, Izzy would have her new job and they could start planning to be married. This, at least, was Frank's assumption. Maybe he could even think of applying for a land-based job. It was by no means certain but he thought that it was a possibility. He had begun to assume responsibilities in the re-victualing arena--the re-provisioning of *Carmania* at its various ports of call. Certainly a job ashore would make for a much more satisfactory married life.

****

Work at the consulate proved not to be as glamourous as Isabel had perhaps expected. Most of the transactions were in English and involved the routine processing of visa applications, renewal of passports for French citizens domiciled in Britain and rendering assistance to distressed French sailors who had fallen afoul of the law or who had missed their ship. On the plus side, her typing had improved immeasurably and she did have the opportunity to hone her French (with the members of the staff who were, in fact, French). Kate's 'heartthrob', the Deputy Consul General proved not to be too large a part of Izzy's life. Isabel found that she was wishing that this were not the case. He was something of an enigma. He managed to convey the impression that he found her attractive but, even after she had worked at the consulate for six months, had made no overture that she could realistically interpret as a 'pass.' Could it be that he was married with a wife safely billeted in France or that he was honouring, by his restraint, her known relationship with a local man? If that were the case, it was very frustrating. She was not formally engaged to Frank and she would have liked to have had positive evidence that other men found her desirable.

The French Consulate hosted a Christmas party every year. The entire staff was only ten in number and so invitations were tendered to the two adjoining office suites to swell the ranks of the merrymakers. It was the one big social event of the year and had acquired a well-deserved reputation for lavish hospitality. The festivities started at the close of business and caterers had prepared a handsome buffet. Many of the invitees from the other offices had started their own office celebrations several hours before arriving and were already in festive mood. The secretaries had changed into their party dresses and the girls from the *Consulat*, with the reputation of French *couture* to uphold, had not allowed themselves to be outshone. Isabel had blown her annual clothing budget on a designer dress in fire engine red, which ended just below her knees and clung to her slim figure thus showing off to their best advantage her pale olive skin and shapely legs. The guests took advantage of the availability of the apparently limitless supply of vintage champagne and the party got off to a rollicking start. Champagne is a surprisingly potent drink.

M. le Comte, the Consul General himself, was in fine form; dancing with all the *jolies filles* and showering them with extravagant compliments. The high spot of his contribution to the evening was his rather rambling speech of welcome in which he extolled the close bonds of friendship between Britain and France that he referred to as *La Belle Alliance*. His deputy cringed. The old buffer presumably meant the *Entente Cordiale* under whose banner the two nations had fought side by side in the recent war and not the name of the farm that had served as Napoleon's headquarters at Waterloo. Fortunately very few of those in attendance either noticed the *faux pas* or would have cared.

There was abundant wine, excellent food and girls in pretty dresses. Isabel was in great demand on the dance floor. She was an accomplished dancer and after several glasses of champagne, she shed her customary inhibitions and let her hair down. Not a few of her dance partners, the bolder ones, contrived to steer her into the alcove where a spray of mistletoe was strategically placed. They were rewarded for their temerity with a modest kiss on the cheek. She was unquestionably the sensation of the evening and she was having the time of her life. Eventually, the energy level diminished and she found herself dancing with the deputy consul. Even though she was wearing high heels he towered above her and when she put her left arm around his shoulder their bodies were close. He did not seem to mind.

"You must really miss your wife at a time like this Monsieur Martin," she said disingenuously.

"I am not married but thank you for your concern," he replied with a quizzical smile. "But for you also Isabel, Christmas must be very lonely with your fiancé away in the middle of the ocean."

"Oh, Frank and I are not engaged. I am a free agent; just a butterfly flitting from flower to flower," she flirted. This was not exactly fair to Frank but she was a little tipsy and feeling the excitement of being sought by so many men and she was in the arms of the most distinguished man in the room.

"In that case, *mon papillon,* allow me to wish you a *Joyeux Noël,*" *the Deputy Consul replied* and steered her under the mistletoe. She prepared to offer him her cheek but at the last moment, driven by some imp of mischief, she kissed him full on the mouth and put both of her arms around his neck which, given the difference in their heights, necessitated a closer approximation of their bodies than protocol would have dictated, assuming protocol covered this situation. When she released him, she realized that she had gone too far and glanced around the room suddenly apprehensive that she had created a scandal but nobody seemed to have taken any notice and, if the Deputy Consul was upset, he certainly gave no evidence of it.

"I see you more as a flower than a butterfly Isabel, and you make a very beautiful flower. Your seagoing admirer had better marry you while he can."

As he was a host of the party he had to continue to circulate among his guests and Isabel had no further contact with him as the party wound down. The evening had been a personal triumph for her and the afterglow stayed with her. Even the prosaic journey home on the No. 10 tram could not completely dampen her satisfaction. She had been the most sought after dance partner and the unquestioned belle of the ball. Even though now she was a little embarrassed by her uncharacteristically enthusiastic response to her boss's kiss under the mistletoe she recalled that he had shown no reluctance to participate. Indeed, if she was not mistaken, during their embrace his right hand had lingered cosily on her left buttock.

"How was the party?" asked Kate when she walked in the door. Her flatmate's question brought her down to earth a little. She and Kate's brother were, truly, not formally engaged but she knew that she had been a little dishonest in downplaying the extent of their involvement. She was not ready, by any means, to drop Frank from her social calendar but, she admitted to herself, it was gratifying to know that there were men, attractive and highly eligible ones, who were eager to take his place.

With the holiday season over, the relationship between Isabel and her boss changed but only subtly. He now addressed her as Isabel and was always ready to make small talk when the pace of business at the consulate permitted but he made no overt advances. She had the impression that he was waiting for her to make the first move and she was not quite ready to do that. *I probably need a couple of glasses of that infernal Veuve Cliquot,* she mused, *before I'll pluck up the courage to try that again.* In the meantime there was Frank: 'old reliable.'

The two girls settled into a cosy pattern of domesticity in the apartment and enjoyed experimenting with meals. Their initial plan was to alternate the responsibility for the evening meal but it generally turned out to be a joint effort. They dined late. Preparation of dinner could not begin until they arrived home together which was generally after six o'clock. Their social lives settled also into something of a routine. When Frank was home all bets were off but they generally spent three evenings a week at Atlantic House with an occasional visit to the cinema. The 'movies' were becoming all the rage. On some evenings they simply went overboard on the cooking and after eating too much went to bed at nine or nine thirty. Their routines were disturbed only by Frank's arrival or by Kate's occasional romantic dalliances. These seemed to Izzy to be lighthearted and not too serious. Kate was still looking for her dream giant.

To the vast majority of Liverpudlians the most important events that occurred during the winter and spring of 1928 were not those involving Frank Kelly and Isabel Iskandar but the exploits of Dixie Dean, the Everton centre forward who was 'finding the back of the net' at a prodigious rate. He looked good to shatter the old goal scoring records.

CHAPTER ELEVEN
The North Atlantic, May, 1928

The football season had just finished in early May and the F.A. Cup final played at Wembley. On board the *S.S. Carmania* about 600 nautical miles south of Newfoundland, Frank Kelly noticed the first waves of nausea. Having been the beneficiary of a British education--albeit a truncated one--he felt nauseated not nauseous but this brought him little consolation. When you're sick to your stomach, you're sick to your stomach. Over the next two hours the waves increased in intensity and frequency and were superseded by a sharp pain in the middle of his belly. He managed to carry out his duties during the evening meal but by the time the last course was served, he felt thoroughly miserable and reported to the ship's doctor. The pain had, by now, moved to the right side. Examination showed a localized tenderness; MacBurney's point, Doctor Grant noted. It was a textbook case of acute appendicitis. The diagnosis was obvious; not always the case with appendicitis, which can present in all sorts of atypical ways but Frank Kelly's appendix would have fooled no one. The diagnosis was straightforward. What to do about it was not.

If they had been on shore there would have been no decision to make; appendicitis calls for surgery; immediate surgery if the diagnosis is certain but they were not on shore and were, in fact, twenty four hours sailing time away from Boston. Dr. Grant was a ship's doctor, not a trained surgeon. He had performed three or four appendicectomies in his first post-graduate year but that had been five years ago, in a fully equipped and staffed operating theatre, with expertly administered anaesthesia and a senior surgical registrar as first assistant ready to leap into the breach should his technique be found not up to the task. The liner had an operating room with a good surgical table and lamp. He had set a few bones there and repaired some nasty lacerations; the inevitable result of crossing the North Atlantic in all weathers, but he had never opened the abdomen there and he was not keen to start now unless the indications were overwhelming.

He was a conscientious young Scot, well trained in Edinburgh and no coward. He had even trephined the skull during the past winter after a particularly nasty fall had caused a depressed skull fracture. On the balance, he decided, the most prudent course of action would be to delay surgery until Boston was reached. He did give serious thought to requesting the Captain to put into Halifax which would have shortened the delay to surgery by several hours but decided that the disruption and expense which would follow such a course of action were too severe. He was not a Scot for nothing. He crossed his fingers and prayed that his patient's appendix would come to the boil slowly.

In the event, the gamble failed by about two hours. As soon as they passed the tip of Cape Cod and were heading for the shipping channel into Boston Harbor, Frank was transferred to a Coast Guard cutter and transported to the quay. In the ambulance, on the way to the Emergency Room at Boston General, he noticed that the intense pain suddenly abated to be replaced by a more diffuse discomfort that involved the entire lower abdomen. The appendix had burst. The diagnosis of acute appendicitis with rupture and generalized peritonitis was made in the ER. The patient was running a temperature of 101 degrees Fahrenheit and manifested the phenomenon of re-bound tenderness. This occurs when pressure is gradually applied and then suddenly released, inducing a sharp pain. It is highly suggestive of an inflamed peritoneum: the lining of the abdominal cavity.

One hour later, Frank had been admitted to Mens Surgical and promptly transferred to the Anesthesia induction room where intravenous lines were established. Anesthesia techniques in that period varied considerably across the world. The use of chloroform was still widespread in Britain where it had received a tremendous boost in acceptance when Queen Victoria had elected to have it administered during childbirth. Boston, however, was 'Ether Country'. Di-ethyl ether had first been successfully demonstrated at Massachusetts General Hospital in the last century, just a stones throw from Boston General and ether was still in widespread use. Its big drawbacks were that it was quite slow to take effect, produced profound nausea and, worst of all, was highly explosive. It had become necessary to build operating rooms with floors capable of conducting electricity, lest static should accumulate, produce a spark and blow everybody up.

This danger was averted and surgery revealed the expected pathology. The appendix, which in Frank's case was about four inches long, is a finger like protrusion emerging from the junction of the small and large intestines. The walls were thickened with inflammation, reddish purple in colour and near the base, blackish green where gangrene had set in and the perforation had occurred. The surrounding tissues were matted together and it was obvious that the entire right lower quadrant of the abdomen was involved. Surgery was carried out with meticulous care by the senior surgical resident under the watchful eye of the Tufts University Assistant Professor of Surgery on-call. This was not an appendectomy to let the surgical intern get his feet wet on. "Appendicectomy" had become "appendectomy" when Frank had left the *S.S. Carmania* and entered the American-speaking world.

In 1928, the world was still in the pre-antibiotic era. The mortality rate for appendicitis could be expected to rise exponentially with every hour that passed between the bursting of an inflamed appendix and its removal. When the offending tissue had been removed all that could be done was to irrigate the abdomen with sterile saline and suction out any residual pus and debris. Wide rubber drains were then inserted into the incision. The wound was packed with sterile gauze and the edges loosely approximated with sutures. The survival of the patient then depended on his vitality and that of his immune system. Frank Kelly was a robust thirty-year-old. He had about a fifty percent chance of survival.

Ether has one very significant advantage as an anesthetic assuming that it doesn't blow up and explosions were, by 1928, very uncommon. Ether is relatively safe even in untutored hands. It is difficult to kill somebody with ether. It is extremely soluble in fat and so the onset of unconsciousness is quite slow. By the end of a lengthy ether anesthetic, the patient's body fat is saturated. The patient emerging into consciousness also does so quite slowly. The only way he can eliminate ether from his body is to breathe it out. The operating room staff themselves inhale a fair amount from the ambient air of the OR, particularly the anesthetist, sitting as he does next to the patient's head and the exhalation ports of the anesthesia machine. This is similarly absorbed into the body fat of the staff. They, too, exhale the gas for hours. Spouses of anesthetists soon become familiar with ether's pungent odor as it is breathed out over the dinner table. For the patient, the major downside is that it makes him sick as a dog during the recovery period.

Frank Kelly's emergence from anesthesia was therefore prolonged and unpleasant. He regained consciousness only after several hours during which he was profoundly nauseated. His mind experienced a whirlwind of unpleasant images. His first coherent thought was that he had a raging thirst and a tube in his nose. The back of his throat felt like it was on fire. He noticed a bandage over his lower abdomen accompanied by a tenderness that he would not describe as pain but which made him reluctant to shift his position in bed. The bed in which he lay was one of eighteen that lined one wall of a long ward and faced another eighteen on the opposite side. It was one a.m. and the ward was dimly lit. He gradually became aware of ghostly female forms moving silently up and down the space between the beds. As his brain cleared the remaining ether fumes, he recognized these as nurses. Eventually one approached his bed: a stout matronly woman with a kindly but business like face.

"Water," he croaked.

"Sorry! You're NPO," she replied inscrutably.

"I'm thirsty," he explained, thinking momentarily that a citizen of Boston might not understand his request.

"You're NPO," she repeated. "You're only allowed ice chips," and she vanished only to return minutes later with a kidney-shaped dish filled with ice chips and a teaspoon. She helped him into the sitting position with gentle and practiced skill and fed him the first few spoonfuls of ice. These provided a momentary relief but what he felt the need for was two pints of water. The ice had at least made speech easier.

"How long till I can have a drink and what about this tube in my nose? I feel like I've got a pencil running down the back of my throat."

Nurse Monaghan, for thus was the good lady named, was not about to permit such importunity from a patient. The arcane mysteries of Medicine were the preserve of the staff. The patients would be told of their fate all in good time.

"We'll remove the N.G. tube and let you drink when the doctor says. Now lie down and try to sleep." With this she vanished into the gloom and, on reaching the nurse's station, charted that Patient Kelly was having an uneventful recovery; BP 110/70, Pulse 96 and Temp 100.5 degrees Fahrenheit. At six o'clock there was a general stirring in the ward as the night shift made their rounds in preparation for the hand over of responsibility to the day shift, which was due to come on at seven thirty. Between six and eight thirty were the busiest and most stressful hours of the twenty-four. The night nurses had to evaluate each patient's status and record it in his chart. Beds had to be made, bedpans distributed, collected and emptied as needed and patients helped out of bed or into the sitting position for breakfast, as appropriate. A detailed report was given on each patient. The day shift nurses were left with the passing out of breakfast trays and with the responsibility for ensuring that the pre-ops were posted as NPO; the designation meaning 'Nothing By Mouth' (*nil per os*), which had so bewildered Frank the previous night. As Frank was still NPO, he was permitted to sleep on after 6:00 a.m., disturbed only by the taking of his pulse and the administration of a few teaspoonfuls of ice that tasted like nectar of the gods to his tortured throat. He was still profoundly drowsy but sufficiently conscious to note that this ministering angel was endowed with a beautiful smile, a generous figure and a nameplate attached to her apron that bore the legend "Josefina Lucca, R.N."

Frank Kelly recovered but he did not recover quickly. The offending appendix had been removed but not before intestinal contents had been released into the peritoneal cavity. That meant that every organ below the diaphragm and above the pelvic floor was threatened with contamination. Only the body's immune system was available to combat this and this meant principally the white blood cells. The result of the ensuing invisible combat was the production of infectious fluids and a matting together of the intestines.

The cardinal signs of infection, as taught to every medical student since Aesculapius, are *Calor, Dolor, Tumor, and Rubor*, (heat, pain, swelling and redness). When the infection occurs on the surface the sequence of events is very obvious. A boil or any superficial abscess is an excellent example. The first axiom of treatment is expressed equally pithily; "Where there's pus, drain it." The application of heat with a poultice to an incipient boil will help to increase the circulation and expedite the flow of white blood cells to the area. Then surgical incision can drain the pus. The teaching however has very little utility when dealing with a potential infection of the entire abdominal cavity.

Frank's surgical wound was infected, inevitably, and a rubber drain had been left in the wound to permit the resulting pus to reach the surface. There the gauze dressings became saturated and had to be changed daily. The stench was appalling and Frank had a feeling almost of shame and disgust that his own body was necessitating this revolting task for the nurses. They, of course, maintained a countenance devoid of expression and he was very grateful for their consideration and professionalism. However, it was the struggle going on inside the abdominal cavity, not on the surface, that would determine the outcome. Within those contiguous spaces the infection was being combated. It could track up as far as the diaphragm or descend into the depths of the pelvis. In either case it would be very difficult for a surgeon to reach an accumulation of pus. The outcome for Frank would be very much in the lap of the gods.

The next four weeks went by and he became attuned to the life and routine of a busy surgical ward in a city hospital. He was not in any serious pain. He had stopped needing narcotics after the first twenty-four hours. He still moved about the bed very deliberately and still needed help getting in and out. The naso-gastric tube remained in place for a full week and was the bane of his existence. He was always conscious of its presence and became almost paranoid in his obsession with it. Dryness of the mouth and soreness of the throat are considered minor irritants by the nursing staff and little sympathy is given but to Frank it was like a jagged tooth; always there and always irritating.

After a surgical insult or in the presence of abdominal infection there is a serious risk that the intestines will cease their normal job, which is to propel their contents onward by their rhythmic contraction; the process known as peristalsis. If the bowels cease their contraction, the condition is known as 'ileus'. In this situation, the stomach and guts dilate. It is very dangerous. It is to prevent this condition that the NG tube is left in place. It provides an escape route for the gases generated by the fermenting intestinal contents. Only when normal bowel sounds have returned can the tube be safely removed. This underlying rationale is not relayed to the patient. That's not his business. It was, however, an enormous relief when the hated tube was eventually removed and oral feeding resumed. He was now fully conscious and no longer in pain but he was affected with a profound malaise; depression and a pervasive lack of energy. Unbeknownst to him, his body was fighting a battle inside him. The battle lasted almost a month.

Nurse Lucca was the first to notice a change in the pattern of his temperature readings. Patient Kelly's temps were starting to peak in a rhythmic fashion and these spikes seemed to coincide with the patient complaining of uncontrollable trembling and profuse sweating. She promptly relayed the development to the surgical intern, Bob Castellano, who after a brief examination passed the word up the surgical chain of command to Nat Ravkin, the surgical resident and Jack Craddock, the Chief Surgical Resident.

"The Ruptured Appendix in Mens Surg. 2 has started spiking a temp. He's four weeks post-op and he's been holding his own. It looks like the infection is localizing," summarized Dr. Ravkin.

"Well, we've been expecting an abscess to form if the infection didn't kill him first. I'll be down to check him out as soon as clinic's over. Shouldn't be more than half an hour. Meet me on the ward. It sounds like it might be a good teaching case. If it is an abscess, we can present it to the students tomorrow if there are any physical signs."

Patient Kelly was duly examined and a diagnosis agreed on; an abscess had formed deep in the pelvis. This was positive news because an abscess in the pelvis is potentially amenable to drainage. Doctors love to drain pus. It fulfills some primordial need to release evil humors. It is also good medicine.

"Let's show him to the students and see whether any of them can palpate the abscess. What's the patient's name, by the way? I'll let the Tufts Attending know. I wonder if he'll want to go in right away or wait it out for a couple of days."

"His name is Kelly. He's the Limey with the glass eye, about half way down on the left side," Castellano contributed.

"If Hillman is the attending on call, he'll want to go in right away," Ravkin mused. Harvey Hillman M.D., not too fondly known by the residents as "Hardly Human" was notoriously quick to reach for the scalpel. The upshot of this discussion was that next morning Frank Kelly was presented on rounds by Dr. Castellano to the Tufts Associate Professor of Surgery, a surgical resident, and six senior Tufts medical students as "Patient Kelly, Ruptured Appendix with formation of Pelvic Abscess." The essentials of the case were recited by Dr. Castellano and all were invited to see whether they could identify the offending pathology.

There are drawbacks to receiving medical care in a teaching hospital, Frank now discovered, as he was subjected to nine consecutive digital rectal examinations. The accompanying nurse gave him a sympathetic smile as he underwent the ordeal, lying on his side with his knees drawn up to his chin. The one female medical student muttered an unintelligible apology as she took her turn for the ninth and last assault on his dignity. Frank, having no reasonable alternative, underwent the ordeal in stoic silence. The result of all the examinations was to confirm the diagnosis but the information was not relayed to the patient. In fact, Frank did not learn of it until later in the afternoon when he was informed by Nurse Lucca that he was on the OR schedule for an I and D (incision and drainage) of a Pelvic Abscess and that Dr. Castellano would be in later to tell him all about it and to have him sign the consent forms. He spent the next few hours feeling a little put upon by the cavalier treatment he felt he had received that morning. *Could they not, at least, have explained what was going on, giving him at least a token request for permission before subjecting him to such repeated assaults on his person?*

Four hours later, as the supper trays were about to be distributed, Frank felt a sudden urge to empty his bowels and made his painful way across the ward to the latrines. Moments later the abscess burst spontaneously into the rectum and was evacuated, in the approved manner, with the normal contents of the bowel. Whether or not this outcome was the result of nine successive digital probings or was merely the end point of a normal patho-physiological process would never be known but the effect on Frank was instantaneous and profound. He had tottered into the bathroom feeling a deep-seated lassitude: sluggish and nauseated. With the drainage of the abscess he almost immediately felt re-invigorated. He felt like a new man and was almost sprightly as he looked to find a nurse to whom he could report his changed condition and to tell her that they could take his name off tomorrow's OR schedule. Frank Kelly spent another two weeks on Mens Surg. 2 as he completed his recovery. It was during this period that he became fully aware of his surroundings, of the ward routines and of the nursing staff. Nurses became individuals with their own names, faces and personalities. It was now that he became fully aware of Josefina Lucca, R.N.

Chapter Twelve
Boston, Massachusetts, 1928

Nurse Lucca was now approaching the end of her second year as a graduate nurse and a member of the staff of Boston General Hospital. She had achieved the status of 'Charge Nurse of the Day Shift' on Mens Surg.; this promotion bringing with it a small increase in pay and a position of authority immediately below that of Ward Sister. It also brought with it the immeasurable benefit of working during the daylight hours. Admittedly the day started at 7:00 a.m. and finished at 6:00 p.m. but it was, at least, predictable and greatly enhanced her social life. During the first six months of her two years at the General, she had worked variable shifts; day, evening and night and in a variety of locations; the Operating Suite, Womens Medical, Mens and Womens Surgical before settling for a more permanent home in Mens Surgical Ward No. 2 on the Tufts Service.

Her social life, though hampered by the early month's frenetic schedule, had not been put completely on hold. She had arrived in Boston with the avowed intention of leading a life full of romantic adventure. A big city hospital in a city like Boston, a city teeming with young adults, was the ideal location for such an ambition. Every day brought a hundred medical students into the wards; ninety-five percent of them male. Interns and residents added approximately the same number; a few years older but still mainly in their mid-twenties. Most were single. The hospital salary scale was risible. Room and board contributed their largest single benefit. Marriage was not therefore a realistic option for those in residency or for those medical students who planned to specialize. None of these sordid financial considerations served to put much of a damper on the sexual comings and goings. The hospital was a seething cauldron of sexual activity. Those nominally responsible for the nursing staff and for the doctors were well aware of this. There were policies promulgated and prohibitions published to check too flagrant behavior but, unlike the nuns at St. Anne's, the administrators at the General knew that they were fighting a losing battle and turned a blind eye to the off-duty behavior of their charges. The wing that contained the doctors' sleeping quarters and the on-call rooms were referred to, even by the Matron and the Dean of the Medical School, as Shangri La.

Into this Rabelaisian milieu, Josefina Lucca, R.N. plunged with enthusiasm. Her new roommate proved to be an astute choice. She presented an image of upper middle class propriety. First impression would place her in a setting of country clubs, tennis parties, the Junior League and the Episcopal Church. The first impression would have been misleading. Like Jo, she had a healthy libido and a strong desire to see what she had been missing in her first twenty-one years. The Bohemian life fitted her like a glove. She became part of an ever-changing population based in the hospital that worked hard and played hard; they smoked; they drank; and they made out. If Jo had any residue of Catholic guilt it was soon overcome. New England, in 1927, was still a bastion of White Anglo-Saxon Protestantism. If Jenny Hudson, daughter of ten generations of Yankee blue-noses, was comfortable with her lifestyle why should she, daughter of Italian immigrants, be any different. The "*dramatis personae*' of any of their parties were very fluid and as variable as the location of their get-togethers. The doctor's lounge in Shangri La or one of the speak-easies off Commonwealth Ave. were popular trysting places.

Frequently, though by no means invariably, one or both of the nurses would decide that some lucky medical student or a resident was sufficiently in lust to merit further attention and would leave the party to see whether that attention was justified in the privacy of their nearby apartment. Their separate bedrooms were an invaluable benefit. There was never any shortage of candidates. They were both very good-looking young women.

'Variety is the spice of life' was their watchword during their first year together. It was only with an exceptionally accomplished or charming lover that the individual liaisons lasted more than a couple of weeks. Jo, in particular, was the more promiscuous in this regard. She loved playing the field and of being lusted after. When several promising young bucks were competing for her, she could drive them into despair by dancing with one and giving the appearance that their bodies were glued together and then abandoning him and flirting outrageously with another. She was a tease and enjoyed it. She would not have characterized herself as such. Teases tantalize but do not follow through. Jo treated the parties as an elimination competition with her as the prize. She was well worth it. It was the most gratifying year of her young life. She had a respectable job that she knew she did well and she basked nightly in the lustful gaze of dozens of young males and in the fevered couplings that followed her selection of the evenings chosen one. There could not possibly be too much of a good thing, she thought, but even the ripest fruit palls after a while. She was becoming aware that she was developing a reputation; perhaps not as a 'loose woman' but certainly as 'fast.' She thought that she was recognizing occasional knowing nods and whispered words in the halls and in the wards.

The decision to modify her behavior was prompted by an event that occurred when her July period did not occur on schedule. Casting her mind back over the previous month she realized that the father-to-be, if indeed she was pregnant, could have been any one of three: two medical students and, ironically, a resident in OB-GYN on whom she had bestowed her favors in the previous month. She realized that she could scarcely recall their individual features. It was astonishing that the risk of pregnancy had not been forever in her consciousness. She was a well-trained nursing professional but her lust for life and her sexual triumphs had led her to believe that nothing bad could affect her. She now was faced with the reality of bearing a child of one of three males none of whom did she care for or even remember. Unwanted pregnancy was not, of course, unheard of or even uncommon in the institution in which she worked. It could hardly be otherwise given the pervasive permissive culture. *Pregnancy does not have to end in the birth of a baby.* The thought went through her mind. Certainly it would be possible to terminate the pregnancy. Surely abortion was available within a community of several hundred medical professionals. It was a tribute to her long neglected religious upbringing that the possibility was immediately discarded with an almost visceral horror.

Jo experienced the worst week of her life; her thoughts in turmoil. How would she support a baby? What would her Italian parents think? Who was the father? The next Sunday she attended mass for the first time since leaving Fall River and promised God that she would reform if only this baby should turn out not to be. God has a very spotty record in responding to such self-serving prayer. If that were not the case, no soldiers would ever die in an artillery barrage. However, in this instance He was alert and on the ball. Jo's menstrual flow recurred two days later. It had either been some hormonal quirk or a very early miscarriage. In either case the experience had shaken her to the core. She desperately needed a trusted female confidante and Jenny was available. She knew the environment in which they both worked and shared the same social mores.

"I've had a really bad scare recently, Jenny. I thought I was pregnant. I'm not but I was a week late."

"Oh God! You poor thing. Are you all right? Who was the father?" she added with unsurprising but unwelcome curiosity.

"That's part of the trouble. I'm actually not sure. It could be one of either of two Tufts boys or Jack Jeffers, you know that stud on OB-GYN."

"Well if it was him you would probably have been able to get a quick abortion. There's nothing to it. I've never told you before but I had one when I was dating Charley Corcoran. It was one of the reasons that we broke up. We had been living together like an old married couple and he asked me if I was sure it was his. I almost hit him, the bastard."

Jo felt herself growing angry. Here she had brought her closest friend into her confidence about a very serious matter, she believed, and her friend was treating it as though pregnancy and abortion were trivial issues. She bit her lip. She needed to hold onto her temper. She needed to confide and there was nobody else she could turn to. The thought of dumping the problem on her mother back in Brockton filled her with cold chills.

"Jenny! I've done a lot of thinking in the past two weeks and you know I think that I've come to some conclusions. There's more to life than one-night stands. I know I'm not ready for the convent; I like men too much. Two minutes in the company with a horny male and I'm ready to tear my clothes off. But I think that I should become harder to get; become more choosy. I don't just mean who's-going-to-be the-lucky-guy-tonight choosy; I mean set out for the long haul. You know the whole love and marriage thing."

Jenny was silent for a few minutes--a remarkable occurrence in itself for she was a compulsive chatterbox. She finally revealed her conclusions. "You know, you might be right. It's been over a year since I had a steady guy and it would be nice to wake up in the morning with someone whose name I could remember."

"So you think I should get myself a steady boyfriend?" asked Jo.

"I do, but don't think that that'll prevent you from getting knocked up. Just look at me and Charley Corcoran. Maybe its time that we both started looking to the future. We can't be playing the field forever. I'm twenty-four and you're twenty-three. Here we are surrounded by a couple of hundred good-looking men who, in a couple of years will have a really good income. Why don't we set out to snap up one each? With your looks you could probably pick off the new Chief Resident," she added with a disarming grin. Irv Schoenfeld was a spectacularly ugly and foul tempered surgeon.

"That sounds a bit cold blooded," admitted Jo as she stopped grinning and gave more serious thought to Jenny's proposal. "I know we won't be the first nurses to set their caps for a doctor. They do say that it's as easy to fall in love with a rich man as it is with a poor one."

The conversation left her feeling much more cheerful. She wasn't pregnant and now she had a plan that would provide the thrill of the hunt. Only now she would be the huntress and the man the prize. Why should men have all the fun? She would scan the field of eligible men with a more calculating eye. Virility which had always, heretofore, been the quality that she had sought in her swain, would no longer be the overriding consideration when she would looked over the prospective men in her life. She was going to get a husband, a prosperous one and one whom she could bend to her will. She knew that she needed sex but she didn't plan on being any man's docile little plaything either before or after marriage. She was going to be in charge. With their new strategy agreed on, the two roommates conferred on tactics. They would concentrate on medical students; the seniors were just entering their final year before qualification.

"We'll have a good chance to look them over. We'll have seen them around last year but this year we should be getting a better idea as to their prospects and their plans," said Jenny.

"How about the residents"? asked Jo, who still rather liked the look of Bob Castellano and who had, at least, an Italian name. Her mother, she knew, would be thrilled if Jo became Mrs. Doctor Castellano.

"There are five or six on the surgical side whom I wouldn't mind climbing into bed with--preferably not all at once--and one of the new interns looks really hot," Jenny said. "You should have seen him giving me the eye this morning but, of course, he's from New Orleans. I don't know that I want to spend my life in the Deep South."

"Don't be too quick to eliminate any of them," Jo replied. "You never know where they'll end up after training but I think that it's not a bad idea to concentrate on the med students. Most of the marriageable residents are spoken for by the time they are reaching the end of their training and the others are just playing the field or are wrapped up in their work."

"Some of those medical students come from well off families too. Maybe I can move in on some of that old Yankee money. Wouldn't those old Boston Brahmins just love it if their 'pride and joy' brought home an Italian girl from Brockton," Jo laughed.

"Don't sell yourself short," said Jenny loyally. "I grew up with some of those prep school boys. Those inbred gene pools could use a little Italian pepping up."

Chapter Thirteen

Boston, Massachusetts, Fall, 1927

J. Roylston Brock was just starting his final year of medical school when he became the object of interest for Jo Lucca. He fit into her long term plans to perfection. He looked arrogant and smug but that would make the conquest all the more satisfying and Jo did not doubt her ability to have any male eating out of her hand. She hadn't failed yet. He was from Gorham, Maine, a small town near Portland and was the scion of an old Maine family whose commercial interests included cotton mills in New Hampshire, thousands of acres of lumber and the Roylston paper mill in nearby Westbrook. He had graduated from Bowdoin College in Brunswick, Maine. He was of medium height and was solidly built. He had been a fair athlete when playing lacrosse at Bowdoin but had put on some weight now that his playing days were over and was a little soft round the middle. He had an apartment of his own close to the hospital. This was very unusual and was a sure-fire indication that he was well funded from home. Most students shared their quarters with three of their fellows and many made do with single rented rooms.

All of this information was widely known and circulated by the nursing staff or at least by its single members. Gossip reigns supreme in a big city hospital. Mr. Brock also had a bit of a reputation as a playboy with a wandering eye. Jo had set about reinventing herself or at least trying to repair her damaged reputation. She still frequented the social gatherings but danced with less abandon and drank rather less. She became less flirtatious and dressed more modestly. She was still the best looking woman in the hospital. She did not need extremes of dress, daring décolletage or skirts above the knee to set male hormones raging. Her body was voluptuous--not even the most modest dress could disguise this--nor did she want it to. Her waist was trim and her legs long and shapely.

She had known since age sixteen that she could excite and confuse lust-filled males with the silent messages of her eyes and lips. She set about honing these already formidable skills. She was striving to present herself as the unattainable prize for the predatory males in their circle. This, she realized, would require a drastic makeover in her public image. She had to reverse the widespread perception of her as a fast and available female. She believed that she could pull it off in a few months. July had witnessed its usual twenty-five percent turnover in both the resident staff and the medical student population and memories are short. She also noted that there was no appreciable diminution in her popularity. Men still flocked around, eager to try their hand. They competed to dance with her and to ply her with alcohol and they attempted to explore those delights that were now so demurely concealed.

Restraint was not easy for Jo. She enjoyed being the most sought after woman in every gathering. It was good for her morale and her reputation but it called for the introduction and re-institution of patterns of behavior that had been cast aside a year ago. She was a young woman with a low threshold for sexual arousal and she had to school her own actions to prevent herself from getting too involved.

Early in the process of reinventing her public persona she danced with an old flame--a now-married surgical resident. She had thoughtlessly permitted her body to move provocatively against his. His resulting erection was prompt and would have been obvious to the assembly were it not for the dim lighting. The temptation to gratify his obvious desire was almost overwhelming. She was, in the elegant parlance of the nursing school, 'creaming her jeans' but she managed to push herself back and fled to the bathroom to allow her pulse to slow. The unfortunate male was left to make as unobtrusive an exit as possible. He went home and surprised his wife with the urgency of their subsequent marital coupling.

Miss Lucca learned her lesson from that and henceforth kept a closer watch on her own behavior. She still delivered hints that she was attracted to the male species but they were subtle and frequently contradictory.

Roy Brock was very content with his life. He was the spoiled only child of his parents and the heir to a sizable fortune. He had been a fair athlete at Bowdoin where he was considered a BMOC (Big Man On Campus). It was an all-male school so his opportunities for romantic interludes with the opposite sex were limited. At college mixers with the pampered young ladies from Smith or Wellesley he fared fairly well given the well-chaperoned nature of such gatherings. There was, however, a State Normal College in his home town with a female student body of several hundred aspiring teachers and Roy realized that his status as a BMOC in an all-male school could not compare with the possibilities provided at home in Gorham. He was presentable, if not handsome. He had his own car and bore the name of the large neighboring paper mill and the family home was the most imposing in the town. Bowdoin was only one hour's journey from Gorham and he made the trip home nearly every weekend in his last year at college.

He met Louise Thibodeau in the coffee shop where she worked three evenings a week to help her pay her way through school. She was of French Canadian stock and she was a second generation American. Her family lived in Lewiston forty miles to the north. Roy had no trouble ingratiating himself with her. She was impressed with his prep school accent and his obvious wealth and agreed to drive out to Sebago Lake the following weekend for a picnic and a swimming party. The swim went off pleasantly. She had been a little taken aback when the party turned out to be just the two of them but she enjoyed her taste of the high life: roast chicken and crusty rolls served from an elegantly packed hamper and chilled white wine. As the evening cooled, Roy proposed that they warm up in his family's summer cottage, which, he told her, was just a couple of miles further along the lakeshore.

Louise, now feeling quite exhilarated by Roy's attentions--there had been a little fairly innocent horse play in the water--agreed and was quite overwhelmed when she discovered that the family cottage was an enormous wooden edifice with ten bedrooms and a huge main chamber complete with deer heads on the walls and a bearskin rug on the floor in front of the fireplace. Roy applied the matches to the logs that were already in place and in a short while there was a blazing fire. He poured each of them a healthy slug of rum and topped it up with Coca Cola and they settled comfortably in front of the fire on the bearskin. It was just too inviting to resist and Louise was feeling mellow. Roy started rubbing her feet on the pretext of restoring her circulation; a pretext neither believed. The rubbing became more gentle and advanced from her feet to her knees and then to her thighs. By this time, Louise, who was neither a fool nor completely innocent, knew what was happening and had weighed up the pros and cons of allowing the liaison to proceed. She had decided that young Roy Brock might be well worth cultivating.

As he slid his hand ever closer to her groin she groaned throatily and moved moistly to meet him. By this time he was fully aroused and was encouraged by her lack of resistance. He struggled to remove her panties and was barely able to withhold his ejaculate long enough to penetrate her. It was not Louise's most satisfactory sexual encounter but she writhed seductively and gave a convincing display of gratification. Roy thought he was a hell of a fellow.

He and his willing partner rendezvoused weekly for the rest of his senior year at Bowdoin. In March, Louise informed him that she was pregnant and informed him that she was willing to become Mrs. Roylston Brock. Roy was not entirely taken aback by this as he had done nothing to prevent such an eventuality and he had no doubts about his potency. Louise's histrionic responses to his lovemaking had convinced him that he was very special in that department. As for the proposal that he should make an 'honest woman' of her; that idea was not even a consideration. That's what wealth and family lawyers were for. With reluctance, but with little fear of the outcome, he informed his father that he had been seduced in his innocence by a dissolute student teacher from Lewiston: a *French-Canadienne*, and she had got herself knocked up. She was threatening legal action if he didn't marry her. Mr. Brock looked appropriately solemn and tut tutted but then gave the son the reassurance that he had been sure he would get. After all, Brock senior had been a 'bit of a lad' himself in his younger days.

"Let this be a lesson to you son," he chided. "Always wear a condom. Don't worry about little Miss Thibodeau. I'll put my lawyers onto it and I'm sure we will be able to come to some satisfactory arrangement. As for you, I think you better keep it in your pants till you graduate."

This would not prove to be too much of a sacrifice as graduation was now only two months distant and, anyway, he was anxious to try his wings on a larger stage than the sleepy confines of rural Maine. As for Mademoiselle Thibodeau who had, in fact, never been pregnant; she was five thousand dollars better off and relieved not to have to continue the charade of her passionate responses to young Brock's unimaginative lovemaking.

****

The first two years of Medical School at Tufts University in Boston were a shock. He had coasted through his undergraduate degree at Bowdoin without ever being pressed academically. He was smart and possessed a good memory. He had graduated *cum laude* but at Tufts his classmates were the intellectual cream of the finest universities in the northeast of the United States. American medical students work very hard. They spend all four years on the wards and in the clinics of the hospital and are expected to be present from 7:00 a.m. till released. Lectures are sandwiched in between hospital duties and the students are required to do much of the scut work: venipuncture, lab work and other even more menial tasks.

Young Roylston Brock found that he didn't have much time for leisure and, when he could squeeze in a few hours for attempting the seduction of the nurses--the prime goal of every red-blooded American medical student--he found that he was at the bottom of the pecking order. Nurses have a well-honed awareness of the hierarchical structure of medical training. First and second-year students are facing two or three years of non-suitability as potential husbands. Their romantic overtures carry very little weight. In his third year, Roy had noted that his success rate was markedly improved. At least when he smiled they smiled back. On entering fourth year he was convinced that he would have his pick of all the female acolytes who, in his opinion, existed solely to serve the pleasure of the demi-godlike doctors whose ranks he would shortly be joining.

He had already set his eye on a particularly attractive nurse on Mens Surgical 2. He had heard that she was hot. She certainly had the body for it. So far she had not responded to any of his opening ploys. She had not responded to his winning smiles and her demeanor on the ward was strictly professional. He had no doubt that in the right setting he could get her to warm up.

He got his first opportunity two weekends later. He had been party hopping all evening and had visited a couple of speakeasies which catered to the hospital personnel. Rumor had it that medicinal alcohol; 190 proof, was regularly supplied from the hospital pharmacy to the bars and the staff received very preferential treatment in reciprocity. Boston was not a hotbed of Temperance fervor. There was always a party in Shangri La on Saturday evening and Brock was feeling quite mellow when he arrived at ten o'clock. The party was in full swing and Nurse Lucca was in the center of an animated gathering that was mainly male, although he noted that a pretty, plumpish blonde had her share of admirers and was making the most of the conversation.

Even in the nursing uniform of 1928, designed, it appeared, to render the female form unrecognizable, Jo Lucca managed to look attractive. In civilian clothing, which this evening consisted of a high-necked yellow sweater and brown silk slacks, she looked spectacular. Her hair, now released from its unbecoming nurse's cap was shining a lustrous deep chestnut brown. It framed her face and, complete with a small widow's peak, formed a perfect heart shape meeting below her chin. She had the classic features of a Renaissance Madonna but this impression was countered by a mouth that Da Vinci would have thought too wide and lips of a sensuous fullness.

She made a quick appraising glance as he came into the room but gave no impression that he was worth a second glance and returned her full attention to the eager men around her. It took him almost half an hour to work his way close enough to be part of the circle of admirers. All appeared to be completely unaware of his presence and he began to feel awkward as the other men in the group made no effort to include him in the conversation. The first person to acknowledge his presence was the pretty blonde who appeared to be a friend of the Italian-looking girl. She gave him an ingenuous welcoming smile and took a step back to include him in the group.

Grateful not to be standing on the outside he smiled and said, "Can I get you a drink?"

"I think I've had enough for right now but I wouldn't mind dancing," she replied coquettishly.

"If you don't mind risking your life. I'm not much of a dancer but I'm dynamite at sitting out," he said with a suggestive comic leer. "I'm Roy Brock, by the way."

"Hello Roy Brock. I'm Jenny Hudson and you don't get to sit out with me until you've earned it on the dance floor."

The music was provided by a Victrola and was up-tempo for the most part and the dancing was not conducive to amorous advances. The Charleston and Dixieland Jazz were by now well established as the popular choice and the knee-length flapper skirt that Jenny was wearing gave her the opportunity to flaunt her legs which were shapely and surprisingly long for a girl who was buxom and barely five-foot-three. Five minutes of the Charleston and the Black Bottom left them quite short of breath and when they sat out Roy found that he was being guided to a dimly lit corner of the room on the opposite side from Jo and her entourage. He was not too put out by this and even smiled to himself at her ploy. She was obviously maneuvering to keep him at a distance from her friend. After they had replenished their drinks she snuggled up next to him on the sofa and did not resist too strenuously when he slid his arm around her shoulder and began a gradual exploration of her breast. She did grab his hand when it made a tentative caress of her knee.

"Not here Roy," she murmured and nibbling his ear added, "Let's dance again. They're playing a slow tune. We can talk while we're dancing. I'd like to get to know you better."

"You know me already. You see me on the ward every day, he replied, slightly nettled. He had thought that he was getting to know her just fine. He suppressed his irritation and was relieved to find that Nurse Hudson was as accomplished a slow dancer as she was an exponent of the Charleston. The evening was getting late and couples were pairing off on the dance floor and in the darker recesses of the room. Shangri La was situated in a separate wing of the building. The main staff lounge was spacious and was the location of the party. Staff bedrooms for the residents and the on-call doctors were on the two corridors that led away into the main hospital building. The well established but unspoken rules of behavior in the main lounge were fairly liberal; a considerable amount of 'necking' as it was now beginning to be called, and discreet fondling were okay as the evening waned but clothes were not shed and overt coupling was not acceptable. On-call rooms, of which there were a half dozen, served that function. These were spartan in their furnishings containing only a bed and a bedside table but they did possess the inestimable asset of a lock on the door. One or two were generally put to use in ways that were not intended when the hospital had been designed. By convention, a man's tie draped over the doorknob served to notify any would be intruders that the room was already being put to good use.

Roy Brock and Jenny Hudson were getting very close to the acceptable behavioral limits. Miss Hudson's breasts had proved to be as abundant as he had imagined and her responses to his kissing gratifying to his ego. The stirring in his loins was becoming more insistent. He had just about decided to suggest that they adjourn to a more secluded location. His plan was frustrated by an unwelcome interruption. Jenny felt an insistent tapping on her shoulder. It was her flatmate who was standing above them wearing a raincoat and ready for departure.

"Come on Cinderella! It's nearly midnight and we've both got to be up by five-thirty tomorrow morning."

Jenny unwrapped herself from her partner's embrace with considerable reluctance. On the whole she was pleased with the interruption. She had definitely planted her hooks into Mr. J. Roylston Brock. He had been on the point of suggesting that they take their lovemaking to the next level and she was not at all sure that she would have declined.

'Leave 'em wanting more' was a strategy that had served womankind since time immemorial and indeed was the master plan that the two women had agreed to. Jenny was not as completely sold on the idea as her flatmate. In Roy Brock she thought that she had discovered her perfect target. When, in her adolescent dreams she had envisaged herself walking down the aisle, it was with such as he: wealthy, handsome and Episcopalian. She had disparaged prep school boys to her friend but the stereotype that the term denoted was precisely what she hoped for. She was from the same Anglo-Saxon race and social class. Her parents were well to do. Her father had a flourishing medical practice in Hanover, New Hampshire and she, too, had been to private schools. Her decision to become a nurse had been her one break with the conventional pattern of behavior of her pampered classmates.

If Jenny could be said to be not too dismayed by the way in which the evening was ending, the same could not be said for Roy Brock. He had been about to add another notch to his belt. He was sure that the nubile blonde now sitting up and adjusting her skirt had been on the point of acquiescing to his suggestion to adjourn to the on-call rooms. He was aware of his all too obviously aroused state. Jo Lucca apparently was as well.

"Well good night, little man," she said ambiguously with a contemptuous smile. "Time to go home and take a cold shower."

Brock was not only frustrated but furious. He was a little sensitive about his height. He was, in fact, of average height, about five feet eight but he had always wished that he were tall. Tall girls in particular intimidated him and Jo Lucca, now seemingly towering above him as he reclined on the low-slung sofa, caused an immediate loss of his tumescence. The next minute the two roommates left leaving him remembering not the seductive blonde but her contemptuous friend. He could not sleep that night.

He had been aroused by his encounter with the willing blonde but it was the image of her dark-haired friend that caused him to toss and turn in bed. In his imagination, he envisaged perfect breasts straining to be released from her sweater which was still golden but now made of fine cotton which revealed the outline of nipples as erect and pulsating as his own phallus. Her lips were parted and she appeared to be in the early throes of orgasm. Her smile, however, remained knowing and scornful. He was filled with an intense desire not just to have her but to take her violently. He saw himself rutting relentlessly as the snooty Miss Lucca yielded to his lust and wrapped her long legs around his back, clinging to him in frantic fervour. He did not want to make love to her. He wanted to take her until she cried out in total surrender. His fantasies were so realistic that, at the temptress's imagined climax, he ejaculated and was finally able to sleep.

CHAPTER FOURTEEN
Boston, Fall, 1927

The next few months were frustrating for Brock. Josefina Lucca was a constant presence in his life but it was an unsatisfactory one. He could see her as his duties frequently took him to Mens Surgical 2 but there, he could only see her as an anonymous member of the nursing staff. She gave no indication that she had ever had any personal dealings with him. Only on a few occasions did her expression vary from one of polite professionalism and then it was replaced by one of amused contempt. He said nothing but was filled with impotent anger every time they passed each other. He was infatuated with her but he was having difficulty finding her when they were outside of the hospital. They both had occupations that gave them little time for leisure. It could be weeks before he might run across her off duty unless he asked her for her plans when he saw her on the ward. He could not bring himself to do that in view of her distant manner while she was on duty and the memory of their last encounter.

It was while on a rotation on the medical ward that he noticed Jenny Hudson who was making beds with another nurse. It occurred to him that here was the key to getting next to the elusive Jo Lucca. He remembered that they were flatmates and how responsive the sexy blonde had been to his overtures. Using her to get to Jo Lucca might have fringe benefits along the way. She had certainly been willing to 'get it on' during their last meeting or his name wasn't J. Roylston Brock. *If that conceited Italian bitch hadn't got inside his brain he could have been having it off with 'Blondie Big Tits' for weeks. Well, maybe if he got lucky he could have them both.* He managed the first part of his plan with gratifying ease. He did not realize how well he fit the profile of her dream husband and assumed that her eager response was recognition of his unique masculine charm.

"Jenny! I've been hoping to catch you for weeks. I've been looking everywhere since you ran off so quickly from the party last month," was his opening gambit.

"I was hoping you would get in touch. I was really mad at my roommate for dragging me off like that. I didn't even get to say goodbye to you properly," she said fluttering her eyes in comic flirtation.

"How about meeting me after you get off duty and we can have a drink and maybe a bite to eat?"

"Sure, Roy. I'd love to. Give me half an hour or so to get cleaned up."

"I'll pick you at your apartment. Where is it?" he asked. She told him and they agreed that he would arrive at seven-thirty. He planned to get there fifteen minutes early. For Jo Lucca the news that Roy Brock had made a date with her friend was not entirely welcome. Jenny was bubbling over with excitement when she told her that he would be picking her up at their apartment. It was not that she was particularly committed to the enslavement of Roy Brock. She had about half a dozen suitable men whom she had set about to entrance, now dangling in the wind. Roy Brock was only one of a small coterie infatuated by her. She played them off, one against the other; alternating alluring glances on one with periods of amused indifference. The problem posed by having him assume the role of Jenny's boyfriend was that it gave him an entrée into her life that she did not want. She knew her friend very well and she had no confidence that she would be keeping Roy Brock at arm's length. That, in turn, would mean that it would be very difficult to treat him with cool indifference. She would be running into him all the time and it would be difficult to avoid sounding friendly. She didn't mind eliminating him from the list of the 'possibles.' She had plenty of those. She didn't, however, want to be sharing a bathroom with him when she woke up in the morning.

Her apprehensions were reinforced that very evening when he showed up at their apartment fifteen minutes early. As he had hoped, Jenny was still dressing and Jo Lucca was left to entertain him. She had been planning a quiet night and was still in uniform having discarded only her cap and apron. She wasn't made up and didn't feel at her best. She felt irritated and her irritation was exacerbated by his frank and lecherous appraisal of her figure. Brock had come to take out her roommate but it was clear that he would not be reluctant to make a play for her too if the occasion should arise. Jenny was a bit flustered when she realized that her new beau had been in the dangerous company of her roommate for some time but she rallied and young Mr. Brock was reassured by the warmth of his welcome that at least one of the two women was eager to please. Jenny had pulled out all the stops and was looking very desirable in a form-fitting dress that accentuated her already ample figure.

As Jo had anticipated and Roy Brock had hoped, Jenny did not play hard to get. He had long since realized that a major factor in his appeal to women was his money and his upper class pedigree and he planned to play to his strength. He had picked her up in his car and taken her to dinner at the Parker House--a very up-market establishment and one in which, for a very handsome tip, they were able to share a bottle of champagne over a very elegant meal. They had a few more shots of Canadian Whisky, courtesy of a bootlegger named Kennedy, in a surprisingly blatantly operated speakeasy. There they had danced a languorous quarter hour before returning to the apartment. They were mildly intoxicated and Jenny made no show of reluctance when they came inside the door.

She was vastly more experienced than Roy Brock and she was determined that she would give him a night to remember. A quick glance confirmed that Jo's door was firmly closed and she led him into her room, seated him on the edge of her bed and had him remove his jacket, tie and shoes. He tried to stand but she pushed him back gently on to the bed and induced him to remain still by undoing the buttons of his fly. His phallus, released from its restraint, became immediately erect and he again tried to pull her towards him. But she wasn't ready to oblige yet. This was her big moment and she was going to give it her considerable all. She slowly undid the front of her dress and revealed her magnificent breasts. She was already feeling excited at the sight of his erection and her nipples were straining against the inside of her bra. She unsnapped her bra and cupped her breasts in her hands as though offering him to drink. His breathing was getting rapid and his face suffused with blood. She decided to terminate the strip-tease before it was too late and, slipping out of her dress and panties, she lay down next to him drawing her knees up to allow him to enter her. He climaxed noisily and swiftly and she, stimulated considerably by her own bravura performance, was able to match him with her own orgasm.

It had indeed been a big night and they immediately fell asleep. They slept till 7:30. Fortunately, it was a Sunday and neither had any hospital responsibilities so they had a leisurely breakfast before Roy left. Jenny had briefly explored the possibility of a second round in the bedroom. It did not appear to be on and Jenny was experienced enough not to push the issue. Far better for him to leave remembering what a stallion he had been the night before.

Jo's apprehension that Brock's presence would encroach into her life was being borne out. She was very familiar with the noises that accompany copulation in the next room.

In her pre-reformation years such sounds had frequently been audible traveling in both directions. But overnight guests were a different story. When she had woken up at five-thirty for the morning shift, she had been all too aware of the disorder in the living room and the unseen presence of a male stranger in the other bedroom. Jenny was obviously embarked on a long-term relationship--indeed a lifetime one if her plans should come to fruition. Jo could hardly object to Roy's visits but she would object strenuously to having him as an overnight guest. That evening, after coming home from work she confronted her roommate. Jenny was in a frenzy of anticipation. She was meeting Roy again, at eight, and did not doubt that the twelve hours of separation from her charms would have re-kindled his ardor. She had been daydreaming of which of her formidable array of enticements should she use to arouse him and she had been feeling a warm glow imagining his amazed gratification. She was taken aback by the forthrightness of Jo's complaint.

"If you're planning on seeing Roy Brock on a regular basis we have to have an agreement on some ground rules. I don't mind seeing him here in the evening and what you get up to in your bedroom is your business but this is my home too," she said.

"Don't tell me that you, of all people, are turning prude on me. I know you too well," she pouted.

"You know that's not what I'm saying. I live here. I eat, sleep, dress and bathe here too. I don't want to have a strange man here when I'm wandering around in my robe."

This last remark was the telling one. On consideration, Jenny, too, did not want Roy here when Jo was wandering round in her robe either. She knew that, despite her considerable endowments, she was no match for Jo when it came to attracting men. They agreed to a midnight to noon curfew for male admirers. For the next three months leading up to the Christmas break the atmosphere in the apartment was strained. None of the three was entirely comfortable with the arrangement. Of the three, Jenny Hudson was the most content. She and Roy Brock were a couple. She was the acknowledged girl of a prize catch among the students and, she imagined, not without some justification, that she was the envy of many of the single nurses on the wards. She did not doubt her ability to keep him satisfied. He was an eager and increasingly competent lover and he had started to hint about establishing a permanent relationship. She had begun to hope that he might propose, perhaps at Christmas or, at least, before his graduation. Her teenage fantasies of marrying into a 'fine old Yankee family' were becoming a real possibility.

The only persistent worry was the unavoidable presence in their lives of her roommate. Jo's behavior gave her no pretext for calling her out. She did not come into the room half dressed when her boyfriend was present nor was her conversation with him more than simply cordial. It was, in fact, cool rather than friendly, but Jenny was aware that Jo Lucca had about her an aura of sexuality that attracted the male of the species without any conscious effort on her part. She could not help but notice that her guy's eyes followed her roommate hungrily when she passed through the living room. She started to consider the possibility of moving out of the apartment and the pros and cons of moving in with Brock. He hadn't asked her to move in but she thought that she could probably induce him to.

For Roy Brock, Jo's existence in his life was both tantalizing and frustrating. He had initially pursued her roommate as a ploy for getting close to her. The tactic had worked. He now saw her several times a week when he called for Jenny. But though she was polite to him she gave no indication that she had any personal interest in him. She still had the ability to raise his pulse rate and to fill him with lust-filled fantasy. He had made one overt pass at her early on when they were both in the kitchen waiting for Jenny to finish dressing. Taking advantage of the confines of the tiny room he had pinioned her body with his and tried to fondle her.

She had handled his clumsy advance with a cool composure that had both humiliated him and enhanced his resolve to have her.

"Keep your hands to yourself, Lover Boy," she said. "I don't need my friend's boyfriends."

"She might not always be my girlfriend," he whispered. "If she wasn't, maybe we could get together."

"Don't get up your hopes, Roy. You've got a great girl. She's crazy about you. You make a perfect couple. Don't worry about the 'what ifs.' Don't ruin a good thing."

He had heard a movement in the bedroom and had quickly returned to the living room. He was content to bide his time. For the time being he would keep his distance but her very physical presence in his life was like a thorn in his side; a chipped tooth that his tongue couldn't help probing. For the time being, Jenny Hudson was eager and available. *One in the hand is worth two in the sweater*, he mused philosophically.

It was for Jo Lucca that the new domestic arrangements provided the least satisfaction. Although her roommate and her paramour abided by the letter of the new rules and Roy vacated the apartment by twelve that still meant that he was a frequent visitor. She was constantly running into him when he arrived to pick her up. They often ate together and exchanged inconsequential chitchat. The regular occurrence of their lovemaking was also a definite drawback. Jenny and her partner weren't quiet lovers and the sounds of their mating through the insubstantial walls of her bedroom left little to the imagination. Jo was generally alone in these situations, slightly embarrassed and vaguely agitated. She was now reluctant to bring her own men friends back to the apartment and her social life was virtually on hold.

As Christmas neared Jenny decided to advance her affair to the next level.

"Will you be going back to Maine over the holidays?" she inquired.

"I suppose so; my folks will be expecting me. I've got to keep them happy you know. That's where my funds come from but I'm really going to miss you, babe," he said.

"Well, you really don't have to. I could take a few days off and come with you."

He didn't look too pleased with this prospect. *Maybe she was coming on too strong*, she thought. She had hoped that he would leap at the idea and take the opportunity to introduce her to his parents.

"You don't need to introduce me to your parents. It may be a little early for that," she backed off. "I could get a room in Portland and then I wouldn't have to do without you for such a long time. You know how I miss you when we can't get together."

This admission still didn't get the desired enthusiastic reply and she was becoming a little nettled. Was she losing her hold on him? Her paranoia brought on by her feminine intuition and her jealous observation of his behavior towards her flatmate caused her to blurt out, "I'll bet you've got your eyes on that slut, Jo. I've seen the way you ogle her when you think I'm not looking. I'll bet you'd take her with you to Maine if you had the chance."

He hastened to make amends. He wasn't ready to take Jenny to meet his parents but he wasn't ready to jeopardize the convenience of regular sex with a nubile and available nurse.

"You must know, babe, that its you I want. Do you think I want to take that little guinea slut to meet my parents? They'd piss their pants. She'd probably want me to take her to Midnight Mass; whatever that is."

"Oh! I don't think that Midnight Mass would be very high on her agenda," the placated Jenny admitted, "but you can never tell with these Wops. First it was the Irish and now the Italians. I don't know what Boston's coming to."

"We've even got a papist running for president," Roy agreed referring to Al Smith, the Democratic candidate. "I just can't wait to see Herbert Hoover clean his clock."

Jenny nodded her agreement. The conversation had been carried out in Jenny's bedroom with voices raised in unaccustomed volume and the door had not been firmly closed. Jo, who had been napping in her bedroom after a particularly hectic day, heard the entire exchange; initially with amusement at her friends attempts to ingratiate herself with the Brock family but then with dismay as she listened to the insulting and demeaning words that followed. As their words sank in she felt utterly betrayed. She didn't have the slightest interest in politics and barely knew who Al Smith was but she was an Italian and proud of her heritage.

That rotten hypocrite, she thought of her erstwhile friend, *telling me how much she despised prep school boys and then taking up with a typical WASP.* 'Guinea' and 'Wop' were fighting words where she grew up. She was not, to say the least, a devout Catholic but Catholicism was part of her Italian heritage too. The term 'papist' was as incendiary as were Guinea or Wop. If the couple now making out sweatily in the next room had set out to make a lifelong enemy they could not have planned it better. Italians are a passionate people; quick to anger and slow to forgive; the race who had given the world the word 'vendetta'. Josefina Lucca was a passionate Italian woman.

Her immediate impulse was to burst in on their lovemaking and do them serious bodily harm but a few moments reflection told her that that was probably not the best course. 'Vengeance is a dish best served cold' was a concept that she recognized and agreed with. She set about deciding how best to wreak vengeance on Jenny Hudson and J. Roylston Brock. It did not take long for her to come up with a plan. It would be subtle but devastating and had a beautiful simplicity. It would play to their weaknesses and to her strengths. Lucretia Borgia would have been proud of her. She would set about seducing Roy Brock. She did not doubt for a minute her ability to do so. This would be a devastating blow to the treacherous Miss Hudson who had so much passion and energy invested in snaring him and was even now daydreaming of a white wedding in St. Mark's Episcopal Church in Hanover, New Hampshire. Then, when she had Brock truly ensnared, she would make his life miserable. She would drive him mad by playing on his fragile male ego. She was already experiencing her own arousal at the thought of how she could manipulate him; tantalizing him but denying him satisfaction. After six months of voluntary self-denial and restraint she could, once again, employ all her feminine wiles.

She went to work promptly. There was to be a party at Shangri La to mark the last evening for the students before the Christmas break. Roy would be leaving the following day and would be away until after New Year. This was no time for a subtle approach. She had to give him something to think about while he was gone. Throughout the early hours of the party she gave him little obvious attention but she was receiving plenty herself. She was wearing a man's thin undershirt without a bra. Over this she wore a snug velvet bolero jacket that covered her shoulders. It was not fastened in the front and her breasts were revealed fleetingly with each deep breath; her nipples plainly outlined. She made a great show of being mildly intoxicated. Jenny had been watching her apprehensively. This was more like the party girl of the previous year, dangerous and predatory. She had kept a close eye on her boyfriend all evening. As the evening progressed she finally had to go to the bathroom. Jo had been watching for this opportunity.

"Come on Roy and kiss me under the mistletoe," she slurred exaggeratedly. He needed no second invitation. He had been hoping for a chance like this for three months. She led him into a dimly lit corner and he found himself receiving a wet open-mouthed kiss. His hands flew instinctively to explore her breast that as he had noted earlier was not encumbered by a bra. They were not rebuffed and with his hands fully occupied he felt her run her hands over his own rapidly engorging organ. Before he could respond to this exhilarating experience she pushed him away and, murmuring "Merry Christmas, Roy," she left both him and the party. The entire episode had taken less than two minutes but, as had been intended, he spent many hours of his vacation re-living the moment.

Unlike the medical students, the nursing staff and residents had very little time off over the Christmas and New Year holidays. The flow of patients passing through any big city hospital is unabated. Nurse Lucca was off duty on Christmas Eve and Christmas Day and Jenny Hudson had time off over New Year. Jo used the opportunity to re-establish her ties with her family. She had deliberately set out to keep her sister and her family at a distance when she had first arrived in Boston and had chosen not to live in the North End where Theresa and her husband, Alfredo Napolitano, were raising a rapidly expanding family. It wasn't because of any personal antipathy. She loved her sister. She just wanted to avoid too close scrutiny of her social life by what she correctly assumed would be the disapproving eye of her big sister. She had visited the Napolitanos only sporadically. It was time to make amends.

"Tessa," she called, "Jo here. It's been ages since I saw you. How are Fredo and the *bambini?*"

"Jo! I'm so happy you called. We don't see enough of you," her sister replied delightedly. Alfredo owned and operated a grocer's shop and delicatessen that served the local population.

"Are you going down to Brockton over the holidays? I was thinking of going to see Mama and Papa over Christmas," said Jo disingenuously.

"Why don't you have Christmas with us if you're off duty? We want to have a big family get-together and I've already invited them. They're coming here."

"Tess! That would be great. I get Christmas Eve and Christmas Day off and I haven't been down to Brockton since last summer."

"Perfect! Come as soon as you can on Christmas Eve. Then we can all go to Midnight Mass together and have a big feast on Christmas Day. It will be a bit of a tight squeeze sleeping. You might have to share a bed with Maria Elena or sleep on the sofa."

"I'll sleep anywhere. Tuck me under the tree and tie a bow in my hair," she laughed.

"Oh Jo! It'll be like old times. You can bring me up to date on all your adventures."

Jo reflected that she would need to give the family a strictly edited version of her adventures but it would feel good to be once again surrounded by a group of people who wished her only well: her loving family. *How dare they--her treacherous friends--condescend to her and her Italian famiglia* she thought fleetingly, but she suppressed the thought. Nothing was going to spoil her Christmas.

Jenny Hudson, similarly, decided to spend her time off with her parents. It was considerably further for her than for her roommate. Hanover, New Hampshire was not as convenient to Boston as the North End. It would be impractical to make the trip on New Year's Eve and then to return to Boston on New Year's Day. By happy chance, her schedule happened to include an off day on January the second as well as the holidays so she would have one complete day at home without travel. She hoped to reassure her hide-bound parents that their golden haired innocent was still unspoiled by three years in the wicked world of Boston. She thought that she might give some broad hints about her Yankee beau: the son-to-be-doctor from Maine. *Who knows?* she thought, *maybe the fact that her father had a busy general practice might prove to be an additional lure to a soon-to-be-graduate looking for an opening. What could be a more perfect outcome all round?* With these idyllic thoughts she

"I suppose I was just so eager to see you. You've been gone two weeks. I've been thinking about taking you to bed ever since you left," he lied. "How about putting off supper for half an hour and I can show you just how much I've missed you." This was the sort of fantasy that she had conjured up in her daydreams. She was excited by his urgency and in their subsequent lovemaking she forgot about her roommate.

Over the next four weeks Jo took pains never to be alone with Roy in circumstances that would permit physical intimacy or even private conversation. She did manage to be a frequent presence in his life and lost no opportunity to appear in as seductive manner as possible. She gave him long soulful glances. She adjusted her clothing in a provocative manner and straightened her stocking seams after placing her foot on a dining room chair. Very little of this escaped the notice of Jenny. Her friend, who had been so circumspect in her behavior, was suddenly behaving like a Hollywood vamp. Why was she suddenly doing this? She had long known that she was no match for Jo if they were in head-to-head competition for the same man, but up until Christmas she had shown no interest in him. So far, Roy had shown no diminution in his ardor for her but she was deeply concerned that she would not keep his interest if Jo really set out to ensnare him.

"What are you up to Jo?" she finally confronted her friend. "You've been making eyes at Roy ever since Christmas. I didn't think you even liked him." Jo played innocent.

"I don't know what you're talking about. You know I'd never make a play for my roommate's fella," she protested.

Jenny was not convinced that her friend was as innocent as she protested. She had lived with her for over a year and a half and had seen her in action on innumerable occasions. Jo was aware of her every move and gesture and of their effects on men. If it looked like she was trying to add

Roy Brock's scalp to her string of conquests it was no accident. Jenny was filled with apprehension but there was not much she could do about it. She continued pretending not to notice her friend's behavior. Roy found himself often bewildered by the oft-conflicting messages that Jo was sending out every time he visited Jenny. Her behavior was provocative; as though inviting him to make an amorous move but the opportunity never came for him to act upon the impulse. He could not understand it. Jo obviously wanted him. Why was she continuing to frustrate him? He had to know what was going on.

Catching her alone for once on the ward he said urgently, "Jo! I've got to talk to you in private. Please meet me after work--just for a quarter of an hour. How about coffee at Brennan's when you get off? I'll wait for you."

"Alright Roy, but I don't want Jenny thinking that we're on a date."

"She'll never hear about it but I've got to know where I stand," he pleaded. "I'll see you at 6:15."

When he arrived at Brennan's, Jo was waiting in the vestibule and kissed him full on the mouth but with the propriety that their public location demanded. He was encouraged and after ordering coffee and two slices of Boston Cream Pie and they were seated in a booth he came straight to the point.

"Jo! You know that I've been crazy about you for six months. I keep getting the feeling that you like me too but nothing ever happens between us. What do I have to do to get through to you?"

"I told you before Roy. You're my roommate's boyfriend. I don't steal my friend's fellas."

"Does that mean we can never get together?"

"I wish it weren't so. Jenny seems to think that you're quite a catch but I won't have her thinking that I took you away from her."

"I'm thinking of breaking up with her," he improvised desperately. "Would that make a difference?"

"Well, it could but don't think you can expect to drop her on Monday and then show up at our apartment on Tuesday. She's my friend and I want to keep her that way. I'll know if you break it off with her. It won't be hard to tell. She'll be devastated and she'll be watching me like a hawk for a while. Once she's got over that we possibly could start over with a clean plate if you behave yourself."

"You want me to stay away from you until she's got over me?" he said with unconscious conceit. "That could take months. Am I not even able to see you during that time?"

"Well certainly not in our apartment. That would be adding insult to injury. Maybe we could see each other after a while; maybe in your place. You have an apartment don't you? But we must be careful. I don't want Jenny to suspect anything. Why don't we just see what the future brings? You know I'm worth the effort," and, so saying, she gave his thigh a squeeze and hurried out into the darkening evening leaving Roy to digest the messages he had received.

He had no idea that Jo had overheard his insulting remarks or that her blandishments were the lures of a mortal enemy playing him like a fish on a line. Consequently, he concluded that she was eager for them to get together and that her reluctance to make the commitment public was truly a concern for a friend; or rather, not so much for her friend's peace of mind, but for her ability to retain Jenny's friendship. Possibly Jo did not want the inconvenience of finding a new roommate, or worse, having to find a new apartment. This was his cynical conclusion but one thing was clear. He had to break it off with Jenny Hudson if he were to have any hope of getting into Jo Lucca's pants. He was, he was surprised to note, a little saddened by the thought. Jenny Hudson had proved to be an ardent and kind partner and he would miss her company and adulation but

Jo Lucca had become an obsession for him. Jenny had to go and must not know that Jo was the reason.

The most obvious course for him was to put the girl's apartment off limits. He would just stop coming around and would avoid, to the extent possible, any contact with her. He knew that in a short while they would have to have a confrontation but after a couple of weeks 'on ice' she would surely have got the message that he was through with her. He could then deliver the *coup de grace*. It was surely characteristic of his sublime self-regard that he considered losing him as a boyfriend comparable to death by firing squad. Jenny was, predictably very bewildered and then upset when Roy did not show up at the apartment for the next four days.

What do you think has happened to Roy?" she cried to Jo. "Do you think he could be sick? Surely he would have called me."

"I've no idea why he hasn't been around. I know he's not sick. I saw him on the wards today. Maybe he's been studying. Finals are coming up in a few months."

When he didn't make an appearance over the weekend Jenny was beside herself. Was Roy cooling off? Has he found himself another girl? Was Jo up to something? She certainly had been acting oddly over the past three months--but no--Jo could be safely ruled out. She had been home safely every evening. Jenny had passed Roy in her ward that day and he had barely acknowledged her presence. She was absolutely distraught. She had no idea what was happening. The young man in whom she had invested so much of her hopes and dreams and with whom she had fondly imagined a life of marital bliss had suddenly turned cold and she didn't know why. Jo Lucca knew and reveled in her friend's consternation even if some residue of conscience caused her to have a faint flicker of sympathy for her distress. This she promptly suppressed by recalling the sense of betrayal that she had experienced when she had overheard Jenny's sneering acquiescence with Brock's insulting slurs about her Italian heritage. The hated words--'Guinea,' 'slut ' and 'papist'--were etched in her memory.

How dare they condescend to her? she fumed. Her forebears had ruled the world when the Anglo-Saxons were still wearing animal furs and painting their faces blue.

For Roy Brock the next weeks were frustrating. He was required by Jo's implied conditions to stay away from the apartment and to treat his former girl friend with a coolness that he did not really feel. He was forgoing the comforts and satisfactions of a cozy relationship with Jenny Hudson and yet he did not seem to be making any headway with the elusive temptress of his fantasies. He now didn't even see Jo except in strictly professional situations, as he now had no reasonable pretext for visiting her apartment.

After a couple of weeks he decided that he could hold out no longer. He had to bring the situation to a head. He knew that he had to make a clean break with his old flame and to make it clear that the breakup was, in no way, precipitated by any actions on her roommate's part. This would call for the confrontation that he had so dreaded. There would be tears, accusations and denials. He would have to be cruel and accept the role of the villain in the melodrama. It was so unfair, he thought. He was not a bad person. He really liked Jenny Hudson. She was his kind of person but that Italian bitch had really got under his skin. He wanted her with a visceral longing. When he called up images of her fleeting nakedness or relived her unpredictable provocations--the glances, the kisses and the fleeting touches--he could feel a stirring in his loins that, even when subdued, left him irritable and frustrated.

He had to stage manage a public break up with Jenny. He decided that the weekly Saturday evening party at Shangri La would be the ideal spot. Jo Lucca could act as co-conspirator to ensure that Jenny was there. He managed to waylay her in the ward as she finished giving out the dinner trays. As always, she was accompanied by two or three convalescing patients who eagerly volunteered to help her with this chore but she dismissed them with a warm "thanks for the help guys" which made them even more determined to volunteer to help tomorrow. Sitting in a hospital bed when you are in the convalescent stage is very boring and watching the nurses was the main distraction. Helping Nurse Lucca with the dinner trays was the high spot of their days and they competed for the privilege on Mens Surgical 2. They knew their place in the hospital hierarchy however-- at the bottom--and they reluctantly trailed back to their beds when the white-coated Dr. Brock hovered in obvious expectation of their departure.

"Jo! I've got to finish this thing with Jenny. It's driving me mad. Can you be sure to bring her to the party at Shangri on Saturday?" he muttered.

"Okay Roy, I'll get her there. If she thinks you'll be there she certainly will come but be sure not to show any interest in me. Maybe you could make a fuss over one of the other girls. Try Patsy Flynn. I've often seen her giving you the eye. But don't get too involved. I might want to check out your apartment if the coast is clear."

It was time to set the hooks a little deeper into Mr. J. Roylston Brock: Maine's gift to womankind. By his sharp intake of breath she knew that she had succeeded. She was hot blooded by nature and not, by inclination, a tease. She had always been straight forward in her dealings with her hosts of admirers. If she liked a man, she liked him and her responses to his overtures were not designed to confuse. He would know where he stood with Jo Lucca. She did not deliberately tantalize simply for the pleasure of brushing off his overheated advances. The case of Roy Brock was different. Revenge was her motivation. Brock had not appealed to her particularly, even in the fall and nothing in his behavior during the familiarity brought on by her roommate's romance with him had caused her opinion of him to improve. To the contrary, she had found him to be crude, conceited and condescending even before she had overheard his unforgivable conversation with

Jenny. To tease, therefore, was to her uncharted territory but she was not naive and for nearly two years, she had been living in the sexually supercharged atmosphere of Boston General's off-duty precincts. She had witnessed, and even participated in, a fairly comprehensive range of male/female interactions.

Teasing, she had observed, involved raising the expectations, generally sexual, of one party, typically the male, with the expectation and intention of denying those expectations. She understood, of course, that many male expectations or at least hopes are rejected and advances spurned not with any premeditation of denying them but out of fright, or prudence or even simply the changing of the female's mind. After all wasn't that a woman's privilege?

Jo Lucca, now, *intended* to tease. She planned to raise Roy Brock's hopes with the express purpose of dashing them and leaving him frustrated and unfulfilled. However, she wanted to prolong this torture for as long as possible and this would pose a problem. It would obviously be a simple matter to 'bring him to the boil' only to leave him unfulfilled. She could do this for an evening or even for a week but she was setting out to keep him on a string until summer when he would graduate and be out of her life forever. To achieve this she knew that she would have to let him have more than just an occasional kiss or pat on the knee. How could she prevent his gratification while ensuring that he kept coming back for another try? To this age-old conundrum she gave much serious thought.

Chapter Fifteen

Boston, January, 1928

"Let's plan on going to the do on Saturday night. You've really got to buck up, Jenny. You look really down. Maybe you'll see Roy there and you can have it out once and for all. He's sure to be there. I saw him chatting with Patsy Flynn on my ward and I know that she's going to be there. You know you're miles better looking than her."

"Oh Jo! I feel so miserable. I don't know what's happened. We were so happy together. It will break my heart if he's taken up with a cheap floozy like Patsy Flynn: damned lace-curtain Irish mackerel snapper," she added with unexpected vehemence. She was not normally given to outbursts of ethnic or religious vitriol. She thought it was beneath her. One may think these thoughts but one mustn't voice them. Jo ignored this and was able, eventually, to coax her to accompany her to the weekend event.

They arrived at 9:00 p.m. with the party going at full swing. Jenny had pulled herself together and was looking very lush and a little apprehensive. She was wearing a snug Angora sweater, an expensive linen skirt and high heels. In other company she would have stolen the show. Roy however found his eyes irresistibly drawn to her friend who gave him a conspiratorial smile across the room.

"How can I get to talk to him, Jo? I can't just walk over to him and ask him to dance. I'd just die if I did and he just walked away."

"Tell you what. I'll get him to dance and then I'll hand him off to you; sort of like cutting in in reverse. After that it's up to you. You can't tell about these things. If he'd rather have Patsy Flynn than you it just shows that he has no taste-- that lace curtain Irish mackerel snapper," she added getting a rueful smile from her friend.

Jo had no compunction about walking straight across the floor and inviting Roy to dance--much to the annoyance of Nurse Flynn.

"Here's where you get your chance, Roy," she said while maintaining a very proper distance between them as they danced a slow waltz. "If you steer me over to Jenny after a bit I'll leave her to you. She's just looking for an opportunity to pour her heart out."

"And when we've broken up finally-- and I'm not looking forward to that process--how soon can we go public as a couple?" he whined.

"I don't want us to be seen together too soon after your break up with Jenny but I don't see why we couldn't get together in your apartment as long as we do it on the quiet. Tell you what; if Jenny dashes off home in tears after you tell her it's over and I'm pretty sure she will, then we can meet in your apartment. It's just off Beacon Street isn't it? Let me have the key and I'll leave quietly right away. You hang around for half an hour or so and no one will be any the wiser."

"Its on Worcester Place: number 24," he mumbled fumbling with his keychain.

"Worcester Place! Oh very ritzy! I didn't realize that I would be hobnobbing with the upper crust," she teased. "Do you think I'm up to it?"

"I know I'll be up to it," he boasted enjoying the risqué turn of the conversation.

"Here we are Jenny. Roy has been dying to talk to you," Jo said as she steered her partner up to her friend. "I'll leave you two lovebirds in private."

She found it almost painful to see the hopeful look on Jenny's face as she smiled timorously at her erstwhile beau as her friend faded away to the other side of the room.

"I don't know where she got that idea from," said Roy deciding to grasp the bull by the horns. "We're not lovebirds anymore. We haven't been since Christmas. I thought you would have got the message by now. I haven't been around for a month."

"But why, Roy? I love you and I thought that you loved me. I even started to hope that we'd be married. I was going to ask you home over Easter. Daddy's so looking forward to meeting you. He's even thinking of asking you to join him in practice when you graduate."

She was getting desperate. Her lips started to tremble and her eyes filled with tears. This was startling news to Roy and, for a minute, he considered reversing his field. To walk right into partnership in a thriving practice in Hanover, New Hampshire--home to the famous Dartmouth College--was not to be sneezed at particularly when it came with the bonus of a doting and very sexy wife who was the daughter of the principal. However, he was too far committed. He had to go through with the plan he had agreed to with Jo. The thought of her waiting in his bed eager to comply with his every wish was too overwhelming and he resolved to end the encounter with Jenny as quickly as possible. It would be cruel to prolong the agony. He would be cruel to be kind, he thought, not too originally.

"You're just making it hard for us Jenny. It's just one of those things. I did love you but it's too early for me to be settling down with one woman. I want to see other girls. I've started dating Patsy Flynn. Besides, I'll be leaving here in a few months. Now don't make a scene. People are starting to look at us," he said as Jenny's tears started to cascade down her cheeks and she stared to sob. "I'm sorry, Jenny. Really I am," he murmured and to his surprise felt a little sad, "but its over," he added as Jenny covered her face with her handkerchief and fled from the room in tears. Jo was nowhere to be seen. The realization that she was now en route for his apartment drove all thoughts of Jenny's distress out of his mind.

The next thirty minutes seemed interminable. He did not want to do anything that would invalidate the bargain he had made with Jo and so he continued to pay obvious attention to Miss Flynn who was delighted and a little surprised. She had been somewhat miffed by the nonchalance with which Jo Lucca had lured him from her side ten minutes earlier and then had been an interested spectator of the drama which had obviously been played out across the room between Roy Brock and Jenny Hudson who, up till this evening had been a recognized couple.

Surely, Jenny's departure in tears could only be good news for her, she thought. *I now have a clean shot.* This thought was reinforced during the next half hour as Roy went through all the motions of courtship: bringing her a drink and chatting animatedly. He was obviously in high spirits and Patsy Flynn allowed herself to hope that she was the reason. As Jo had mentioned, Patsy had had her eye on him for some time. It was, therefore, quite a surprise and disappointment when he bade her a cursory 'good night ' and hurried from the room thirty minutes later. *Surely he's not going to try and make up with that Jenny Hudson,* she thought. *I've got a much better figure than her; that fat, insipid, Yankee bitch,* she added spitefully. Vitriol is not limited to any one ethnic group, color or creed.

Meanwhile, Roy was making his way to his apartment in an agony of expectation. This was to be the culmination of months of plotting and the reward for which he had given up a comfortable, if unexciting relationship, and undergone the discomfort of an embarrassing and painful breakup. He was not disappointed when he reached his front door he found it unlocked and went in. Jo had been through his closets and had shed her clothes. She now stood, leaning back slightly against the kitchen table wearing only the top half of his pajamas and a pair of high heels. Soft music was playing on the radio and the place was dark except for a light escaping from the bedroom. He stood in awe for a few moments trying to take her in. She was all he had ever imagined in his wildest fantasies: a lush body, the more exciting for being partially covered, the pajama top barely reaching her upper thighs and then those magnificent legs rendered even more improbably long by the high heels. She left the table and walked slowly toward him and, before he could move, wrapped her arms around his neck and pulled herself into him till she was standing on tip toe with their bodies locked together. He had been becoming aroused from the moment he saw her and now his erection was becoming painfully evident to him and also, though not painfully, to Jo as well. This was exactly what she was striving to achieve.

"Wait a minute, Jo," he panted. "Let me get out of these clothes. This belt is killing me."

"Don't be in such a hurry, lover. We've waited so long for this. Let's take our time and enjoy it properly," she murmured throatily. "Let's go into the bedroom," and she led him in by the hand.

She turned him around to face her with his back to the bed and gave him a languorous kiss and with their bodies close together she sank down onto her knees and with her head nestled against his stomach she released his belt and slid his trousers and underpants down to his ankles where he frantically kicked them off. He was now in a state of extreme sexual excitement: his phallus engorged and pulsating. He was getting frantic. He realized that unless he took her immediately he would soon not be able to. Jo was well aware of this too. She had made love to many men and knew that there was a wide range in the duration of their excitement before they achieved orgasm. She had become something of an expert in gauging their reactions and she knew that Roy was about to ejaculate. Her ability to make this almost clinical assessment was enhanced by the fact that she was not involved emotionally with him. In fact, she disliked him and her actions since his arrival had been as calculating as they were convincing.

He was starting to breathe rapidly and was trying to push her down onto the bed. This was the moment that she had been waiting for. She allowed herself to be pushed backwards and as he scrambled towards her, she opened her thighs and wrapping her legs around him she locked her heels behind his back and allowed him to penetrate. His orgasm was almost immediate. He was spent in seconds. He soon realized the futility of remaining impotently between her legs. His body was no longer filled with lust-filled craving. He was not happy as he collapsed down beside her on the bed. He could hardly believe that he had made any impression on her. She had barely had time to realize that he was inside her, never mind being excited and fulfilled by his virility. He knew for sure that he had not caused her to climax. Jenny's orgasms were frequent and noisy. To make matters worse, she was being nice about his shortcoming.

"Never mind, lover," she consoled, "there'll be lots more times in the future."

"Can't you stay tonight," he pleaded. "In a couple of hours we could try again."

"You know I can't do that Roy. I'm sorry but if I leave now I'll be home before midnight and Jenny will be none the wiser but if I don't get home till breakfast she'll be sure to smell a rat. The least you can do is to fix me a drink while I have a shower and then I must go," she added.

He reluctantly agreed and half an hour later, the evening in which he had placed such expectations ended on a downbeat note. He couldn't blame Jo. She had been all he had ever imagined: incredibly gorgeous, sexy and even eager but somehow the evening had not lived up to his expectations. He had unconsciously envisaged himself as the dominant figure--the priapic male subduing his reluctant mate with his rampant masculinity and ending, triumphantly, with her completely overwhelmed, exhausted and grateful. That was not what had transpired. Jo had been in complete control at all times and part of him resented that. He was even more resolved than before to bring her into his thrall. Half a mile away his erstwhile lover was having very different thoughts. The evening had gone just as she had planned and she reveled in the thought of his humiliation.

When she arrived home, Jenny's door was closed. She had cried herself into an exhausted sleep. The disordered state of the apartment--discarded clothes strewn across the furniture and unwashed dishes in the sink--was testament to her agitation. She was normally a meticulous housekeeper. Climbing into bed she set out to review critically the events of the evening. She figured that he would not be forgetting tonight any time soon. That should keep him drooling for a while. *He'll be all too eager to show what a stud he really is*, she ruminated. *I'll let him stew over that for a while.* She also had to prevent getting pregnant. She had absolutely no intention of getting knocked up. She had had that scare once before and she didn't need a repeat performance. Tonight she had not taken any precautionary measures but she reasoned that she was only five days after the start of her period and, according to her understanding of female physiology, this was the 'safe period'. She would have to be more careful in her future trysts. She was sure that she could keep out of his way for a week without being too obvious but beyond that, he would undoubtedly become aggrieved and importunate.

To maintain the charade that she was now an eager partner in their relationship she would have to give him another ride. Unfortunately, that would put the timing right into the middle of the most fertile days of her cycle. The only solution to this dilemma, she decided, was that Roy would have to use a condom. She guessed that he would not want to. Most men, in her experience, didn't. They found them awkward and they drastically reduced the spontaneity of the lovemaking. She was not a big fan either. When she had, in the past, partnered with a man to whom she was physically attracted she had generally ignored the risk. She delighted in the last seconds of her partner's climax with its gush of semen serving as a testimony to her desirability as a woman. She had, so far, in the past dodged the bullet with only one scary exception but she shuddered at the thought of being impregnated by Roy Brock. Still that was ten days into the future. For the time being she had to keep him interested but unhappy. This should do it she decided as she wrote him a short note to be delivered to his apartment.

Dear Roy,

Thank you for a wonderful evening. I am re-living the moments of our lovemaking as I sit here in bed penning this note and remembering the thrill of our bodies coming together. I am counting the days until we can be together again but, darling, we must still be careful. I know that we cannot keep our affair a secret forever. We live in a goldfish bowl but I still want to keep Jenny as a friend. In a few weeks, if we are seen together, she won't be able to make any connection between your breakup and our getting together but, till then, we must be discreet. I am sorry that I will not be able to see you for a week or so. I have promised to help my sister in the evenings all next week. She lives in the North End and she's painting the kitchen but we could get together a week from Wednesday. If you promise to take me out for a decent meal you could probably persuade me to stay overnight. One note of caution: I don't want to get pregnant. Bring a condom. Better yet, bring a box!!

Yours till then,
Jo
xxx

Looking this over, she wondered whether or not she might be laying it on a little thick, particularly in light of his less-than-inspiring performance but she left it unchanged confident in her knowledge of man's capacity for self delusion. She particularly liked the patent unlikelihood of her helping to paint her sister's kitchen. There was nothing quite so effective as an obvious lie to fill a suitor with fury. How often had she turned down an unwelcome date by telling the presumptuous suitor that she had to wash her hair?

During the next ten days Jenny moped around the apartment. She rallied enough to carry out her nursing responsibilities and to keep a brave face to the world but, even on the ward, her fellow staff members noted that she was not her ebullient, chatty self. The very public breakup with her medical student was public knowledge. It had occurred in the midst of a large gathering of the unmarried segment of the hospital staff. Opinions varied but the consensus among the nurses was that Roy Brock was a louse. Jenny was popular with her fellows. She was normally a cheerful and outgoing colleague, conscientious at her job and always willing to accommodate a request for a shift swap or to help out with one of the less pleasant duties that are the frequent lot of the nurse. Patsy Flynn was looked on with disdain for a day or two as she was believed to have betrayed the code of the nursing staff by moving in on a fellow nurse's man but this was short lived. Enough people had witnessed Brock's departure to know that she was not responsible for his abandonment of Jenny Hudson.

It was during the hours off duty that the depth of Jenny's unhappiness was most evident. Jo had set about to achieve this very result and should have been delighted but she was not. It was one thing to plot the shattering of dreams but quite another to be a close up witness of your victim's distress, particularly when the victim was a friend with whom you had lived for nearly two years. She and Jenny had shared innumerable adventures together. They had partied together, laughed and cried and shared triumphs and disasters. Now she had to watch while her friend moped around the apartment listlessly; her silent gloom punctuated by bouts of quiet sobbing. Even Jo had not realized the extent to which her friend had pinned her hopes and her affections on Roy. She had been head over heels in love and couldn't shake off the effects of his rejection. Jo was staying out of the public eye when not at work to limit Roy's opportunities to accost her. She was therefore exposed to the full extent of her friend's unhappiness. She was even starting to experience twinges of guilt and regret at having been its cause.

In retrospect, Jenny's contributions to Brock's sneers had been minor. Perhaps she had overreacted but it was too late for second thoughts. Brock was the real target of her vendetta. She could not reveal her part in his betrayal without undoing all the effort she had put into ensnaring him. She did everything to console her friend short of revealing her involvement in the plot. She listened to incessant reliving of the climactic break up and accounts of the depths of her distress. She put her arms around her and allowed her to sob against her shoulder until she cried herself out.

"I don't understand what happened, Jo. I love him. I was sure he loved me. We were so happy together," was the theme repeated over and over with minor variations. Jo made all the right noises and gave her words of encouragement.

"There now, baby," she crooned. "There'll be plenty of others coming along or maybe Roy will realize how much he misses you. I don't think that anything is coming of that fling with Patsy Flynn. She's been walking around looking like her nose is out of joint."

"But Jo! I love him," she wept for the thousandth time.

Silently, Jo reflected that she had not counted on being the consoler-in-chief when she had plotted her revenge. She was 'hoist by her own petard.' This was not the exact way in which she would have expressed her thoughts. Petards had played little part in her life to that point but that was the gist. She realized that she was not as tough as she had imagined, at least where Jenny was concerned.

"Tell you what, Jenny. Let's wash our hair. I'll set yours and you can set mine. I'll even paint your toenails. Then we'll make a batch of oatmeal cookies and a pot of coffee, add a slug of rotgut. Then we'll have a feast and make an early night of it."

It was almost a relief when the evening of her assignation with Roy finally arrived. She was a healthy and energetic young woman and sitting around doing nothing with her lachrymose friend was wearing her out. The long evenings had given her ample opportunity to consider how best to manipulate him. The first consideration was that she was almost exactly half way through her menstrual cycle and, that being the case, she was at her most fertile. It was of paramount importance that Brock's spermatozoa did not get the opportunity to mingle with her eggs. She was not letting Brock get her pregnant. That gave her two options. She would either have to contrive to make him ejaculate before he could gain access to her vagina or ensure that he did not come while he was still inside her. Neither of these options was a good bet. It looked like a condom was the only solution. This had to be non-negotiable.

She decided to attempt to achieve option one, with a condom as the fall back strategy. With this in mind she met him at eight o'clock at Brennan's wearing her most seductive outfit and a lavish amount of her friend's Chanel. She knew that she could bring him to the boil but she also knew that she had to pace herself. They would not reach his apartment for a couple of hours. She therefore limited herself to snuggling up next to him in the booth he had booked and treating him to a chaste kiss while ensuring that his hand was tantalizingly close to her breast now thinly covered with a silk blouse and unrestrained by a bra.

The evening was starting off very well for Roy. He felt that he was on his home ground and playing to his strength. Jo would not be the first girl to be swept away by his *savoir-faire*, an elegant meal in a famous restaurant and the judicious consumption of illicit alcohol. He was careful not to drink too much himself. He wanted to be wide awake when he took the elusive Jo Lucca to his bed. It was a fine meal and in other circumstances Jo might have enjoyed it wholeheartedly but she too was intent on her role-playing to fully enjoy the meal or the wine. As he drove her back to his apartment she turned up the heat by nibbling his ear while informing him of the delights she was planning for them both. As soon as they entered the apartment she gave him a wet kiss exploring his mouth with her tongue. He reacted as she expected by running his hands over her breasts and thighs. He was already erect and eager to bed her.

"Let's go to bed. I need to come into you," he urged throatily.

"I want it too, Roy. Just give me a minute to get ready," and she went into the bedroom pausing at the door to say, "I'll call you when I'm undressed."

A minute later she called, "I'm ready Roy." He entered, half expecting to find her standing naked by the bed or perhaps lying on her back. She was, in fact kneeling on the bed facing him as he entered the door. She was wearing only a minute pair of panties. When he came within arms reach she pulled him to her so that his face was pillowed between her two magnificent breasts. He had been determined to mount her as soon as he entered the room but he could not resist taking a while to cup her breasts and nuzzle her nipples.

Jo was on the edge of achieving her goal. In another few minutes he would be unable to control himself. Option one would have been achieved. She was excited by her success and having a mouth on her tits had felt good even if the mouth belonged to a real bastard. Roy had learned his lesson though. He wasn't going to lose control too soon. He broke away, pushed her down onto the bed and started taking off his pants.

"Wait Roy!--the condom. I don't want you to get me pregnant--unless you've decided to marry me," she added with a sly suggestive smile.

He had hoped to avoid a condom. He had used one only twice before during his affair with Jenny. They found them frustrating to handle and she had agreed to forgo their use, confident that they were destined for marriage anyway. He was therefore very clumsy in opening the packet and grumbled and fumbled as he attempted to put the sheath on his penis.

"Let me help you, Roy," she said and grasped his erection gently between her fingers.

This was her last chance to avoid actual intercourse and her ploy almost succeeded but he pulled her hand away and pushed her back onto her back. She resigned herself to the inevitable and opened her legs invitingly and he entered her with a shudder of satisfaction. He did not climax quite as soon as he had done on their first encounter and Jo was able to give a very convincing impression of a woman in ecstasy. When she felt him reaching his climax she dug her nails into his shoulders and, clinging to him with her feet, raised herself to meet him as he let out a loud groan and collapsed on her like a deflated balloon. He fell asleep almost immediately and Jo felt a little smug; congratulating herself that she had managed him quite well. She had, in fact, rather enjoyed the sex too. She had faked her orgasm. She thought she had been very convincing but she had found that it was almost impossible for her to fuck even Roy Brock without enjoying it, somewhat, herself and she had.

At that alarming thought she pulled herself together and was able to rekindle her loathing of him by gazing at him snoring softly by her side with his mouth open and a trickle of drool dripping from the corner. She had already planned that he should not leave her in the morning feeling any sense of conquest. After their first disastrous coupling he had begged for a second chance. "Let me try again. I'll be ready in a couple of hours," he had boasted. Jo had known a fair number of men and knew that the ability to have sex several times a night was not a common characteristic. She had promised him that she would stay overnight and she had decided to find out if Roy Brock was one of the exceptions to the rule. If she couldn't arouse him before she left in the morning she would leave him nursing another blow to his ego and if he proved her wrong then his virility was something she needed to be aware of in planning their further sexual forays. She set the alarm clock for four a.m. and when she awoke she nudged him awake as well and ran her hand up his thigh to his flaccid penis.

"Wake up Roy. I've got to be at work by seven and I'll need to go home and get ready. But I want you now. We've still got two hours before I have to leave."

He was delighted by this acknowledgement of his performance the previous evening but he felt an abrupt sinking when he felt that his body was not reacting in the usual way. He could normally become erect at the thought of Jo's lush body and here she was leaning over him with her breasts inches from his face and he felt nothing stirring. His body felt as though it had lost all sensation from the waist down. He tried to conjure up the sensations that had filled him so urgently the evening before. He nuzzled her breasts and fondled her groin--nothing. Jo was insistent. She writhed convincingly under his touch. He imagined that he could see that she was getting desperate to have him possess her. She certainly acted the part giving him ever more licentious access to her body. She massaged his feet and slowly proceeded with her hands and mouth up his thighs. She rubbed her nipples against his face and teased his with her tongue. She finally, in apparent desperation, stood above him with her knees on either side of his thighs and slowly sank to straddle him with his still flaccid organ cuddled between her breasts. He was still a spent force. It had become obvious that further intercourse with him was not on the breakfast menu and Jo left after a quick shower.

As she left him, humiliated and angry at himself, she murmured in false consolation, "there'll be other times, lover. Not every man is up to a second round. I'll never forget how you made me feel last night." *Now I've really got him where I want him,* she gloated to herself. *He won't forget last night in a hurry,* and then filed in her memory bank, one strike and he's out for future reference.

One incidental benefit of the early morning disaster was that Roy was no longer interested in her staying overnight. He would content himself with a single amatory interlude with Jo in those evenings when she consented to go to his apartment. This enabled her to live a more predictable existence and she was able to delay her roommate's discovery of her treachery.

****

It was early April before it finally dawned on Jenny that her roommate's comings and goings could only be explained by her having a man seriously in her life. How else to explain her regular absences after dinner, departing perfumed and with full makeup or her returning in the late evening, disheveled and smiling smugly to herself? Without the torpor brought on by her depression, she would have put two and two together long since. Inevitably, she had heard that her former lover was now heavily involved with her best friend. Suddenly, everything fell into place. Jo had, quite cold-bloodedly, set out to steal her lover, she realized, and she had succeeded. Horrified, she relived the events of the last four months since Christmas. She could not recall the date of her breakup with Roy or the exact sequence of events before and since that awful day. Jo's carefully calculated stage management of her delay in taking up with Roy had been wasted effort. For three months she had been living in such misery that very little that was going on had made much impression.

Jo had obviously mounted a deliberate campaign to lure Roy into her clutches. She had sent out the signals of her availability and of her eagerness to receive his advances. She had all the weapons on her side and Roy had succumbed to the temptations. He was scarcely to blame at all, she rationalized. She had seen so many men, over the last two years, falling over themselves to vie for Jo's attention and to ingratiate themselves with her that she was willing to believe that Roy had been helpless and was not responsible for his desertion. She was so desperate for a happy resolution of their split that she was willing to forgive him anything if he would only return to her side. She wanted 'happy ever after'. The nagging thought that remained in her brain; why had Jo decided to win him away from her? She had never before made a move on any of her other boyfriends and she had never, prior to last Christmas, indicated that she found Roy at all attractive. She had been polite but cool and distant, while Roy and I were hitting it off so well she thought. Jo's behavior had been beyond reproach. Never once had she sent out any indication to Roy that she would welcome his attentions. What had happened around Christmas time that had turned her most loyal friend into the shameless siren she had become? She had to have it out with her. The decision to bring the issue to a head brought her a degree of relief. Nothing could be worse than the sensation of bewildered despair. At least I'll know what's been going on, she thought even if it doesn't get Roy back to me.

"Jo, stay a while after dinner. I've just got to talk to you. I think you know you owe me a few answers," she said, as they were finishing up the evening meal.

"Sure Jenny what's on your mind?" Jo replied. She knew full well what this had to be all about. She had known that this had been coming for weeks and she had not been looking forward to it, particularly now that the reason for her anger towards Jenny had almost been forgotten: not so much the actual words but the intensity of her reaction to them.

"I know that you and Roy are having an affair," Jenny said at the conclusion of the meal. They were seated face to face in the apartment's two armchairs. Jenny was succeeding in maintaining her composure. She had resolved not to become hysterical and she was trying to sound judicious rather than accusatory.

"What I don't understand is why you suddenly changed. You don't particularly like Roy and it seemed like you wouldn't give him the time of day. Then all of a sudden you're all over him; flashing you tits and wandering through the room half dressed. You could have any guy that you set your eye on and yet you decided to make a play for the one guy who loved me. I thought you were my friend, Jo." With every word she became more emotional and as she finished she began to cry and sobbed brokenheartedly.

"I heard that you had called me a guinea and a slut and I just wanted to get back at you," Jo admitted. She realized that flat out denial would not work and hoped that the partial truth would be sufficient to satisfy her friend. By not mentioning the actual circumstances in which she had heard the words she hoped that Jenny would not realize that Roy had been the other participant in the insult. She hoped to give her enough information to placate her. She still hoped to keep hidden her antipathy towards Roy and her plans for his continued humiliation.

"I never called you a slut," Jenny insisted. The mental turmoil of the last four months had long since swept any memory of the conversation from her mind. "You know I don't talk like that. It's just not like me."

"Oh! I don't know," said Jo hoping to lighten the tone of the conversation. "How about calling Flynn a 'rotten, lace curtain, Irish mackerel snapper?'" This recollection brought a slight wan smile to Jenny's face and when Jo followed up by throwing her arms around her and whispering "I'm sorry Jen," she allowed herself to be comforted. That brought the dreaded confrontation to a happy conclusion but it still left unresolved the fact that Jo was still spending several nights a week in Brock's apartment and, Jenny presumed, in his bed.

"I just can't break it off like that," she said snapping her fingers. "It just wouldn't be fair to him," she added disingenuously, "but I've been thinking of breaking it off for some time. There's a really good-looking intern, you know--

Mogsie Peacock who's been giving me the come on. I'd just about decided to give him a run after the Easter break. I hear he's hoping to do a radiology residency here next year so he'll be around for a while. I'll ease Roy out of my life by then and we can go back to being best friends. I've really missed that. If you forgive him, I know he'll want you back. He's always talking about you--really pisses me off," she embroidered.

Jenny was a little bit nettled at the cavalier manner in which Jo proposed to sever the relationship with her idol as if casting off a worn out shoe but she could hardly complain at the objective. She would just have to put up with his infidelity for a few more weeks. Neither girl was entirely happy with the outcome but they had at least agreed to a plan to put the past behind them and get on with their lives.

Jo was now faced with the problem of how to make the last months of her affair with Brock as unsatisfactory for him as possible. After his difficulties with the condom he had become adamant that he would not use one again. This provided Jo with a pretext for preventing the complete subjugation to his needs that she knew he craved. She insisted that they observe the practice of *coitus interruptus* or as it is more generally known 'taking the kettle off the stove before it boils over.' This had never been a very effective technique and had accounted for much of the surge in population in countries all over the Catholic world. It called for enormous self-control by the male at a point in the coupling at which he was least inclined to uncouple. This was a most unsatisfactory situation for most couples but one perfect for Jo's purposes. When a 130 lb. girl is pinioned on her back by the phallus of a 180lb. male in the heat of a sexual climax she has very little option but to accept his decision whether to vacate the premises or not.

Knowing this fact well after several unsuccessful episodes in her past, she took care that the first time that they attempted *coitus interruptus* she was safely in the middle of her non-fertile period. As she had expected, when she recognized the signs of Brock's imminent ejaculation and called on him to pull out, he ignored her words and her squirming resistance and climaxed noisily. This was his most satisfying moment in his four month long relationship with her. He had not only completed the sex act with her but he had done so over her manifest resistance, overcoming her apparent objection by his overwhelming masculine power. He could see himself as a veritable caveman and he could not resist a smug smile of satisfaction on his face as Jo furiously berated him. He did not exactly want to have impregnated her but he felt an inner satisfaction that she knew that he could have done so--or so he thought. Jo knew that she had given a virtuoso performance. He was not even too annoyed when Jo punished him by shutting him off for a couple of weeks. She would come around, he was sure. Now that she had coupled with the real Roy Brock she would be panting for more. Her protests were merely attempts to disguise her true feelings. Jo had been angry at the necessity of giving him the satisfaction of one complete sex act; *coitus ad terminum* you might say. It does not mean 'making love at the bus stop.'

Indulging him had been regrettable but an essential part of her strategy. She was now ready for stage two. She eventually allowed herself to resume her liaison and when they had reached the point of retiring to the bedroom, she put her plan into effect. They had had a particularly lavish evening on the town as Roy had tried to charm his way back into her favor and her bed. She had him lie naked on his back. He cautioned himself not to become excited too soon. It was not easy because she was as desirable as ever and he soon found himself aroused by her near nudity. He was relieved therefore when she promptly straddled him and positioned herself over his erection so that he could feel her moistness with the tip of his penis.

"Remember Roy, if you come into me it will be the last time you ever do," she murmured and lowered herself fractionally until she engulfed the head of his penis. He was intensely excited and he strained his hips upwards to plunge deeper into her but she pressed his hips down with her hands, immobilizing him and squeezed his penis with the muscles of her pelvic floor. Before he could either climax or drive further into her, she pulled herself upwards and disengaged from him leaving him to ejaculate messily on the sheets. It had been an intensely erotic experience for him but it again left him unfulfilled. This was the pattern of their sex life as the month passed by and Easter approached. He yearned to possess her but she was completely in control of their lovemaking. He could not deny himself those final seconds of intense sensation even though he knew the climax was to be denied him. He wanted her but he hated her too; the teasing bitch.

Chapter Sixteen

Boston, May, 1928

It was all well and good for Jenny to agree to live with the promise of Jo's eventual shrugging Roy off but the reality of living with it on a day-by-day basis made her miserable. She had to know that when Jo left their apartment dressed to kill she was going to end up in his bed. She could not help reliving her confrontation with her; dredging back every word with obsessive concentration. *"I heard that you had called me a guinea and a slut."* Did that explain her subsequent behavior? Suddenly, the circumstances in which these words had been spoken came back into her memory. Roy had actually been the one to utter them and she had merely agreed with them. If her memory was accurate, and she knew with certainty that it was, then it had been in the bedroom that they had been spoken and Jo must have overheard them; not only hers but Roy's as well. How then to explain her subsequent behavior? She could understand how Jo might, out of anger at her, have contrived to steal her boyfriend but why, when she had also heard his snide remarks would she have chosen to throw herself at him. She knew that most of the men in her circle of acquaintance lusted after Jo so why was she apparently rewarding his nasty words by giving herself to him.

Jenny was, by nature, a straightforward girl at heart so it took her a while before considering a more devious explanation for Jo's behavior. Could it be that Jo was set on entrapping Roy into marriage? Hardly likely if she hated him.

But how about if she was only toying with him with the idea of dashing his hopes; leaving him at the altar perhaps? This wasn't precisely what Jo was trying to achieve but it was close enough to have the feel of truth and it convinced Jenny. Roy was trapped in the coils of a treacherous seductress. Jenny was filled with a cold fury and a righteous anger; the heartless hypocrite, pretending to be sorry for me while she was conspiring to destroy my perfect love affair and hurting me so. She had to get close enough to Roy to lay out the details of the whole conspiracy and she knew that he would not be happy to learn that he had been gulled so comprehensively. She would need to give him some incentive to talk to her and to do so in private. After much agonizing she decided to write him a note.

Dear Roy,

I hope you will forgive my presumption in writing to you. Perhaps you will forgive one who has loved you so deeply. I promise that I do not want to make a scene. Daddy does not yet know that we are no longer together and he is still interested in having you join his practice. Please meet me after work on Wednesday or another day if that does not suit you --say six thirty- at Brennan's. I only need thirty minutes of your time.

With love as always,
Your Jenny

The letter duly arrived at his apartment and Roy found himself intrigued by the possibilities that it suggested. Could he possibly have his cake and eat it too? When he had dumped Jenny, somewhat reluctantly, he had imagined that all prospect of joining her father's practice was gone. Heck, he was only weeks from graduation! He could surely forego half a dozen bites at that tempting apple, Jo Lucca, to keep alive his prospects with the Hudsons; father and daughter. He was still simmering with the realization that Jo wasn't going out of her way to make him happy. He'd find out what Jenny had to say.

He met her as she had requested and they found themselves a booth, away from prying eyes. She had made herself up and was smartly dressed. She looked very attractive. He had forgotten how exuberant her figure was but Jo Lucca still had the power to send him into paroxysms of excitement or of frustration. He knew that he could not abide much longer in this ambiguous state. His ego was in tatters. He, at times, felt that he was going mad when she brought him to the brink of sexual gratification only to leave him disappointed again; used and defeated yet again. As he looked at the young woman sitting next to him, gazing at him like an adoring puppy, he realized how content he had been when they had been a couple indulging their mutual desires without inhibition or restraint. Not with Jenny had he been tantalized and then rejected. She had yielded her body up to him generously and unreservedly. He was almost ready to make up to her even before he had heard what she had to say to him. The chance of a partnership in her father's practice was an additional consideration but Jenny would make a very welcome sight to return to in the evening if he played his cards right. He had treated her cruelly and she had every right to hate him but her letter had sounded as though she was a still in love with him. He reached out and tentatively put his arm around her.

Any doubts about his reception were swept away when she promptly responded by pillowing her head against his chest and sobbing, "oh Roy I've missed you so much."

Brennan's was as busy as always at that time of the evening so they had to keep their reconciliation restrained and Jenny launched into her account of what had preceded their break up and of her interpretation of what had transpired since.

"Don't you see Roy? Jo heard us when we made those remarks about her. We didn't mean them and she completely over reacted. She has set out to get her own back. By stealing you away from me she has hurt me terribly. I'm not sure exactly how she is planning to hurt you but I know she is and that she doesn't love you. She has just been playing with you, taking advantage of your loving nature. I know she's got some scheme to injure you; maybe she's trying to have a baby with you and trap you into marriage."

At this appalling thought she again burst into tears and Roy decided that they should continue the conversation in the privacy of his apartment. He had come to the restaurant straight from the hospital and so they had to walk. It was only fifteen minutes away and his mind was furiously churning trying to digest the information that Jenny had given him. He didn't doubt what she had told him and her interpretation of Jo's behavior had the ring of truth. It was a hard nut for him to swallow that she had been playing him for a fool. She had had him dancing on a string for four months. All of her behavior, in and out of the bedroom, had been a sham and fitted Jenny's theory. He cringed as he remembered the many humiliations that he had endured in the course of their lovemaking and how easily she had made him jump to her bidding. In contrast, he recalled the satisfaction that he had experienced when he and Jenny had been a couple.

What a fool I've been to allow that sexy slut to lure me away from Jenny; his lover of the lush body and compliant daddy. By the time they had reached his apartment he had come to a momentous decision. He would not only reconcile with Jenny he would cement the deal by marrying her. It was very drastic but he would be graduating in six weeks and he had not yet decided on his future plans; should he become an intern or look for a job in Southern Maine? A cozy billet in Hanover, New Hampshire was appearing very attractive.

"Jenny," he said when they had arrived and shed their coats. "I've missed you. I don't know what I ever saw in Jo

Lucca. She's just a low class floozy; an over-sexed tramp. She came on to me when you were coming back to Boston last Christmas and, like a fool, I let myself be taken in. You're the only girl I've really loved. I was happy with you and I think that you loved me too. I want to marry you as soon as I'm through with school. I graduate in six weeks. Do you think that'll be too soon?"

"Too soon Roy! I'd marry you tonight if you wanted me to." She was beside herself with joy. She had hoped that her unmasking of her rival's nastiness would result in Roy's disenchantment but she had not realized that he had already considered extricating himself from her clutches. He had bought into her every accusation and now (Could this be true?) he had asked her to marry him. He wanted her back and to have her forever.

"Yes! Yes! Yes!" she sobbed and folded herself into his arms to give him a foretaste of what he had to look forward to and a reminder of what he had been missing. If Mr. Royston Brock had had any second thoughts about his decision they were soon banished as he experienced the most satisfactory sex he had had in over four months. Jenny was not aware of it for nearly four more weeks but on that night J. Royston Brock Jr. was conceived.

When they finally simmered down and tidied themselves up they sat in bed and discussed some of the practical details that would have to be attended to if they were really going to marry in June. First they would have to introduce Roy to her parents and tell them that they wanted to marry. Jenny suggested that she take him home over Easter. It would give them the news and also give Roy a chance to ingratiate himself with her father as a potential partner. She didn't doubt, with stars still in her eyes, that they would be overjoyed. Her mother, particularly would be relieved to have her rackety daughter safely wedded, and to the scion of one of New England's wealthiest families no less. There was still one fly in the ointment. Jenny couldn't bear the thought of sharing an apartment with Jo until her wedding. She never wanted to see her again. Roy suggested a solution for that problem

"Why don't you resign from the hospital before you leave for home? You'll have so much to do getting ready for the wedding and you wont be needing to practice once we're married," he said masterfully. "You need to see Jo Lucca only long enough to clear out your stuff. Think what a wicked blow that will be to the rotten slut. She won't be able to afford the place by herself and it's the wrong time of year to be getting a new roommate. She'll be lucky to find one by mid-July."

This was not the kind of small mindedness that would have normally occurred to Jenny but tonight her hero could do no wrong and she agreed to his proposal. The Easter break was only a week away and with her accumulated leave she could give her two weeks notice now and never have to return to the hospital. She would miss being a nurse, she thought a little sadly, but perhaps, one day, she could help out in Roy's office or at the Mary Hitchcock--Dartmouth's hospital. Maybe she would--after she had had a half dozen kids--she thought complacently, not realizing that she had already made a head start in that direction.

That evening she managed to avoid Jo. She decided that she would not give her any warning that she and Roy had discovered her faithlessness. *Let her find out when I don't come back from home after Easter. I'll just tell her I've resigned--tired of nursing. I won't even mention that I'm marrying Roy. She'll go crazy wondering what's happening and then--Wham!--I'll send her a wedding invitation just for spite.* She called her parents the next morning and told them of her plans to visit them next week. She asked them if she could bring Roy along to visit and hinted broadly that she had very special news to give them. They agreed and were suitably intrigued. They had not heard much from their daughter about the young man she had been so agog about at Christmas and had assumed that their romance had run its course. That, apparently, was not the case and once again they prepared themselves to be suitably enthusiastic about young Dr. Brock were he to turn out to be a future son-in-law.

Jo had to be told something. She and Jenny shared responsibility for the apartment. This was not true in the strictly legal sense as Jenny was the sole lessee. Jo had been reimbursing her directly for her share of the rent and the lease ran through September. It would be Jenny's liability as long as Jo kept making her contribution. In that regard Brock's assumption that Jenny's departure would be a formidable blow to Jo's finances was incorrect. That, however, was the last thought that was occupying Jo's mind when she learned that her long-time friend was planning to give up her career and return home. She was still unaware that Jenny had broken the code to her mysterious behavior and so took her friend's startling decision at face value; Jenny was still depressed at Roy's abandonment of her and had decided to return to the solace of her home and family. Now she felt even more remorseful at being the cause of her friend's distress.

Things moved fast and by Easter, Jenny had departed for New Hampshire. Her notice had been regretfully accepted with assurances that she would be gladly re-hired if she were to decide to re-enter the work force. She had packed up her clothes and books and shipped them home. Her furniture she left in place pending its potential acquisition by some future tenant. Jo was happy that she was not required to fill all the gaping spaces that would have resulted if she had elected to take it all with her. She was a little hurt by the lack of warmth of Jenny's farewell after their lengthy friendship but did not give it much thought. *Poor Jenny is still pining over Roy,* she thought. *I hope she gets over him soon. She's much too nice for him.*

Chapter Seventeen

Boston, Summer, 1928

For the first time in months, Jo found that she had a void in her social life. Brock had gone to visit his parents in Maine, he had informed her, and would be gone from Boston until shortly before his graduation. It felt odd to have the apartment to herself but she was relieved to have a respite from having to deal with him. She was actually becoming quite tired of the entire charade and would be glad when he graduated and she could put the whole affair behind her. Revenge was just not worth the trouble, she decided. Maybe I don't belong with the Borgias after all she thought to herself ruefully. She could now scarcely remember the incident that had caused her fury but she would let the play run its course; it would only be a couple of weeks. Meanwhile with no Roy to bamboozle, she was able to spend a little time with her family and to think about re-ordering her priorities.

One aspect of her life that never failed to give her satisfaction was her work. She enjoyed the daily challenge of being responsible for a busy surgical ward. Even though the days were long and some of the individual duties distasteful--not even Florence Nightingale would have found flushing bed pans pleasant--she never failed to leave the hospital without the 'gratifying feeling that her duty had been done.' There was always a new problem as there was a constant turnover in the ward's thirty-six beds.

Most of the patients in a surgical ward are not hospitalized long enough for them to register on the nurses' consciousness as individual human beings. Patients who needed hernias repaired, gall bladders removed or varicose veins stripped tended to flow through the ward seamlessly and uneventfully. Jo treated them with her customary efficiency and good cheer but it was the patients who needed longer hospitalization who impressed the nurses as individual human beings with their own quirks and personalities. In the main it was older men and those with more serious conditions who required longer stays in the ward; patients convalescing from cancer surgery or diabetics learning to walk with prosthetic limbs after amputations. Jo was always cheerful, helpful and caring. Especially with the terminally ill she was upbeat and encouraging. Along with delivering a narcotic for the relief of pain she brought her charming smile and a solicitous, if unnecessary, 'tucking up.'

The patients adored her. They loved to watch her progress up and down the ward and competed for the right to help her distribute the meal trays or shift the beds or screens when those maneuvers were required. She ran her ward almost like the conductor controlling the mood and tempo of his orchestra. On the day of her return to duty a patient with terminal cancer of the bowel died. This was, of course, not an uncommon occurrence for the nursing staff but, for the current occupants of the patient beds, it was a particularly depressing experience. There develops in an open ward a certain *camaraderie*. The longer-stay patients get to know their fellows, their diagnoses and their progress. When the death occurred that day with its attendant grim rituals and the eventual removal of the corpse under a sheet, a pall of gloom descended over the ward. Conversation between the patients virtually ceased as the patients were reminded of their own mortality.

It is in this sort of situation that the best nurses show their true mettle. Jo circled round the ward with great animation making lighthearted banter and giving out her most winning smiles as if she had just won the 'Irish Sweep.'

She was refusing to acknowledge the validity of their gloom and, for a few seconds, an air of resentment followed her but her good humor was catching and her smiles irresistible. She was soon the center of a lively storm of badinage and primitive repartee and when she returned to her more prosaic duties the ward had returned to its normal condition.

Late that afternoon Frank Kelly was admitted for the beginning of his lengthy stay in Mens Surge No. 2 at Boston General hospital. Jo was a nurse of some five years experience. She had taken care of, literally, dozens of patients who had undergone appendectomy. She had even stopped wondering why the procedure was so illogically named. The 'append' was not an organ found in *Gray's Anatomy*. Major complications such as generalized peritonitis were less common and far more interesting. Over the next four weeks of his body's internal life or death struggle with the infection going on inside his abdomen she and her colleagues became interested spectators of the battle and not just spectators but participants.

Of the very ill patients on the ward, Frank was one of the younger ones and his facial scars and eye patch made a memorable impression on the nurses. That his missing eye was the result of a world war battle injury contributed to his fascination. Jo found herself hoping to find signs of improvement when she checked him at the start of each workday. Of course, she was, in her professional capacity, eager to see all her patients get better but with Frank she developed a more personal interest. She admired the uncomplaining manner in which he accepted the indignities and discomforts of his illness. He was very undemanding; almost apologetic when his condition required him to request help and he treated the routine attentions to his needs as though he had received a great favor. He was obviously very ill and not up to the lighthearted chatter that the convalescing men loved to indulge in. Jo was the nurse who noted the first evidence of abscess formation and passed the information along to the surgical staff and it was to her that Frank had reported its spontaneous drainage four weeks into his hospital stay. She felt an almost personal satisfaction in his recovery.

During the next two weeks, as his body was throwing off the residual effects of his prolonged infection, Frank became more conscious of his surroundings. Inevitably he fell in love with Nurse Lucca. Men who have faced death or serious injury almost always do fall in love with their nurses. Frank had observed the phenomenon when he had been hospitalized in Flanders. With their defenses down and an acute awareness of their own vulnerability even the toughest of his fellow 'Tommies' treated the nurses with an almost reverent regard. No thought of romantic involvement crossed his mind. His love was not entirely platonic. Jo's 'female' appeal was simply too strong not to have some impact to the male in him but to Frank she was a ministering angel and to think of her in a romantic context was simply beyond the powers of his imagination. She couldn't help but notice his infatuation. He was, by no means, the first patient who had fallen for her and she recognized the signs but there was not the slightest trace of flirtatiousness in his conversation. His eyes followed her adoringly when she walked the ward but it was the look of one who gazed at an unreachable prize. She was flattered but not entirely happy. As a woman she was warmed by the affirmation that men did not just admire her but want her. Especially was this so when the man was young and not unattractive despite his resemblance to Captain Morgan the pirate.

Frank's convalescence was uneventful and over the last two weeks of his hospitalization his body regained most of the weight that it had lost and color returned to his cheeks. He gradually overcame some of the awe in which he had held the nurses and occasional managed a mildly flirtatious remark to Jo, to which she might respond with "Oh thank you kind sir! You are too kind," with a comically exaggerated fluttering of the eyelashes which made his heart race and his face blush.

He was so obviously smitten that it was almost comic to watch but, even though she laughed off his clumsy gallantries, she was quietly quite touched. He was such a nice and decent man. On the day of his discharge, he returned from a visit to the shop in the hospital lobby with a bouquet of roses for Jo and a five-pound box of chocolates for the whole nursing staff.

"Miss Lucca, I think that you're the nicest nurse in the whole world. I am really going to miss seeing you each day," he stammered blushing to the roots of his hair.

"You're not a patient any longer, Frank. You can call me Jo now" and with that she gave him a kiss on the cheek. Think about us American girls once in a while as you cruising the ocean waves."

"I don't think I'll ever forget you Miss--er Jo. Thank you for everything."

"How soon are you going back to Britain?"

"In about ten days. Cunard has me booked on Mauretania sailing out of New York on the ninth. I'll be staying at the Seaman's Hostel on Front Street until I leave. Maybe we'll run into each other," he said and then, overcome by embarrassment at his temerity he fled, leaving Jo smilingly ruefully at her reluctant admirer's shyness. He really had been rather cute.

****

Roy returned to Boston with only one week remaining until graduation and his right to bear the title 'Dr. Brock' after its rather ironic usage during his last two years in school. He told Jo the necessary lies to account for the time of his absence in New Hampshire by recounting fictitious anecdotes about his stay in Maine with his parents. He had been on his best behavior while visiting Jenny's parents and this had required him to keep his hands off their daughter except in the most restrained fashion. Jenny too reverted to a more demure style of dress than had been her custom when out and about in Boston. Roy had not wanted to jeopardize his chances of success with the parents and he and Jenny had decided, rather belatedly, to 'save it for their wedding night.' Jenny's parents were suitably impressed.

At Bowdoin Roy had learned to comport himself as a gentleman. He had the look, the accent and the manners of a proper blue blood and they congratulated themselves that their daughter had finally regained her senses and had abandoned her quixotic ideas of nursing among the great unwashed masses of Boston. She could now return home and marry her rich Yankee and claim her rightful place in the country club and the Junior League. The marriage date had been settled on: two weeks after Roy's graduation. It was a shorter period than Mrs. Hudson would have preferred what with the thousand details that custom decreed needed attention for a proper wedding but she agreed to compress the schedule given that her husband wanted Roy to join the practice as soon as possible. Having practiced solo for twenty-five years he couldn't wait to take the month-long tour of Europe that they planned to take as soon as Roy was installed in the practice.

Roy had therefore had not had any sexual release for several weeks when he returned to Boston. Prudence, not to mention any remnants of conscience, would have prompted him to put aside forever any further contact with Jo, but he did not believe that he was adequately revenged on that Italian strumpet who had made such a fool of him during the previous six months. Why jeopardize the chance of a fairy tale marriage and a life of happy ever after for one last fevered encounter with Miss Josefina Lucca R.N.? He knew that it was foolish but he could not resist the chance of getting the upper hand, just once more, before he left Boston for good. She still knew nothing, he believed, about the changed chess board on which the game was to be played out and his bride to be was a hundred miles away, up to her neck in plans for wedding dresses, decisions about brides maids and orange blossoms. Even in the worst-case scenario, her discovery of his final fling, he was confident that he could charm his way out of trouble. *She worshipped him,* he congratulated himself.

"Jo," he said when he eventually found her in her, now half empty apartment, "I've really missed you. All the time I was up in Gorham I was looking forward to being back. I've made all sorts of plans that I'm dying to share with you. While I was up north I decided to go for an internship--just to flesh out my education before I go into practice. I have been accepted at Maine General in Portland--a really fine hospital. Don't be sad. We don't need to be apart. You could easily get a job there and we could be together."

"I don't know about that, Roy," she replied. "I really like it here in Boston and I've already got a good job at the General. I'll be a head nurse in a year or two. Ask me to marry you and I might give it some thought," she added. She was sure that that would cause him to drop the subject and it did.

"Well, think it over anyway. I'd like our last evening together to be really special. You're Italian. Why don't I take you to your favorite Italian restaurant? We'll wine and dine and then we can say our goodbyes here. I've been saving myself so that we can give each other a night to remember. If we make love here you can just roll over and go to sleep in your own bed. I'm planning on wearing you out."

"Make sure I don't fall asleep while you're trying to," she replied. She had never allowed him to become too cocky and she wasn't about to start now that there was a light at the end of the tunnel. *I just need to be careful one more time,* she reflected. *I believe that I'm 'safe' but, last hurrah or not, this last romp is not going to be a home run for Brother Brock.*

True to his word, in this regard at least, Roy had made reservations for 8:00 p.m. at arguably Boston's finest Italian restaurant. Boston is inordinately blessed with institutions of higher learning. Many of them were holding graduation ceremonies and the town was full of families gathering to celebrate the great event. Reservations were hard to come by but money is a great persuader. Jo amused herself by thinking that, if Brock had been somebody she didn't detest, she could have saved him a lot of money; the owner of the restaurant was her second cousin once removed. She resolved to indulge herself with no regard for his bank book. He could afford it anyway.

They started with *Pollanca con Risotto* and followed up with *Lombatina di Vitella* accompanied by *Carciofi Vignarola* and rounded off the meal, which would have satisfied Lucullus, with *Zabaglione ala Marsala*. They had knocked back a bottle of *Aziano Chianti Classico Riserva* during the course of the evening and Jo had to admit to herself that it had been a damn fine meal. *Don't get careless* she cautioned herself as she realized, piling into his car, that she was not quite sober. Brock had kept her glass filled and had drunk less than a third of the wine. He had his own agenda and remaining sober was a part of it.

In the apartment Jo still played the vamp. She wanted to give him one more futile climax and then send him out of her life forever. She had not quite decided whether or not to taunt him, once he was through, by letting him know that she had been playing him for a fool but she decided against it. Just let me get it over, she thought. With this in mind, she performed the maneuvers that she knew excited him most. It didn't take much. Jo, undulating her hips in the near nude, would have given the statue of a saint an erection. True to form he promptly became erect and pulled her down on the bed next to him.

"Lie down, Roy," she breathed. "You know I like it when I ride your cock," she breathed. He liked it when she 'talked dirty'.

She positioned herself to receive him. She preferred to have him under her as it enabled here to control the tempo of the coupling and to end it in time to avoid insemination. This was the moment that Roy had been pointing towards all evening and how he intended to end Jo's infuriating dominance. Without warning, he pulled her down onto his chest and spun her onto her back. She was wet. Even with a jerk like Roy Brock, Jo responded to male excitation. He threw himself on top of her, his body between her spread-eagled thighs. She was unable to stop him entering her deeply. She struggled frantically and for a minute he was content not to move but held still, enjoying the sensation of her body writhing helplessly against his motionless penis. Then when her struggles had started to subside he started pumping rhythmically and within seconds she felt his phallus convulse and his semen spurt into her. He did not fall asleep as he normally did after sex but sat back on his haunches and sneered at her devastation.

"Now you know what it feels like to be taken for a ride. Jenny and I have known about your dirty tricks for weeks. We've been back together for two weeks. She's a wonderful lover; knows how to make a man happy; not like you, you teasing bitch. We're getting married next month. So *arriverderci*! If I never sleep with another 'wop', it will be too soon."

Jo lay motionless for several minutes. The expectations for the evening had suddenly been turned on their heads and she had difficulty grasping what had happened. She had in fact been raped but she knew that she would have absolutely zero chance of getting anybody--layman or police--to sympathize with her plight. She felt violated and yet she had been a party to her own violation or, at least, had been partly responsible for it. Most of all she felt the loss of her feeling of invulnerability; of being mistress of her own fate. Then came the gut-wrenching realization that Roy Brock might have impregnated her. *Please God, don't let that be*, she prayed and sobbing heartbrokenly, she finally fell into an exhausted sleep.

****

Graduation from medical school is a profound experience and one that is, potentially, a life altering event. Henceforth, the new doctor becomes a member of the ancient and honorable brotherhood of healers. Only ordination into the priesthood brings with it such a profound change in the very essence of one's existence. Even the most prosaic of new physicians must feel on this day that he has become a member of a noble profession and find himself resolving to be worthy of it. Tufts University had placed its seal of approval around his shoulders. J. Royston Brock enjoyed his justifiable success but couldn't help the unworthy thought from entering his head that the ceremony gave him one last opportunity to publicize Miss Lucca's humiliation to the world. In addition to his parents, Roy had invited Jenny Hudson and her mother and father to the graduation. Within the circle of the unmarried staff of the hospital, Roy's break up with Jenny and subsequent affair with Jo Lucca was common knowledge. They were known as a couple by all their acquaintances and had even been seen together only two days earlier. The very public reconciliation with Jenny Hudson was considered by many to be a real 'kick in the teeth' for Jo. Her comeuppance received a mixed reception. Both girls were popular colleagues. Speculation ran rife that the presence of two sets of parents at the ceremony must mean that a wedding was in the offing. Jenny confirmed this gleefully when a friend enquired. There is nothing like the engagement of one of their number to a member of the medical staff of 'their hospital' to delight the hearts of the nursing staff. It is the last scene of "Sleeping Beauty'; the fairy tale finale. Despite Roy's degree, Jenny was the heroine of the hour and by extension, Jo Lucca was the villain, doomed forever to weeping and wailing and gnashing of teeth.

Had they been privy to Jo's inner thoughts they would have been surprised. They presumed that Jo was devastated by Brock's apparent *volte face*. This was not the case. When she awakened on the morning after her violation she was still in a state of shock. It was not so much the actual physical trauma of the assault that bothered her. That had been negligible but the possibility that she might be pregnant was terrifying. That she might be bearing Roy Brock's child produced waves of nausea. That possibility was remote however. She had still been 'safe.'

Within hours, her natural resilience asserted itself. It would take more than one losing skirmish with life to send Jo Lucca into a permanent decline. She could not even feel a deep sense of injustice. She had been raped. When a man forces sexual intercourse on a woman when she indicated her unwillingness to participate, he has raped her. The law is very clear on that point. There was no doubt in her mind that she had registered her unwillingness to continue but her innate sense of fairness made her accept that she had left it rather late to object. She even noted the beginning of a grin creeping over her face at the thought that the man had not yet been born who could voluntarily disengage at that point in their foreplay.

By the graduation day itself, Jo was ready to get on with her life. She realized that she had wasted six months pointlessly with a man whom she had disliked from the start. Into the bargain she had incurred the loss of the closest friend she had had in her adult life. Maybe, she thought, just for once I can fall in love with some one who doesn't just see me as a good lay. She knew that she would always be happy that nature had given her the face and figure that men found irresistible but she was more than that. She was a woman with a brain and a good education. She could hold her own in conversation. She could laugh and make others laugh. She now hoped that one day she would meet someone whose child she would want to bear. He would love her in return and they would be married. At age twenty-four, Jo Lucca had finally grown up.

Chapter Eighteen
Boston, July, 1928

The Seaman's Hostel in Boston served much the same function there as Atlantic House did in Liverpool. It provided respectable entertainment and inexpensive accommodations for seafarers. The hostel was within walking distance of the quay where the Cunarders customarily berthed and Frank was familiar with it and the area immediately surrounding it from numerous previous voyages. It was not the most scenic area of the city and after a couple of days residence in the hostel Frank was ready to wander farther afield. He still had a week before he had to get himself to New York for the voyage home. Boston was, unlike most American cities, blessed with an extensive public transportation system and so getting around was no problem. On the third day after his discharge he ventured further into the city.

There was, apparently, something going on as evident the flow of the crowd. He followed and found himself outside Fenway Park. This proved to be the home of one of Boston's two baseball teams and they were playing an afternoon game against the New York Yankees. He had heard a lot about baseball during his two weeks convalescence at the General and he decided to spend two bits and a couple of hours and see what all the excitement was about. Two bits, he had learned, were equal to twenty-five cents. This he calculated made each bit to be worth twelve and a half cents, which struck him as an odd unit of currency, but 'when in Rome' he reflected and shelled out the silver coin to gain admission. The Yankees, he gleaned, were the Red Sox' bitter rivals; rivalry that had been exacerbated when the Red Sox had traded a certain Babe Ruth to New York; a trade which had proved disastrous to Boston. Ruth had become the best player in the game and had in 1927 hit an incredible sixty home runs in one season. Frank could imagine how the Bostonians must feel each time 'the Babe' came back to Boston in a Yankee uniform. It would be as if Frank's hero, Everton's Dixie Dean, had been traded across the park to Liverpool and having him return to Goodison twice a year in the despised red shirts of the Liverpool F.C. Dixie, too, owned a record: his was for goal scoring and had been established only the past May. It was also sixty, in this case, goals in one season.

Frank did not understand the subtleties of the game but he easily got the general idea and was impressed by the athleticism of the fielders and the prodigious power of the hitters. Ruth obliged his fans and further infuriated the Red Sox faithful by hitting a ball over the enormous wall in what he learned was called left field. The Red Sox prevailed 6-2 and it was with a contented crowd that he emerged from Fenway shortly after five-thirty. It was getting on towards dinnertime and so he started to look for a place to eat. He couldn't afford an expensive restaurant and had walked for almost half an hour when he recognized the massive concrete outline of Boston General Hospital and ran into Jo Lucca R.N. who was emerging after her day shift. It was the Fourth of July Weekend and she was looking forward to the three-day holiday. She was wearing her familiar uniform and looked as good as ever. He had no way of knowing it but this was the first day of the new gentler and sweeter Jo Lucca. She was eager to get home but happy to see him. He struck her as a decent man, neither arrogant nor cocky; in fact the exact antithesis of Roy Brock.

"Good evening Miss Lucca. How nice to see you," he managed to say.

"It's Jo. Remember, Frank? Are you out seeing the sights of our fair city? I thought you'd probably seen enough of Boston General to last a lifetime."

"You're right about that but I've been watching the Red Soxers play baseball. It was quite a game. Now I'm looking for a place to get a good cheap meal."

"Well if you can wait for a few minutes till I get out of this uniform we could go out and get a bite together. I live just a few minutes from here."

The thought of such an undemanding companion and an innocent evening seemed like a good way to start her new life. She didn't think that she would be fighting for her honour with Frank.

"It's not much fun seeing the sights when you're by yourself; no one to talk to," he said. He could not believe his good fortune. This lovely girl on whom he had developed a hopeless crush was offering to spend an evening in his company. "If I'd known I'd be taking a pretty girl out to dinner, I'd have worn my best suit."

"Don't worry about the jacket, Frank. The place I have in mind, you'd be overdressed in a clean shirt." They walked amiably the five blocks to Jo's apartment. Jo felt comfortably at ease with the young Englishman and he wore the slightly dazed expression of a man who could hardly believe his good fortune.

"It's great to see you healing so well, Frank. I almost considered you my special project. I was the nurse who admitted you. You won't remember that. I was the one you first told when your abscess burst and I was the last person you spoke to when you left. I almost feel like you're my patient."

"You were wonderful, Jo. Even when I was half conscious I knew it was you looking after me. All the guys in the ward were in love with you," he confessed.

"How about you Frank?" she said flirtatiously. Old habits die hard and any way her morale needed a little boost after the blows it had suffered over the previous few days.

"Me most of all, Jo. If I wasn't leaving for home in a week, I'd be trying to make you my girl."

She was a little disconcerted by his artless words and patent sincerity and decided to keep the conversation on a light plane.

"There you have it, Frank. We're just two lonely hearts destined to be separated forever by the wild Atlantic Ocean."

They soon reached the apartment and Jo changed out of her uniform. She re-appeared in a few minutes wearing a simple sweater and slacks. As she had promised, she was not dressed for a big night on the town. Frank had never before seen her wearing anything other than the notably shapeless uniform of the BGH nurse. Now, even dressed for a casual evening, she was heart-stoppingly beautiful and for a few moments Frank was speechless. Jo was quite familiar with the impact that her appearance had on unsuspecting males. She always got a kick out of it but tonight she wanted to keep the tone light. She found Frank attractive even if his looks were unremarkable but the evening was to be a pleasant and innocent way to spend a few hours while helping to get her life back on an even keel.

"Tell me a little about yourself, Frank. You must have a glamorous life sailing back and forth across the ocean in a luxury liner," she said.

"Oh, its not too glamorous if you're part of the crew but I'm glad to have a job and I do enjoy the stopovers," he replied.

"Oh! You sailors--a girl in every port, eh? Am I going to be your girl in Boston?" she said teasingly. "How about back home? Do I have a rival in Liverpool?"

She could tell that she had hit a nerve. Frank paled. He had not thought about Isabel very often in recent weeks and he now felt a small rush of guilt that he was *tête-a-tête* with such a glorious creature as Jo Lucca and enjoying it so much.

"Come on, Frank. Tell me all the romantic details. You know us girls. We all like a love story." There was no better way of keeping an interplay between a guy and a girl from getting too mushy than by introducing the guy's other love into the conversation and Jo wanted to keep the conversation lighthearted.

"I've got a girl at home. Her name is Isabel Iskandar. I call her Izzy. We've been going out together for almost two years. We'll probably be getting married one day. She's very beautiful," he admitted.

"I'll tell you what. I've got to hear all about this. I'll make you a deal. Instead of going out, I'll make us both something to eat and you can tell me the whole story. Have you ever had a BLT? Never heard of it? It's an American delicacy; a Bacon, Lettuce and Tomato sandwich on toast," she said and retreated into the kitchenette to work on the masterpiece.

"Oh a bacon butty. I love them. I can't turn down an offer like that."

They enjoyed their BLTs and Frank conceded that the lettuce and the tomato were worthy additions to the basic bacon butty. After the main course, Jo managed to unearth a packet of Fig Newtons lurking at the back of a cupboard. They were rock hard and provided a perfect dessert when dunked in a cup of tea. There is nothing like a shared meal for promoting the conversation and, with Frank's acknowledgment of his Liverpool sweetheart, each felt that all the cards were on the table. They spent a couple of innocent hours exchanging life stories; in Jo's case rather censored ones. They told silly jokes and generally enjoyed each other's company. Shortly after nine, Frank thanked his hostess for a lovely evening. He still had to find his way back to the docks and was still unfamiliar with the MTA. Frank had been enormously surprised but delighted to have discovered that Miss Jo Lucca was not just a beautiful but unreachable ideal but a warm and approachable real live girl. The evening had been innocent. He did not owe Izzy any apologies but he definitely wanted to see Jo again.

"I'd better be off," he said, "but you've got to let me pay you back for such a wonderful evening. How about letting me take you out to dinner tomorrow evening?"

"You don't need to do that, Frank. It was only a couple of BLTs."

"Best ones I've ever had and certainly the prettiest cook--but I'd certainly like to take her out for a meal--just to say 'thank you'."

"You do know, don't you, that tomorrow is the Fourth of July? The town will be bursting at the seams. There'll be fireworks and a free concert down by the river. If you like, we could make a day of it. Meet me tomorrow afternoon and I'll show you the sights--be your tour guide. Then we can have a picnic on the Esplanade, listen to the music and watch the fireworks. Frank was eager to see her again and somewhat to her surprise she was pleased at the thought of seeing him again too. It would be almost a patriotic duty, she rationalized, to show this young Englishman how much his country had given up when they decided to tax tea back in…well, way back then. History had never been Jo's strongest subject in school. The truth was that she found him attractive and would have welcomed a little more masculine aggression from him. It would take a while longer for this female leopard to change her spots. Frank could hardly believe his good fortune. Not only would he get to see this amazing girl again but she was proposing to spend a whole day with him.

"Jo! That would be terrific. I'll pick you up here at two." He was so excited at the prospect that, as he said goodbye, he gave her a chaste kiss on the cheek.

"Come on Frank. Even a couple of BLTs deserves a better kiss than that," she smiled and gave him a resounding smooch before murmuring, "sweet dreams," and pushed him out of the door.

The fourth of July 1928 would undoubtedly rank as one of the most memorable in the young life of Francis Xavier Kelly Jr. He arrived promptly at two pm. He was wearing his best (and only) suit. The weather was quite warm and he was perspiring slightly when he arrived. Jo was feeling very good about herself. A day of wholesome pleasure stretched out before her. She was part of a national day of celebration and in the company of a nice young man who was obviously quite smitten with her, even if he was incredibly reticent. She knew she was looking at her best. Her summer dress of pale yellow set off her lightly tanned complexion and she planned to wear her big floppy straw hat adorned with a band of matching yellow ribbon.

"You look stunning, Jo," he stuttered.

"Well, thank you, Frank. You're looking pretty sharp yourself but I think you'd better leave the jacket here. You'll roast. You can pick it up when we come back tonight."

"Did you change your mind about dinner? I still want to thank you for last night."

"Don't worry about that. I've made us a picnic. We can eat while we're listening to the music. You can treat if we need to pay to see any of the sights and maybe we'll need to pick up something to drink along the way. We can always get a Coke or some lemonade if we get too hot. I'm a Moxie girl myself." She was pretty sure that most of the sights were free but even an impecunious sailor has his pride. I must really be beginning to like the guy, she reflected.

They had a wonderful day. As is true of many residents of cities famed for their historic sites, Jo had never visited most of them. She probably enjoyed the history associated with Quincy Market and Faneuil Hall more than Frank. He was simply delighted to be in her company. At the Old North Church on Salem Street she declaimed several stanzas of *The Midnight Ride of Paul Revere* to an amazed group of fellow tourists who applauded her patriotic fervour. It was only when she found that she was declaring 'Shoot, if you must this old grey head, but spare your country's flag, she said' that she realized that she had better leave poetry to the guide. Frederick, Maryland was a little further south and that was a different war. Frank wouldn't have cared what she said. She could have recited the Gettysburg address as long as she was smiling at him while she did it. They passed up on Bunker Hill but made the longish trip to Cambridge to walk through the Harvard Yard with its ivy clad walls. They watched the rowing shells on the Charles and then, tired from walking they found a coffee shop in Harvard Square where they rested their feet. They each had an ice cream.

"Don't spoil your appetite now," chided Jo. "I've made us a nice meal. By the time we're back at the Esplanade, we'll be tired again and we can have our picnic on the lawn. We'll be able to hear the music and watch the fireworks from there. It'll be a popular spot so we better not be too late."

It was a fair stretch from Cambridge to their destination and they were happy to rest on the grass and eat the repast that Jo had prepared. She had again demonstrated the mastery that she had shown with the BLTs and they were both full and rather drowsy when they had finished with her efforts. Jo had provided two bottles of Moxie to wash it down with. Frank drank his manfully. It must be an acquired taste he decided but not even Moxie could detract from his sublime feeling of well being. Jo was obviously enjoying his company and he was touched when she demonstrated her comfort in his presence by falling asleep with her head in his lap.

It was a quietly contented couple who made their way back to Jo's apartment that night. They had been stirred by the patriotic songs. Somewhat to Frank's surprise, the band played 'God Save the King'--(nobody else seemed to know the words)--and the concert had finished with cannons and the 1812 Overture. They were, by now, completely comfortable in each other's company and walked, hand in hand, from the MTA station after the ride home to pick up his jacket. When they arrived Frank felt no hesitation in pulling Jo towards him and kissing her full on the mouth. He knew that she wanted to be kissed. Jo was such a sexually charged creature that it was difficult for her to dissemble. She responded willingly and enthusiastically to him. They sank into the armchair and for twenty minutes Frank made her tingle with his kisses. He had overcome his early reticence and as each of his advances failed to draw a rebuke he gradually extended his explorations of her body to her breasts. He was in familiar territory now. He and Isabel had spent many 'goodnight' embraces in precisely this sort of situation.

Jo was thoroughly enjoying the encounter. May be this young Brit was not so inexperienced as he had seemed. He had gently unbuttoned the front of her dress and unsnapped the front clasp of her bra. Her breasts were released and he gently nuzzled her erect nipples. She was becoming eager for him to extend his explorations when he suddenly and abruptly gathered himself together and said "I'd better be going, Jo. It's late and I've got to be getting back to the Hostel." He had been reaching the limits of his self-control and there was no Izzy to keep him in check. He had never experienced a girl whose sexual appeal was so intense and he didn't want to disgrace himself by going too far.

Jo was taken aback. She had been living in a young adult society in which self-control was not considered a virtue and she had never before been put off by a suitor in the middle of an embrace. Her pride could hardly allow her to ask him to keep making love to her but she was put out and not ready to bring the evening to such an untimely close. Frank's caresses had had almost the same effect on her as they had on him.

"It's way too late for you to get to the docks tonight. They're way across town. Why not stay here overnight and go in the morning? My roommate's room is vacant. She's on her honeymoon. You can sleep there. I'll say goodnight. It was a wonderful day. You can have first shot at the bathroom. I'll see you in the morning."

She poured all this out in a rush and with a sad smile she went into her bedroom. With her departure Frank tried to get his emotions under control. He felt some relief. He had resisted the temptations of Jo's abundant charms and he had not betrayed Isabel; at least not irretrievably but every nerve in his body was crying out in anguish. He had so wanted to keep making love to Jo Lucca.

The self-restraint that it had taken had left him exhausted. Even now as he slipped out of his trousers and climbed into bed his body was quivering with suppressed desire. Meanwhile, Jo was struggling with mixed emotions too. She had been in the process of falling in love with Frank. In some inexplicable way he had gotten under her skin and she had been willing and indeed eager for him to make love to her. She felt herself becoming indignant. How dare this ordinary English sailor turn up his nose at Josefina Lucca whom the cream of the Tufts medical school pursued so avidly?

She put on the top half of a pair of pajamas and slipped quietly into his room and into bed next to him. Frank's pulse that had finally slowed down immediately started to race again. He was unable to move or speak as he felt a pair of soft hands deftly unfasten the front of his shorts. His erection was instantaneous and rock hard. The room was dimly lit but Frank could see the outline of Jo's body as she straddled his thighs and leaned forward to bring her breasts close to his face. She was still very aware, even in her fevered state, of the risk of pregnancy and she was now in mid-cycle. She wanted to have sex with Frank but she planned to 'take the kettle off the stove just in time' as she had so often with Roy Brock. One thing she hadn't counted on was her own level of desire. She had despised Roy and had not had any difficulty in willing herself to bring copulation with him to an end. Frank was different. She was powerfully attracted to him. She thought that she could learn to love him. During their foreplay in the armchair she had found herself wanting him not to stop.

Now as she lowered herself onto his phallus she felt her labia moisten profusely and her pelvic muscles relax to accommodate him. He groaned in ecstasy and reached up to gently cradle her breasts. Her nipples were erect and she started to move her pelvic muscles rhythmically, up and down. He did not respond immediately by thrusting frantically against her but gradually timed his movements in counterpoint with hers. She could feel his tempo quickening and knew that it was time to disengage. Her body would not listen. She had to ride this wave of ecstasy to its nature driven conclusion. They climaxed together with Frank crying out her name and encompassing her body in a bear hug. They lay together for ten minutes, side by side and then she turned away and they spooned and fell into an exhausted sleep.

It may appear to be wildly inaccurate to describe the next four days in their life as first love but it would not be too false. Jo Lucca had been sexually involved with many men over the previous three years but they had been purely physical affairs; promiscuous young adults whose interest in each other was limited to physical gratification and never, before she had met Frank, had she cared for her lover beyond mere physical attraction. She thought that, perhaps, it was having known him when he was so vulnerable as a patient in her care that had generated the desire in her to please as well as to be pleased that is the essence of true love. It would not be accurate to describe what Frank felt for Jo as first love. He had been genuinely in love with Isabel Iskandar and in his heart he knew that he would be again once this incredible romantic bubble burst, as he knew it must. Beauties like Jo belonged on the covers of a magazine not in the arms of ordinary blokes like Frank Kelly. Still the bubble had not burst yet. Jo was still right there, when he woke in the morning, beautiful as ever in a silk robe and making bacon and eggs for them both.

They made love in the afternoon and fell asleep in each other's arms at night. They were delighted just to be together. They held hands and kissed as they walked through the park. Jo finally allowed Frank to take her out to dinner; General Tso's chicken in Boston's small but vibrant Chinatown. On Monday, the bonus holiday in the weekend, they went to the North End so that Jo could show Frank off to her sister and her family. If proof were ever needed that Jo was in the throes of first love, this was it. Theresa, with an older head on her shoulders, approved of the young Brit. He was obviously besotted with her 'baby sister' but she couldn't help but realize that this romance was doomed to end and end sadly. What were the chances of success for a love affair between a couple that would be repeatedly separated by the Atlantic Ocean? She prayed that Jo had not fallen too heavily.

On Tuesday morning Jo had to go to work and Frank wandered sadly around the apartment and started to organize his belongings for his inevitable departure. He closed out his account at the Seamen's Hostel and retrieved his suitcase, then took the MTA to South Station to pick up his ticket for New York. He was to travel by train. The New York, New Haven and Hartford would get him to Penn Station and from there it would be a short cab ride to Mauretania's berth on the west side of the city. He hadn't been at sea for almost two months. They stayed at home that evening and had a melancholy meal. Jo's apartment had become home and the site of their love making during their brief affair and neither of them felt the urge to have a final night on the town. They both realized, sadly, that their golden hours were drawing to an end. They lay on the bed fully clad in each other's arms, painfully aware that this was goodbye. There wasn't much left to say. Jo snuggled close to him and Frank realized that she was crying. He wrapped his arms around her and gently caressed her face. They made love one last time, not with the wild passion of their first three days together but with great tenderness and ineffable sadness. Next day he was gone.

CHAPTER NINETEEN
Boston and Liverpool, July, 1928

The voyage home gave Frank eight days for reflection. The entire stay in Boston, starting with his burst appendix and culminating in his brief affair with Jo Lucca, had lasted for almost two months. So much had happened and yet it had acquired an almost dream-like quality. He could hardly believe that it had happened. First the confused month in which his body had been battling with infection. Then the two weeks of convalescence in which he had come to idolize the selfless and nurturing 'angels' who had made his recovery so interesting and so pleasant, and finally, and most astonishingly, the final week spent with Jo Lucca. This had started as a harmless romantic fling but it had brought about a mutual passion which had taken them both by surprise and which had caused a profound re-alignment in all his hopes and aspirations.

By the time they docked he had almost come to believe that none of it had happened. Such extremes of emotion did not happen to the Frank Kellys of this world. He thought of himself as an ordinary, hard-working, decent man, not the sort to have had a wild fling with an exotic and hot-blooded Italian/American beauty like Jo Lucca. He must have dreamed the whole thing. He knew, of course, that it had happened but he also knew that it was over. There would be no further encounters with the fabulous Josefina. She would surely have got over, by now, whatever madness had caused her to have fallen for him and to make him fall, so unnervingly, for her. He resolved to put her out of his mind and to get on with his mundane but tranquil life. Not that he had anything to complain about, he reminded himself. *I've got a good job and I'm well on the way to marrying a beautiful and wonderful girl. Two months ago, all I could think of was Isabel and in twenty-four hours more that's who I'll be thinking of. I just need to see her and hold her in my arms again. Josefina Lucca was just a figment of my imagination.*

Twenty-four hours later, Isabel's welcome confirmed these happy conclusions. She had met him at the quayside. He had not made the trip home as a member of the crew. The company had sailed him home in passenger status and so he disembarked with the other third class passengers shortly after docking. She threw herself into his arms with unaccustomed abandon. She was not normally this demonstrative in public but she too had had two months of separation to cope with and she had missed him.

Holding him at arms length after they finally unraveled, she said, "You look so thin. You must haves lost weight. Didn't they feed you in that American hospital?"

"I just missed that home cooking. God! It's good to be home."

"I love you Frank. I've really missed you," she said renewing the embrace.

"Hold that thought, Izzy, and after I've said hello to my folks and to Kate I'll show you how much I've missed you."

"Oh! You sweet talker. Where did you get that smooth line? Have you been trying it out on those Yankee nurses?" she joked.

"No! Of course not," he said a little too defensively.

A momentary alarm bell rang in her brain, to be dismissed equally quickly. This was, after all, Frank Kelly: old Mister Reliable. His reception in Garnet Avenue was, as expected, warm but the news from home was mixed. The good news was that Brendan had earned a Junior City Scholarship, an award that would grant him admission to the Irish Christian Brother's college on St. Domingo Road and thereby open up the possibility of eventual university education. Frank senior was the source of the bad news. His health was markedly worse. He was visibly short of breath, even at rest, and his cough was almost constant and moist. Mrs. Kelly's happiness at her son's homecoming could not erase the worry lines that were becoming etched in her face.

Later, Frank escorted the two girls to their flat and Kate made a tactful prompt exit to leave the young couple some privacy. They settled comfortably into the big armchair and Frank soon was reminded why he had fallen so completely for the beautiful Isabel. They kissed passionately. His brain had forgotten Jo Lucca but his body had not. His lovemaking with Jo had been uninhibited. Without making a conscious decision he ran his hand inside her skirt and caressed her thigh.

"What's got into you Frank?" gasped Isabel grasping his hand. Frank's reaction was to recoil with guilt written all over his face.

"You met someone while you were over there. Didn't you?"

His face was giving him away. He did the best he could to laugh it off.

"You know how it is with guys. They always fall in love with the nurses. I took one out a few times after I got out of the hospital and was waiting for my ship."

Isabel was not entirely convinced. Frank's incursion beneath her skirt did not really conform with his description of a casual date with a friendly nurse but she didn't choose to make an issue of it. The interruption took some of the steam out of their reunion but, by and large, Frank was happy to put the whole episode with Nurse Lucca behind them. He had been in the wrong but he had been forgiven.

His complacency lasted for a week. Four days after Frank had sailed for Liverpool, Jo Lucca RN had realized that her period was late and by the time he docked and reconciled with Isabel she was fairly certain that she was pregnant. Early morning nausea followed and a visit to an obstetrician confirmed that she was with child. The father could only be Frank Kelly, her former patient. The only other partner that she had had in the previous months was Roy Brock. It surprised her that, when she ruled Brock out as the father, her feeling was one of relief. The thought of bearing his child filled her with disgust. Jenny Hudson could keep her Yankee boyfriend. Frank Kelly was a decent man.

She felt a little ashamed at the way she had seduced him but he hadn't been reluctant to continue their affair. *In fact I know he fell for me head over heels. You can't fake that. Maybe I even started to fall for him too. He certainly made me feel like I've never felt before.* Reality set in as she weighed up her options and considered her predicament. As on the previous occasion when she thought that she was pregnant, she ruled out the possibility of abortion. She would carry the baby to term and then put it up for adoption. Though she quailed at the thought of involving her family in the solution she imagined that her mother would arrange it so that she could be quietly delivered in a discreet clinic out in the country. *I suppose that there might be one or two of the studs who have been hotly pursuing me for the past two years who would be willing to marry me even if they knew I was carrying another man's child. Do I really want to enter a lifelong partnership for better for worse with some one who thinks that he is doing me a favor and that I'm damaged goods?* Her pride rejected that option.

How about Frank? She was overwhelmed by the impracticality of that idea. She knew very little about him. She knew that he was an Englishman with an Irish name and that he worked on a transatlantic liner--a Cunarder, she remembered. He didn't make much money and he was in Boston for only a few days each month. *For all I know he's got a wife in England.* To her surprise she found that she was trying to imagine ways in which this unlikely outcome could come to pass. She remembered that he was quite good-looking in an offbeat way and that, despite their passionate coupling, he was gentle and considerate. He was well spoken and polite. She had looked forward to his arrival during their brief affair and not just for the sex. They laughed a lot when they had been together. She loved the trace of Irish brogue in his speech. She could see herself falling in love.

She pulled herself sharply. *Stop daydreaming, Jo,* she told herself. *You know you've seen the last of Frank Kelly. Still I better let him know that I'm carrying his baby,* she added to herself. *I owe him that. A man should know that he's responsible for another human life. What he does with that information will tell a lot about him.* Her thoughts were still in turmoil and she decided that she needed a sympathetic ear. Jenny Hudson was out. She had proved to be a faithless friend (almost as faithless as I was to her, she thought ruefully) and her casual attitude to abortion had horrified her. I need to let my sister know. I know she'll read me the riot act but I know I can trust her. She'll give me sound advice and she'll help me to break the news to Mama and Papa when I decide what to do. Theresa proved to be more sympathetic than Jo had feared might be the case. She enfolded her baby sister in a hug and said that she'd do every thing that she could to help. Jo had always considered herself to be pretty hard-boiled and was quite astonished when at the completion of her tale she burst into tears.

"The father needs to be told," she agreed and together they composed a cable:

    To: Francis Kelly %   The Cunard Shipping Company
                                                   The Cunard Building.
                                                   Liverpool.

    From: Josefina Lucca % Theresa Napolitano
                                                   27 Harris Street.
                                                   Boston, Mass.
                                                   USA.

Frank. I'm pregnant. We are having a baby next April. Please advise. Josefina Lucca.

With this bombshell on its way there wasn't anything to do but await developments. Tessa promised to keep her secret and see what happened. Oddly, now that the dice were cast, Jo felt better.

CHAPTER TWENTY

Liverpool, late July, 1928

The arrival of a telegram at Garnet Avenue was, in itself, a major event. Nobody on the street had ever received one. The telegram boy's arrival on his bike at No. 25 was enough to set the neighbourhood's tongues wagging.

The message contained had a far more profound impact on Frank. His brain churned with conflicting emotions. His initial reaction was horror; how could he tell Isabel? She would be bitterly disappointed in him. He had managed to convince himself that his affair with Jo was an aberration--a one time dream-like occurrence--sublime and sweet but somehow not real. It had recast Jo as an almost mythical figure; her image to be treasured but restricted to his memory. His relationship with Isabel was real. He loved her. He had fallen for her at first sight and, although the progress of their physical relationship had progressed only at a snail's pace, which was what real life demanded, he knew that they were on course for marriage and the full intimacy that it promised.

The days that he and Jo had spent together had been the most fulfilling of his life. They had spent almost all the hours of the day together and each had brought him exquisite joy. Just being with her, watching her pottering around the kitchen or brushing her hair had filled him with ineffable pleasure. He had not been able to resist touching her as they passed by and she, in return had been, apparently, equally eager to respond to his touch. How often had the most casual caress ended in a passionate romp--on the bed, in the armchair or even, on one memorable occasion, in the shower. These treasured images he had locked up in his memory. He had willed himself to forget Jo Lucca. He owed it to Isabel to insulate himself from any memory of her and he had determined to devote his whole life to making Isabel his wife and being a devoted husband.

The telegram brought him back to reality. Jo was pregnant. He had fathered a baby. This was the one immutable fact. He was horrified at the thought that he had let Isabel down and that she would be bitterly disappointed in him. He had won her heart, almost against her wishes, by his persistence and devotion and now that she had finally fallen in love with him he must own up to his own infidelity. There could be no reconciliation. She had tacitly decided to overlook his self-described fling with his pretty nurse in Boston but she could not be expected to overlook an illegitimate child. 'Illegitimate child!' The term, stark and ugly, caused Frank to refocus his thoughts. Isabel was not the person whose life he had most selfishly endangered. It was Jo who was carrying his child.

He had to break the news to Isabel. He knew that it would devastate her and he was weak kneed at the thought of telling her but he would marry Jo Lucca. He was almost overwhelmed by the contemplation of the difficulties that such a solution would entail. There was the most obvious problem that they were of different nationalities and lived on opposite sides of the Atlantic. Jo was from the middle class, he definitely a working class lad, albeit Americans did not seem to take such classifications too seriously. She was certainly better educated and probably earned more money. At least they were both Catholic, he thought wryly. Their torrid weekend had not been interrupted by attending eleven o'clock mass at St. Brendan's. He had never considered not marrying a Catholic girl or raising a family outside the faith. Would she even want to marry him? That thought now hit him. He was no catch, he admitted, with his scarred face, one eye and modest financial prospects.

For a fleeting moment, he considered that if he were to propose and Jo were to reject him he could carry on his life undisturbed, not even mention the cable to Isabel and expunge thoughts of Jo and his unborn child from his memory. This unworthy scenario was no sooner envisioned than it was banished. Frank Kelly was, at heart, a decent man. He had been genuinely in love with Jo Lucca. He had fallen for her, at first almost platonically during his hospital stay and, although in the fevered days of their affair he had been intensely attracted by her sexual magnetism (what male wouldn't be?), he had come to genuinely like her; her generosity of spirit, her cheerfulness and her *joie de vivre..* He would ask her to marry him. Even if she turned him down he would still be her child's father and he couldn't just walk away from that. He still had to break the news to Isabel. The thought nearly unmanned him. Would she burst into tears? Would she scream at him and call him out for the selfish rotter that he now felt himself to be? In his heart he knew that she would do neither of those things. She would be deeply wounded but she would greet his abject apologies with dignity.

Like the other members of the family, Kate had been intrigued by the arrival of the telegram at No. 25. Telegrams were rare in the extreme in their neighborhood and were inevitably the harbingers of bad news. The last telegrams to arrive in Garnet Avenue had carried the dreaded news of death of a son or husband during the war. Frank had opened his and turned pale but had immediately closed himself into his bedroom to digest the news. He emerged after half an hour, still pale but with the appearance of a man who had made a decision and was content with it.

"Come for a little walk with me, Kate. I need someone to talk to."

He was unusually serious with none of the bantering tone of his usual remarks to her. They set off round the park; their customary stroll. He stopped after a few seconds and handed her the telegram. She read it and took a minute to digest it.

"What does this mean Frank? Who is this Josefina Lucca? How can you be having a baby? Oh, my God, Frank," she cried as the implications of the message hit her. "This is going to kill poor Izzy."

"I know that Kate. This has just come like a bolt from the blue. I fell for one of the nurses while I was in hospital and we had a few days together while I was waiting for my boat home. She's really a wonderful girl but I never dreamed that she would be a permanent part of my life or that we would have a baby together."

"A permanent part! Why? Are you thinking of marrying her? How would you live together? And what's to become of Izzy? Oh Frank! What a mess you've made of your life and not just yours. No matter what you choose to do, you're going to have to hurt one unfortunate girl terribly."

"I know it all too well, Sis, but there's really no decision to make. There's a real live human being growing inside that girl and I'm the father. If she'll have me, I'm going to marry her. I have to tell Izzy and I'm going to tonight. Will you help? I know I have to tell her face-to-face. If I know Izzy she won't carry on and scream but I know she'll still need a friendly shoulder to cry on once I've left. Would you, please Kate, be there for her tonight. Kate had never seen her brother so distraught. They were very close and, despite their constant banter, Kate loved him dearly and though she would never admit it to him, held him in a regard bordering on hero worship. Now he needed her and she would, of course, do what he asked. Besides, Izzy was her best friend and confidante.

His confession to Isabel that evening was as painful and humiliating as Frank had feared.

"Frank! You told me that you had a couple of dates with a nurse after you got out of hospital and now you're telling me she's pregnant. I thought you loved me. You've even said you did since you been home. I never took you for a liar, Frank. I don't think I ever want to see you again. Please go away. Don't say another word. Spare me your excuses."

She ushered him out of the flat wordlessly and only the quivering of her lips showed how close she was to breaking down in tears. She was devastated. Kate came out of the bedroom, took Izzy in her arms, and the two friends consoled each other in a tear filled embrace. Each had discovered that a man whom they had loved deeply was only a flawed and fallible male.

Frank was deeply ashamed; sorry for having been the cause of his erstwhile lover's distress but at least he was not tormented by indecision. He would ask Jo to marry him. She had informed him of her condition by cable but this was too exotic a means of correspondence for him. His next stopover in the USA was scheduled ten days hence and it was in New York. A letter sent out in the morning mail would arrive in Boston before he would and so he wrote Jo a note. He was no writer and was daunted at the thought of expressing on paper the thoughts that were teeming in his brain. He could have told her that he loved her. It was true. Now that he was over the shock of his impending fatherhood he was excited and happy at the thought of resuming their relationship. But 'I love you, Jo' seemed so banal and even insincere coming from one who had said just those same words to Isabel just two days earlier. He therefore modeled the note on the expense-per-word consciousness of the cable that he had received.

Miss Josefina Lucca
℅ Theresa Napolitano
27 Harris Street
Boston, Mass. USA.

"Dear Jo,

I will be arriving in New York on 11 August. I will take the train to Boston as soon as I can. Please meet me. I should be able to get to Boston by the time you get off work. I'll be at the front door of BGH at 6pm.

Love,
Frank."

Nine days had passed before Jo received Frank's response to her cable. Her thoughts were even more conflicted than his. There was, first of all, the lingering hope that the absence of her menstrual flow was some hormonal quirk and that, any morning now, it would resume and she could put the whole episode behind her. But did she really want that to happen? Part of her felt a glow of fulfillment. She was living out the primordial function of woman: bearing the child of a man she had been in love with. The stark reality of the situation brought warming thoughts to a screeching halt. Would she ever hear from Frank again?

It was now over a week since she had telegraphed him the news and even if he responded and was willing to marry her, did she actually want to be the wife of an uneducated British sailor who would only be with her for a few days every month. She had fallen for Frank quite hard and very unexpectedly but could they be happy married together? His letter, short to the point of being terse, had re-awakened all the questions that had been swirling around in her brain since she first was aware that she might be 'late.' On that point she was no longer in any doubt. She was feeling a slight tingling in her breasts and she had thrown up her breakfast three times in the past week. What did Frank's letter portend? He had given no indication as to how he felt about the news. He had signed the letter "Love, Frank" but that was a fragile branch on which to hang the hopes for a resumption of their brief love affair; and, more importantly, for that passionate affair to grow into a lifelong partnership.

S.S. Carmania was due to dock in New York on the morning tide in two days, she learned by consulting with the Cunard office in Boston. She learned that Frank would not have to sail again until the 14th. He could be in Boston only for three days even if he took the overnight train back to New York on the 13th. The note--(it hardly qualified as a letter)--had said that he would meet her after work at the hospital. How typical of a man, she fumed. She was to face the most critical moment of her young life in her dowdy nurse's uniform. For once her sublime self-confidence in her attractiveness deserted her. She was going to meet the man who had fathered her child and whose reaction to her would alter the course of her life. She wasn't sure that she wanted to marry Frank Kelly but she was certain that she would be devastated if he didn't want her. In those circumstances she knew that she must look her best. She resolved to bring 'civilian' clothes to work with her. She would change after her shift and before leaving the hospital. If Frank had to cool his heels for ten minutes then so be it. She'd had far more moments of anxiety than he.

****

It took Frank about thirty seconds to dispel any anxieties that Jo might have had about his feelings for her. He had arrived outside the doors of the hospital at ten to six and by ten past six, when she emerged, he was in a fever of anxiety and anticipation. She saw him first; pacing back and forth with a worried expression on his face. When their glances met, his face broke into a boyish smile of such sweetness that her heart melted and she felt tears come to her eyes.

"Jo, my darling, I love you," he murmured in her ear as he wrapped his arm around her waist and swung her off her feet in a big circle. The people still emerging from the building gave them a wide berth but passed smiling. They made a handsome couple; love's young dream. Even the hard-boiled citizens of Boston smiled their approval.

One question in Jo's mind had been resolved within the first minute of their reunion. The physical attraction that had so dominated the first days of their affair was as strong as ever. With their first embrace, even here on the public street, she felt a strong tingling throughout her body and a strong desire to respond to the intensity of his kisses and the impassioned words that he was murmuring. But, she was the woman. She was the one carrying the baby in her womb. She must be the one to be practical. There was so much to discuss--so many decisions to make. Frank would only be in Boston for three days before he had to return to his ship.

"Lets go to my apartment. I still have the place to myself, Frank. I've made us a quiche. We can eat there. We have so much to talk about."

"Well, just so you know, my darling, that I want so much for you to be my wife. I never dreamed that I could ask you before. I'm not good enough for you; not smart enough but maybe God meant us to be together and our baby is how He's letting us know."

"Let's go home Frank. People are stopping to stare."

Linking arms she steered him homeward. The walk was only ten minutes long and they didn't talk much. They were both contented with the warmth of their linked arms and the afterglow of all their remembered endearments. For Jo there had really only been three questions to be resolved when she met Frank. Was the fire still there? That had been answered for her in their first embrace. Second: Did Frank want to marry her? He had answered that with a fervor that had amazed and warmed her heart. As they walked home arm in arm, she already knew the answer to the third question: Yes! She would marry him. She wanted nothing more than to be his wife and to raise their children together. Certainly there would be difficulties to overcome and hard days to endure. Surely the baby growing inside her was not a punishment for their sins but God's blessing on their union. As they climbed the stairs to her front door she had made her mind up.

"I want to be your wife Frank. Let's get married."

They ate the quiche. Jo was a good cook but the meal didn't get the attention it deserved. The couple was too wrapped up in details of their impending wedding.

"I'll have to let Tessa know what we plan. She likes you Frank. I think she's hoping we'll get married. Let's go up to the North End tomorrow. I'm going to call in sick for the next three days. I haven't missed a day in two years. I'm pretty sure my OB-GYN will cover for me."

"I never saw anyone looking healthier, sweetheart, but we could certainly use the extra time that it would give us. How soon can we get married? Where? Do you want to get married in Boston or Brockton? Is there any problem with me not being American? Where should we live? What can we afford?" Frank had a million questions.

"Would I like it if we lived in England? Could I get a job there? I'm an R.N. Would they recognize my qualification in England?" Jo had a few questions of her own.

"I think you'd find that the Royal Navy has first claim on the letters RN over there."

These and a myriad other related questions gave them much material for discussion but, since they all presupposed that a wedding was in the offing, the discussions were suffused with happiness. It was late in the evening when they decided to put off further discussion until morning but not too late to deflect them from the culmination for which they had been waiting since their first embrace at the hospital font door. Frank took her into the bedroom and, as she stood in front of him, he slowly and gently undressed her. He kissed first her lips then her neck and then, almost reverently, her breasts.

Laying her down on the bed he removed her remaining clothes and kissed her belly murmuring, "sweet dreams little baby."

They made love slowly. Their lovemaking was not practiced or skillful. It was the coming together of two mature young adults committing themselves to each other for life; better or worse, richer or poorer. The actual wedding was two months into the future but that night they sealed their union in the way of lovers since the dawn of time.

****

Theresa, Jo's sister Tessa, proved to be a tower of strength.

"You've got to get married in Brockton, Jo. Mama and Papa would be crushed if you don't. You can't deny them the chance to have a big Italian get together. We'll need to give Father Baldini as much warning as possible. Bring back a copy of your Baptismal certificate. When are you back next in the States, Frank?"

"I'm due back in New York in three weeks " he replied.

"That's not enough time. We've got a million things to take care of. How about after that?"

"I'm due back in Boston in late September. I'll have to lookup the exact date." He addressed his answer to his future sister-in-law. She was in full take-charge mode. Nothing was going to be overlooked for her little sister's wedding.

"Late September will work out just fine. Jo will be barely three months along and we'll have plenty of time to book Saint Anthony of Padua's and the K of C Hall. Are you going to carry on working, Jo, and where are you going to live once you're married?"

"I'm going to keep working as long as I'm able. We're going to need the money. My lease is good thru September but after that I think we'll need to look for a cheaper place to live."

"I think you should try the North End. Rents are much cheaper and you'll be nearer family if you need help later when the baby's born. Will you always be away at sea, Frank? Is there any chance that you could get a job ashore? Surely, a company the size of Cunard must have some folks based in the USA. Now that you're marrying my sister, have you given any thought to settling in America?"

This suggestion was real shocker for Frank. He had been angling for a shore-based job with the prospect of marriage to Isabel but, of course, that was with Britain as the 'shore' in question. He had been confident that his chance of a transfer to land was a possibility. He had already been given some responsibilities in the overseeing of the re-victualing of *Carmania* at its various stopovers. He resolved to approach the company about transferring to a land-based job in the USA, preferably Boston. It was the idea of permanent residence that stopped him in his tracks. Despite his seafaring history he was a Brit and a Liverpudlian at heart. He had worn the King's uniform for four years and had shed his blood. The Kelly family had been British for three generations. Heck! His mother's maiden name was Rigby and the Rigby family farm was registered in the Domesday Book.

One look at Jo convinced him that these were considerations that simply carried no weight. He was responsible for Jo's condition. He was the one who had come to her country and got her pregnant. He knew that she would not be happy in Liverpool with its austerity and its awful weather and separated by the ocean from her tight-knit Italian family and friends. He would just have to see how he could live here, get a job and move here permanently, become a Red Soxer and forget Everton. *Forget Everton! Well, let's not lose our heads completely,* he cautioned himself.

"Jo! I'll see whether Cunard can find a place for me on shore in Boston. I think I have a chance. I actually have a small pension from the government on account of my injuries in the war but I'm afraid that it wont keep us in luxury," he admitted wryly. "It might just keep you supplied with 'Moxie'." he added.

Jo grinned. At least her Frank wasn't letting all these domestic problems get him down.

Later that evening, when his shop was closed, Fredo (Alfredo), Tessa's husband arrived home and the children assembled in platoon strength and for the first time, Frank Kelly was absorbed into the midst of Jo's extended family. He had become Uncle Francesco; Aunt Jo's husband to be.

CHAPTER TWENTY-ONE
Liverpool, July, 1928

Ten days later, on his arrival in Liverpool, Frank found the family in mourning. Two days before he had docked, his father had finally succumbed to his emphysema. A lifetime of smoking had destroyed his lungs and he had not been able to ward off the last of his recurring bouts of pneumonia. His death had not been unexpected but Meg was distraught. They had been married thirty-five years and she had borne him five children. She had married the young, red haired Irishman when she was only seventeen years old; the youngest of eight children of the farmer of a small holding in Gill Moss. Frank Sr. had been a devoted husband and father whose only vice had been his addiction to 'Woodbines.'

At least, thank God, I'm home in time for the funeral, his son thought. *Mam will need the support of the whole family.* His father was buried out of St. John's; the Requiem Mass being surprisingly well attended. Monsignor Kieran gave a moving eulogy and the parish chapter of the Union Of Catholic Mothers rallied around and provided refreshments for the friends and neighbours who visited the home after the internment to pay their respects. By eight p.m. the flow of comforters was over and the family was finally alone in the house. Frank found himself the *de facto* head of the family. It was a position he had not wished for and it was coming at a particularly difficult time as he was about to make them aware that he was going to marry an American girl and settle in Boston leaving them, to some extent, in the lurch. With the two male breadwinners gone from the scene, drastic revision of their domestic arrangements would be required. They gathered in the parlour.

"We have some important decisions to make as a family. Can we afford to keep the lease on Garnet Avenue now that we don't have Da bringing home a wage? I know that Kate has told you that I have got a girl in America. Well its true. She's a nurse. Her name is Josefina Lucca--Jo, and I've asked her to marry me. In fact we're getting married in September. I know that this couldn't come at a worse time but it has to be. I'm sorry to spring it on you, Mam, at a time like this but I'm only home for three days and there's so much to decide."

This unwontedly lengthy speech brought on an immediate flood of questions.

"Who is this girl, Frank? "What has happened to Isabel?" from his mother.

"I don't see how we can afford to stay here with you and Da gone," added Bridget. "Where are you going to live? Will you still be working on the boats? Will we still see you when you come back to Liverpool? Why don't you bring your wife back here? We need nurses too. She could get a job at Walton."

The conference that ensued was confused and emotional but, eventually, it subsided. There was a general consensus that it would be possible and highly desirable to retain the tenancy of their home at least for the next year. They were all horrified at the thought of having Mam forced to leave her home so soon after losing her husband. The top family priority had to be to leave her undisturbed. This course would bring the additional benefit of keeping Brendan within walking distance of his new school. They were all secretly very proud of the scholastic prowess of the baby of the family. Frank committed himself to continuing to send his allotment home for as long as he stayed employed and Kate agreed to give up her share of the flat that she occupied with Isabel and to move back into the family home. She was saddened to do so but the relationship between the two girls had become a bit strained since Frank's 'defection'. Bridget had, by now, completed her apprenticeship and was now a qualified hairdresser and was looking to open her own shop. She would continue to live at home and contribute to the family budget. Mary, too, had no incentive to move. Garnet Avenue was a comfortable tram ride from Hartley's Jam Factory and, while she was now seriously involved with a young police constable, a wedding was still in the distant future.

When, inevitably, the question was raised as to why Frank's wedding had to occur with so little warning in an era when engagements lasted up to a couple of years, the explanation was deferred until Brendan was sent 'creeping like snail, unwillingly' to bed. Kate had already made her sisters aware of the circumstances of their brother's precipitate engagement, but for Margaret Kelly, with thirty-five years of scrupulous monogamy behind her; her elder son's fall from grace was a bitter pill to swallow. She did, however recall that Frank Sr. had wooed her fairly lustily and she remembered trysts in the hayloft when he had been a day laborer on the family farm back in '93.

"Rest in Peace, Frank, my darling," she prayed, "and as for you, you American hussy, you better be good to my son or you'll have Meg Kelly to deal with," and, with these pious thoughts, the eventful day drew to a close.

The three days before his return trip to New York went by like lightning. He was, to a very considerable extent, severing his ties with his homeland, not perhaps with the finality of earlier emigrants who, when they set out for the New World, would never see their native shores again, but henceforth he would be a visitor. He made a point of having a few minutes alone with each of his three youngest siblings.

"Tell me about your young 'copper', Mary. Does he have big feet?" he teased.

"He's a big lad all right--feet and all--a real farm boy at heart. He grew up on a farm, out in the country, past the racecourse. We can watch the Grand National from his bedroom. I mean, you could watch the Grand National IF you were in his bedroom," she corrected herself.

Ignoring her blushes, he asked, "How did he end up on the Force?"

"He didn't like getting up with the birds so now he only has to work forty eight hours a week" she laughed. He works out of the Aintree Police station, near the Black Bull. We met at a church dance; 'Blessed Sacrament.'"

"Are you serious about him, Mame?"

"I think so. He's an awful dancer but he's really sweet-- calls me his 'wild Irish Rose'."

"He's certainly got a neat turn of phrase," he deadpanned.

"Oh! Go on Romeo," she replied, punching him on the shoulder. Like her sister Kate, she would never let her brother have the last word.

Bridget was full of plans for her new business venture. She had had enough of working for wages and she was ready to branch out on her own. She had been surveying the terrain within striking distance of home and had her eye on a recently vacant store that was located just opposite Walton Hospital that was an enormous sprawling edifice with over 1000 beds. With that largely female staff and a large nursing school, she thought her new business would be well situated and with no shortage of potential customers.

"I've been saving like mad ever since I got out of school and I'm going to try the Midland Bank for a loan for the equipment," she admitted.

"I'll chip in five pounds towards the shop," he offered.

"Oh Frank! You mustn't do that. It's you who should be getting wedding presents from us."

"This'll make up for all the birthdays I missed," and he produced a five pound note from his wallet and presented it to her with a kiss on the forehead. Bridie had never seen a five pound note before. It was an impressive document; about twice the size of the pound and it represented about three weeks wages for a workingman. On to Brendan.

"How are you liking your new school, Bren? I hear that you don't want to give those Brothers any lip." The Irish Christian Brothers had a well-deserved reputation as disciplinarians.

"You know, Brother Walsh stands inside the main door at nine o'clock and it's 'two of the best' for any one who comes in late. I'm lucky I don't have to rely on the trams but I love St. Ed's. The Brothers are tough but they're a lot of fun; never a dull moment. We've got Brother Bewley for English. He's got an accent you could cut with a knife.

If any one gives a wrong answer he shouts, "Ye are a pack of illiterates. What are ye?"

And we all have to shout, "A pack of illiterates, Sorr."

"I can't hear you."

"A PACK OF ILLITERATES, SORR!"

It was with Kate that he had the most serious talk. They were closest in age and it was through Kate that he had met Izzy. He knew that his breakup with Izzy had placed enormous strain on the friendship of the two flatmates.

"I feel so bad that my marriage is causing a rift between you and Izzy. I'd really like to make it up to you. I'd like you to come to America and be a part of the wedding. Jo wants it too. I know that it would cost a fortune but I'll split the expenses with you and maybe we can get Cunard to give us a break on the fares. They don't often get round trippers."

"That would be fantastic, Frank. I've often dreamed of seeing America but I always thought that, if I did, I would be emigrating. You know I'd love to be a part of your wedding. Do you see me as 'Best Man?' This Jo Lucca must really be quite a girl if you'd give up a girl like Izzy for her.

"She's really special, Kate. I know you'll hit it off. Please see if you can manage it. You'll be the only one on my side of the aisle. You know you've always wanted to meet a giant. They grow their boys tall in the US of A."

"You've talked me into it, little brother. Let me check my savings account. I'll need to talk to Izzy soon. If I'm to move back in with Mam, I'll need to give Izzy some warning about getting someone to share the flat."

Isabel had learned about the death of Frank Sr. and her parents had attended the requiem and tendered their condolences to the Kelly Family. Isabel had not been able to bring herself to attend and run the risk of meeting Frank. The Iskandars knew, of course, that there had been a falling out between the couple. Now Frank was to marry an American girl. They did not know the details. They differed slightly in their reaction to the split up. Both liked the young Kelly boy but Adlai had always wanted a better-educated and more urbane husband for his daughter. Marie had always been able to see the qualities in Frank that would appeal to a young woman. She was saddened that Isabel was taking the breakup so hard.

The evening after the funeral and the family pow-wow, Kate asked Izzy to sit together for a while.

"With Dad's death and with Frank moving to America it's put the family into a financial squeeze. If I don't move back home they won't be able to keep up with the rent on Garnet Avenue. Do you think that you can get someone else to share the flat?"

"As a matter of fact, Kate, I was going to ask you the same thing. So may be it'll work out just fine."

Frank's guilty revelation had stirred up a complicated set of emotions in Isabel. She had felt the fury of a woman scorned. She had been ready to commit herself to marriage with Frank despite his lowly position in life and the distance between them in social standing and education. Her memory had selectively eliminated the recollection of her indiscretion at the Christmas party and her disappointment that the deputy consul had made no further advances in the ensuing months. She had become certain that all she had needed to do to have him declare his interest in her was for her to give him a little encouragement. She had, over the winter months, made herself as pleasant and as obviously available to the Frenchman as her pride would permit but to no avail. She now had convinced herself that she had been a model of restraint and this was the reward for her self-denial.

"How dare he?" she stormed inside. "The infernal cheek! To turn up her nose at Isabel Iskandar, BA, the beautiful daughter of the wealthy Iskandars when she had spurned (she now fantasized) a handsome diplomat out of some misplaced sense of obligation."

Admittedly, in between paroxysms of fury and self-pity, she remembered that she had not always been as enthusiastic as Frank about the idea of their marriage. Looking on the bright side, she now was released from any expectations and without any angst on her side; she could enjoy the role of the injured party and rejoin the ranks of the available. Now she could, with a clear conscience, see whether M. Martin might respond to a little more overt encouragement. With this in mind, it would be preferable if she had a place of her own. Kate's offer had come at the perfect time.

****

True to her word, Sister Clementine had given Isabel a glowing recommendation to append to her application to teach French at the new Broughton Hall Convent High School in 1928. What neither had reckoned on was that the school would not be springing to life in September with a full roster of pupils. The Sisters of Mercy planned to open the school with only the lower two classes in place. They would then grow incrementally, year by year, until five years later they would be up to full strength. For the first year they could only offer employment for three days per week. They would be delighted to sign Miss Iskandar to a contract. She was eminently qualified and would be guaranteed full employment for the academic year 1929/1930.

Isabel had been quite taken aback by this development and Sister Clementine was quite mortified that she had not foreseen such an eventuality. I think that we could probably arrange with the Board of Education to have you work as a stand-by substitute teacher. This option was singularly unappealing to Isabel. The thought of walking in on a fresh bunch of hellions every day gave her cold chills but it did spark an alternative idea. She had now worked for a full year at the French Consulate. By now, she virtually ran the administrative and secretarial sides of the operation. The work was not difficult but she knew that she was now regarded as irreplaceable. She requested another interview with the Deputy Consul.

Her intuition and their Christmas kiss had told her that M. Martin had a more than strictly professional interest in her. While she and Frank had been so heavily involved she had given the suave Frenchman only the most subtle signs of encouragement and, in turn, he had scrupulously avoided all but the most innocent elements of flirtatiousness to enter their dealings in the office. She had noticed that he cast more than the occasional appraising glances at her. *Who knows?* she thought. *Maybe I'll show Frank Kelly that he was not the only fish in the sea. Certainly, if I can keep working here on a part time basis, then a little harmless flirtation with a wealthy Frenchman would add a little sparkle to my dull life.* She requested an interview.

"Monsieur Martin, you have known for some time that I have planned to leave my position to start my teaching career in September. I have just learned that, for the first year, they can only hire me three days a week. Would you consider keeping me on on a part time basis? You know that

I can do the job. You can hire another girl part time and I can teach her the ropes and she will be able to move in full time when I leave."

The Deputy Consul had indeed been very much aware of the beautiful Mlle. Iskandar over the past year but he had prevented any lecherous thoughts to reveal themselves in his dealings with her. He suspected that she would be receptive to a move on his behalf. Ever since their brief tryst under the mistletoe she had been gone out of her way to present herself to him as available but he had deliberately given no obvious response. He had been content to play a waiting game.

He was no novice in the art of seduction. Now, he had learned through the office gossip that she was unencumbered by a local attachment, and here she was asking for her old job back. If he agreed, she would not only be somewhat beholden to him but he would have two whole days every week to work his charms on her. Yvette was at home in French Algeria and he had needed to be very discrete in his amorous forays in stuffy provincial Liverpool. *We handle 'affairs of the heart' so much better in sophisticated Paris*, he thought.

He remembered his 'salad days' as a rising young diplomat in *Le Ministère des Affaires Etrangères*. He had lived a double life then; proper, studious and industrious by day and, by night, throwing himself headlong into the bacchanalia that had erupted in Paris after the gloom of the war years. He had graduated from the *Ecole Spéciale de St. Cyr* just six months before the Armistice and had come through the war unscathed. He was wealthy, well educated and handsome in a nation that had lost four million of its male population in the abattoirs of Metz, Sedan and Verdun. The sun shone and he had made hay.

For two years he had lived a life of self-indulgence. He had been equally accepted in the salons of the upper crust and the parties of the *Corps Diplomatique* as he was in the dance halls and bordellos of the Left Bank. Then he had met Yvette Houssa. She was a Moroccan Arab from Rabat, the capital of French Morocco. She was a student at the Sorbonne, fiery and exotic. They had fallen in love and he had found that he no longer had any desire for *La Vie Boheme*. He continued to advance in the ministry and his nights were filled with Yvette. He set her up in a small but elegantly furnished apartment in the Latin Quarter near the Church of St. Germain de Prés and she became his mistress. Marriage was out of the question for a rising young diplomat. Jacques was a French *colon* from Algeria, a *pied noir*.

Algeria was, theoretically, an integral part of France but Algerian Muslims were not full French citizens. Despite Arabs comprising ninety percent of the population, only seventy thousand Muslims had the franchise to vote. It would be the end of a promising career for a diplomat to marry an Arab. To take an Arab mistress was an entirely different matter. In the *Ministère des Affaires Etrangères* it was almost *de rigeur*. For three years they lived in cosy domesticity and during that period Yvette bore him two daughters. He had continued to progress at the ministry and had worked on his doctorate at the Sorbonne.

Inevitably his tour in Paris ended. He had been very fortunate to have stayed so long in the City of Light. He would be spending the next two years in Saigon; French Indo-China. This brought about a radical revision of their relationship. It had long been brewing. Yvette had to speak. They were, de facto, a family after all. The present situation had become intolerable.

"Chéri! The children need a permanent home. We cannot travel all round the world. I don't want to ruin your career Build a home for me and our children in Algeria amid your vineyards. We will have a home for you to return to when you come back from overseas."

Almost all of the arable land in Algeria was in the Coastal plain. Ninety percent of it was owned by the *colons*.

It was almost exclusively devoted to vineyards. Algerian wine was abundant and served as the *vin ordinaire* for much of France. The Martin family holdings, which he had inherited, were extensive and had made him a rich man. It was a simple matter for him to establish Yvette and his children in comfort before his departure for Saigon. They lived in a handsome villa with a complete staff of house servants.

He spent two years in Vietnam and thoroughly enjoyed the hedonistic existence of a French diplomat in the 'Pearl of the Orient'. The work was undemanding and the French rule virtually uncontested. What little amount of unrest existed among the native population was suppressed efficiently and the soldiers, mainly French Foreign Legionnaires, considered their tours in Indo-China to be plum assignments. Jacques' social life revolved around the *Cercle Sportif*, its pool and its tennis courts, and the constant round of diplomatic receptions and dinners. Female company was readily available in almost infinite variety and Jacques felt no need to enter a long-term affair in gratifying his libido. A one month leave in the middle of his tour enabled him to visit his 'family' in Algeria and during that delightful re-union Yvette conceived their third child: a son--Jean-Claude.

His assignment as Deputy Consul General to the busy Northern English port of Liverpool was considered to be a promotion by his contemporaries. He was definitely a young man on the rise. The reality of living in the north of England in the 1920's was not so glamorous. The weather was colder and wetter than France and the moral climate still almost Victorian. Prostitution existed but it was largely confined to the most disreputable sections of the city and to establishments that the middle classes did not frequent.

By the time of Isabel's request to extend her employment at the Consulate, Jacques Martin had been celibate for more than a year. The now-available Mlle. Iskandar was a very attractive young woman and Yvette and his children were a thousand miles away. With Isabel spending a couple of days a week working at the consulate, he could foresee limitless opportunity to ingratiate himself with her. The fact that she was a very proper young woman; a schoolteacher and the daughter of a prosperous local businessman, would only add spice to the chase. After the casual availability of women in Saigon, the seduction of Isabel Iskandar would present more of a challenge. He had no doubt that the prize would be more than worth the effort, or that he was up to the challenge.

"Isabel! You have been an excellent member of the staff and I'd like to give you the chance to stay on part time. Let's give it a trial for three months and see how it works out," he offered. *Let's continue to make her eager to please*, he reasoned to himself.

"You can work directly for me as my administrative assistant and we'll take on an additional typist for the routine secretarial duties."

"That's wonderful Monsieur Martin. I love it here. I'm going to find a new place to live, closer to the school but I'll be sure that its close to the tram route so I can get down town in under half an hour."

"Don't worry about that. If it's raining too hard, I can run you home. I have a new Citroen. I can have you there in ten minutes and, by the way, when we are outside the office, please call me Jacques," he added with a smile.

This was an unexpected development and Isabel felt a jolt of apprehension. The deputy consul had never before shown any interest in her and his last remark felt like a tentative invitation to a more personal relationship than she had bargained for. *Still*, she thought to herself, *Why not? 'We're both unattached. I lost my head once over a man. I'm not going to make that mistake again but I can certainly stand to widen my social horizons. Besides when he smiles, it completely transforms his face. He is really quite good looking.*

By early August, Isabel had completed her move and was ready to start her new careers. Her new home was a small, two hundred year old cottage within two hundred yards of the tram terminus in West Derby Village. West Derby was now a suburb of the city of Liverpool but antedated it by a hundred years. The gates of the Earl of Sefton's estate opened onto the village square and a set of iron stocks gave testament to its antiquity. Isabel decided to buy a bike to manage the commute to her new school--a pleasant ten-minute rustic journey along Leyfield Road.

The start of her career as a teacher of French was a delight. The new convent was situated on what had been a large estate with the main house remaining intact as the residence of the nuns with newer construction for the classrooms. The grounds were beautiful and included a small lake. Isabel's only previous teaching experience was as a student teacher and this had taken place in the elementary schools in the city centre. There, the children had been unmotivated, boisterous and, given the slightest chance, unruly. For a slight, shy and rather non-assertive student teacher like Isabel, it had been torture. By contrast, her first classes at Broughton Hall felt like paradise.

Her classes held only thirty girls each, all between ten and eleven years old; neat and demure in their uniforms. They were attentive, well mannered and eager to learn. Admittedly the subject matter was not terribly stimulating consisting as it did of the verbs *être* and *avoir* and explaining the logic of why a pencil needed a masculine pronoun; *'le crayon'*, while a pen took the feminine; *'la plume.'* Isabel, even after a few weeks, was looking forward to the years ahead when she would be able to introduce her young charges to the delights of Victor Hugo and *Le Chanson de Roland*.

Ah well! Il faut ramper avant qu'on marche, she thought, cunningly avoiding the subjunctive. (You must crawl before you can walk.)

The downside of her new living arrangements was that she desperately missed Kate. With both of the Kellys effectively out of her life she was quite lonely. She loved her cosy little cottage but had not yet made any new friends in the neighborhood. All the school staff and pupils were female. She found herself looking forward with unexpected eagerness to her days at the consulate and to her markedly more personal relationship with the deputy consul. Jacques Martin, in turn, made no further pretense to disinterest in her. There was no change in his behavior in the presence of other members of the consular staff but when they were alone together in his office he called her by her first name and contrived a light flirtatious tone in their conversation that permitted her to fully realize that he found her attractive.

He did not cross the line by making her uncomfortable. *Au contraire*, she found that she really enjoyed the game. Her self-esteem, bruised by Frank Kelly's abandonment, was consoled by the attentions of the dashing Frenchman. As the weeks went by she found that her feelings towards Jacques were becoming ambivalent. On one hand, having the flirtatious tone of their dealings limited to the confines of the consulate prevented any messy complications but after a while she began to wonder whether or not the banter was going to lead to anything. She was ripe for Jacques to make the first move. Isabel had had only one love in her life. Jacques Martin was the veteran of innumerable romantic liaisons and was eight years her senior. He was the *Compleat Angler* and Isabel the fish nervously nudging the bait. With the school year underway and Isabel comfortably installed in her new job, he decided to intensify his campaign. A torrential downpour of rain occurring at 6:00 p.m. provided him with his opportunity.

"I can't let you go home in this Isabel, *ma belle*." (Was he the first Liverpool resident to realize the rhyming potential of *'ma belle?'*) "You'd be drowned before you reach the tram shelter. Come on! I'll give you a ride home."

"*Merci, mon chevalier'*. I didn't even bring an umbrella," she replied, eyelashes aflutter. Jacques managed to get himself fairly damp himself by the time he retrieved his car and picked her up at the *porte cochère*. The storm had abated considerably by the time they arrived at Isabel's cottage. When they pulled up, they sat silently for half a minute. The ball was obviously in her court and Martin thought fleetingly that he had got soaked for nothing and Isabel wondered what kind of a mess her house was in. Should she or shouldn't she invite him in? Swallowing, she took the plunge.

"Come in Jacques. Dry off a bit. I can have a fire going in a few minutes and I'll fix us a cup of tea.," she offered.

"Oh, you English and your tea. Next time I bring you home I'll carry a flask of cognac," he joked.

She set a match to the coal fire that was set in the grate and set about the tea-making ritual.

"Next time you bring me home," she said, greatly daring, "I'll be sure to have more to offer than a share in a piece of haddock. That was going to be my dinner tonight."

"Well, if we're talking about dinner, I don't want to impose but how about we find ourselves a nice cosy pub and eat there? You can save your haddock for tomorrow."

They finished their tea while Jacques' coat toasted in front of the fire and then they ventured out in search of a meal. Not, by any means, did every English public house serve a decent meal in 1928 but they were able to find one that did and it was within walking distance, right on the village square: the Sefton Arms. In view of the uncertain weather they drove anyway. They had a healthy meal--meat pie and chips--and Isabel had a couple of glasses of 'port and lemon' that she had heard was a 'ladies drink'. Jacques proved to be a charming companion who kept Isabel amused with tales of the high life in post-war Paris and an expurgated version of the delights of the Orient. There was a big open fire and she felt quite mellow by the time he drove her home at closing time: 10:00 p.m.

She invited him in and hung up her raincoat. Without waiting to shed his, he pulled her close and kissed her emphatically and expertly. She found herself responding to his caresses and was about to consider the propriety of such intimacy after such a short courtship when Jacques disengaged from the embrace and, thanking her for a lovely evening, bade her goodnight. He was too shrewd a veteran of the ebb and flow of *l'amour* to expect to take an innocent like Isabel Iskandar to his bed at the first encounter. Her body had conformed to his when he had kissed her and he had broken off the embrace before she could gather her wits. It would be very hard for her to put that genie back in the bottle.

For Isabel it was the first physical contact with a man since Frank had sailed on his fateful journey six months ago and there was no doubt in her mind that she had found the evening very enjoyable even if it had ended rather abruptly. M'sieu Martin, driving home, felt that he had put in a good night's work. Those brief seconds during their kiss had told him that Isabel Iskandar concealed plenty of passion behind her demure exterior and was ripe for the plucking.

The genie did, in fact, prove impossible to return to the bottle. Isabel could not realistically reject her boss's offer to drive her home from work without appearing ungracious. Truth was, she was not reluctant to accept his offer. It was tacit acceptance of their new status as potential lovers and she found the prospect exciting if a little frightening. Jacques Martin would bring a sophistication to a relationship that she was not sure that she could control. During the years of her affair with Frank Kelly, she had always felt confident that their physical intimacy would stay within well-defined, if unspoken, limits. She suspected that if she entered into a serious affair with Jacques, she would be playing with fire. She recognized that she had accepted that risk when she was selecting her outfit for her next scheduled day at the consulate. If, as she suspected would happen, Jacques offered to drive her home and the lift should develop into an evening together she wanted to look her best.

She experienced a fleeting wave of anxiety that she had gone over the top when the Consul General himself greeted her appearance by taking her hands and holding her at arms length and, ever the gallant, saying, "Why! Mademoiselle Iskandar, you look particularly lovely today. Are you sure that you're not French?"

"You're too kind Monsieur le Comte but I'm just a simple Egyptian English girl."

The deputy consul, also, was very aware of the pains that Isabel had taken to look her best and congratulated himself that she would welcome his continued interest.

"I hope that you will allow me to drive you home again this evening," he said as the consulate locked its doors. "You look far too beautiful to be riding the trams."

"I was hoping you'd ask me. I've bought a couple of *bifteck anglais* and a bottle of claret on the off chance that you'd ask. I didn't want you to think that 'meat pie and chips' was the best that British cuisine had to offer."

"Thank you, ma belle. I would love to dine with you. So you can cook too. I have discovered a treasure."

Once out side the confines of the office they rapidly fell into the gently flirtatious habit of speech which they had enjoyed during their first evening together and this continued comfortably throughout the evening. Isabel's bifteck *anglais* was duly applauded, helped along by the shared bottle of claret. Jacques helped with the washing up and pulled his own surprise contribution to the evening by producing a hip flask.

"You see, Isabel, you were not the only one with happy memories of our last evening. I have brought a little Cognac to drown the taste in case you offered me tea."

"Oh! I think I can probably rustle up some coffee. In fact, I think Café Royale would be the perfect end to a perfect evening."

"Well not quite the end I hope."

They both knew that the evening would not end with coffee; even diluted with Courvoisier. It would be difficult to say with certainty who made the first move but as soon as the coffee cups were cleared away, they were in each other's arms in an armchair by the fire. As had happened during their first embrace Isabel felt her body respond as he kissed her but this time he did not stop and when he felt that she would not resist, he slid his hand beneath her blouse and caressed her breast. She became very excited; her breasts were tingling and she could not fail to notice his aroused state. This was the boundary where all her previous sexual encounters--those with Frank Kelly--had been brought to a halt. Jacques Martin was a far less pliant suitor. He placed his hand on the inside of her knee and began to slide it up beneath her skirt. Isabel gasped and gripped his wrist.

"Stop, Jacques, please. We're going much too fast. It's been a lovely evening. Don't spoil it."

He was disappointed but not too surprised. He was too old a hand at seduction to have expected a desirable, but conventionally-raised girl like Isabel to jump into his bed at such an early stage in their relationship. He accepted his rejection with as good grace as he could muster.

"I'm sorry, darling. I just got carried away. You are a very desirable woman and I can't help wanting you. Please let me continue to see you. *Je vous en prie, ma chérie.*"

She was all too ready to agree to this plan. She had brought his caresses to a premature halt but her body was still glowing and she was experiencing a throbbing deep in her pelvis. When she finally kissed him good night at the front door she threw her arms around his neck and drew herself up against his body. He was very tall and she was barely five feet four. When he responded by pulling her into his embrace her feet completely left the floor and their bodies were locked tantalizingly close. She was well aware that he still wanted her. Perhaps it was not too fantastic to start thinking that Jacques Martin was 'the One.'

In the face of such exciting developments she really missed having Kate to confide in. They worked in the same building and so it was inevitable that they would run into each other periodically. There had been no falling out when they had stopped sharing the same flat but Kate had been reluctant to intrude on what she assumed was her old friend's desolation. She was experiencing guilt by association even though she could hardly be blamed for events that had taken place three thousand miles away. She imagined that she was serving as a reminder of her brother's existence. She was just about ready to depart for Frank's wedding, which she feared, Isabel would consider a further betrayal.

The reality was that Isabel, in no way, blamed Kate for her unhappiness. She was a rational girl and was well aware that Kate was genuinely sympathetic. Even Kate's impending trip to America did not bother her unduly. Family was family. The next time they met during the workday, Kate could see that Isabel's spirits had revived considerably and that she would welcome a resumption of their closeness. Jacques Martin's attentions and romantic overtures were balm to her bruised self-esteem. She had needed re-assurance that she was an attractive woman and the deputy consul's calculated campaign of seduction was welcome. Her appearance told her friend that something was happening in her life that was getting her out of her funk. Her eyes had regained their customary sparkle and her face its animation. She looked like the Isabel of old and Kate decided that the time was ripe for a reconciliation.

"Let's meet after work; maybe ride home together," suggested Kate. We haven't had a chat in ages. I want to know what's going on in your life. How's the new teaching job going--everything?"

Isabel was also eager to resume their intimacy but she was expecting Jacques to be driving her home and she wanted to be available.

"I'm sort of expecting to be given a lift home," she admitted with a blush. "My boss has started taking me in his car."

"Izzy! You sly dog! You mean that somebody finally got through to that skinny Frenchman. Now we have to get together to spill the beans."

"He's not skinny," Izzy laughed. It was great to be friends again. "I prefer 'slim'. Kate, I really missed you. What say we hit the 11:00 on Sunday at St. John's? Then we can go to my folk's place and spend the rest of the day catching up. I've been coming in from West Derby on Sundays since I started teaching. That way my parents know I haven't fallen off the edge of the globe."

****

"Kate! We haven't seen you for ages," said Mrs. Iskandar when they gathered on the steps after Mass. "I know Isabel has missed you since she moved out to West Derby."

"Oh Mother! You make it seem like West Derby's at the end of the world. It's only about four miles from here: fifteen minutes on the tram."

"We hear that you're going to America next week," said Adlai, "and your brother's going to marry an American girl and settle in Boston. What's the world coming to? Next thing we know you'll be telling me that you're off to Australia to settle in a 'billabong farm' and raise 'jolly jumbucks.'" Adlai's knowledge of Australia did not extend much further than the first few verses of 'Waltzing Matilda.'

"What can you tell us about Frank's fiancée?" he continued, rather insensitively given that this was the girl for whom Frank had jilted his daughter.

"Is she Italian then?" Isabel said quietly. Izzy seemed to be taking the reference to Frank with equanimity so Kate decided to get all the details off her chest.

"It's an Italian family. I think they come from Genoa. Jo works as a nurse in Boston and I think that they're planning to live there. Jo has a married sister living in the Italian district. I believe they call it the North End. Frank will be working at Cunard's bonded warehouse."

"I hope that that situation holds up," said Adlai ruminatively. "I have heard some rumblings at the Chamber of

Commerce that the North Atlantic passenger business has been decreasing drastically over the past few years. The flood of emigrants from Europe to America has shrunk to a trickle. I believe that Cunard may cut back on some of its passenger ships and convert them to cruise ships. There's even talk of moving the company headquarters to Southampton."

"Surely not, Adlai," Marie cried. "Cunard has been a Liverpool company for nearly a hundred years."

"I know that, chérie, but business is business. Southampton is much more convenient for London and the Continent and the exodus from Ireland is long since over. As a matter of fact, much as I hate to be a prophet of doom, I am very worried about Britain's future, not just Liverpool's. We've never recovered fully from the war. We sold off billions of pounds worth of our overseas assets to sustain our troops. Now the factories that were our industrial strength--the mills, the foundries and the mines--lack the capital to compete in the world markets. I think that we're facing some very lean years."

"Oh come on, Gloomy Gus," Marie interjected. "Izzy and Kate didn't come here to listen to your dire predictions. So tell me Isabel, I overheard Kate calling you a sly dog. Don't tell us you're engaged to a mysterious foreigner too?" Marie didn't miss much.

"Nothing as romantic as that," she admitted. "Jacques Martin at the Consulate has taken me out to supper once or twice. That's all."

"Martin. Isn't he the deputy Consul General; a tall skinny chap with black hair, combed straight back?" asked Adlai. "I've seen him at some civic affairs at the Town Hall."

"He isn't skinny, Captain Iskandar. He's slim and soooo good-looking," Kate chimed in, pretending to swoon.

"That's the last time I'll be telling you any of my secrets, Kate Kelly," Isabel laughed.

"Isn't he a bit old for you? He must be in his thirties," her father worried.

"Oh Adlai, and how old were you when you snatched me from the cradle?" Marie countered. "Isabel's twenty-three. I was only twenty-one when you first saw me and fell madly in love."

"How true, my dear," he said complacently. He was in fact not at all dismayed by Isabel's news. A member of the French Diplomatic corps was much more in line with his marital ambitions for his daughter than was a working class boy like Frank Kelly. Later that evening, when they climbed into bed, the Iskandars reviewed the news that they had heard that day.

"I'm a little worried that Isabel might be placing too much importance on this new romance," Marie confided. "She had a nasty blow when the Kelly boy left her. We both saw how upset she was. If this fellow, Martin, is still single well into his thirties, Isabel can't be the first girl he's paid court to. Isabel is twenty-three but this Monsieur Martin is only the second man whom she's ever been involved with. I just hope that she doesn't fall too hard for this Frenchman."

"Isabel is your daughter, my darling. She's got a level head on he shoulders."

"Adlai, you sounded very serious when you were talking about Britain's finances. Do you think it's going to be as bad as all that."

"I'm afraid I do. I've been thinking about it a lot. Britain's had a great run of luck. We got off to a fast start; the first industrial nation in the world and we've had the Empire to supply us with raw materials and to provide us with markets for our goods but the war has nearly bankrupted us and other nations are eating into our business. We're already seeing thousands of men out of work and it's going to get much worse."

"What do you think we should do about it? I don't mean Britain. I mean us: Adlai and Marie Iskandar. Do you think that we're at risk?"

"Most of our money is invested in industry. We've got shares in several cotton mills mostly in the Ribble valley and we have a significant stake in the Cronton Colliery. Our only other assets, apart from this house, are our tobacco shops."

"They don't bring in a huge amount of income but, at least it's steady," Marie said. The tobacco shops were her particular interest. She had been responsible for recruiting the tenants and she had gradually assumed responsibility for that part of the family finances.

"I think you've got an important point there," agreed Adlai. "We can't do much about the fate of the country's heavy industry but we can pull out our funds and invest them where they won't be so vulnerable. Look at our tobacco shops. Even if the workingman has to cut back on things, he is not likely to stop smoking. He'll still want his Woodbines and his St Bruno. We should think about expanding our little empire but I think that we don't want to get too spread out. It will be too hard to manage if our shops are scattered all over the city. What other businesses are essential? What are the shops that will stay in business even in the worst of times? Think about it. I'm afraid the big breweries have got a lock on all the pubs in the city so they're not a possibility."

"Well, people can get by without luxuries. They can get by without new clothes or new furniture but they've got to eat. I think that we should put our money to work by buying up grocery shops just like we did with the tobacconists."

"Marie! I always knew that you were the financial brains of this family. We don't need to do it all at once. In fact, it will be better if we don't, but I'm going to liquidate our industrial holdings over the next month and we can start looking for opportunities to acquire two or three more retail tobacconists. Then we can see about buying a local grocery shop. That way we can learn the ropes before we get too heavily committed."

"You know, Adlai, I'm quite excited about all this. I've enjoyed being the 'lady of the manor' but I'll enjoy getting back into the real world where you can provide an honest service and make an honest profit. I think I'm just a simple Lebanese shopkeeper at heart."

CHAPTER TWENTY-TWO
Boston, September, 1928

The re-supplying of ships when they are away from their homeport was a very efficient and tightly controlled operation. A large organization like the Cunard Line, which needed to repeatedly and predictably service its transatlantic liners, maintained permanent bonded warehouses in Boston and New York. The need for 'bonded' warehouses was made even more critical than in other parts of the world because they contained enormous stocks of top-of-the-line alcoholic beverages in a country in which even bathtub gin commanded top dollar. A victualing bill was a custom house warrant that permitted the shipment of bonded stores. In Britain, a licensed victualler was the person authorized to run a pub. A reputation for reliability and scrupulous honesty was a vital element in the selection process when Cunard recruited staff for their US operations. This was undoubtedly the reason that the company reacted positively to Frank's request for a transfer to the victualing team in their Boston warehouse. He had ten years of impeccable service with the company as a steward; an occupation in which the opportunities for petty theft were legion.

The Liverpool to Boston voyage in late September was to be Frank Kelly's last as a steward. He would leave the ship after its last docking and assume his new duties ashore a week later after his wedding. His sister, Kate, was a passenger too. Although her share of the round trip ticket had virtually wiped out her life savings she had not been able to resist the opportunity to participate in Frank's wedding and to see the fabled United States of America. The voyage had been magical. She had turned out to be a good sailor, untroubled by the motions of the boat, and even in Third Class, accommodations and dining were luxurious. Any girl as striking as the vivacious Amazonian redhead would have been assured of first-class attention from the staff but the fact that she was the sister of a popular longtime crewmember ensured that she was treated as a minor celebrity.

On the evening of their last full day at sea, the Kellys were treated to a party in the Third Class dining room. The Captain himself put in an appearance and made a short speech recounting Frank's service to the company, his upcoming wedding and his good fortune in having such a charming sister. At the last remark, the stewards cheered enthusiastically and Kate astonished the bluff old mariner by kissing him on the cheek, which provoked even louder applause and laughter in which the passengers joined. Altogether it was a memorable maiden voyage for the young Miss Kelly and a very satisfactory conclusion of his seagoing career for Frank, he still had shipboard duties to complete on docking and so it was Kate, by herself, who first disembarked with the other passengers, reclaimed her luggage and made her way through Customs.

The Boston Quays, like docks the world over, were functional rather then decorative. In the winter they would be positively bleak but it was September and, to Kate's pleasant surprise, the sun was shining warmly and the sky was cloudless. She scanned the crowds milling around and searching for relatives, friends and transportation. She soon spotted two attractive young women, obviously sisters, one of whom was brandishing a large placard on which was, hand printed, a large 'KATE'.

They made eye contact and drew close with tentative smiles and the younger one of the two said, "Kate! It is you, isn't it? There can't be two women who match Frank's description of you on one small ship."

"I'm Kate. I'm going to be Frank's 'Best Man' but you didn't need the sign. I could have recognized you from Frank's description too. He said that Jo was the most beautiful girl in Boston. So tell me, which of you is Jo?" she added disingenuously.

Tessa was amused. Obviously Frank's young sister could obviously hold her end up. Theresa Napolitano was a handsome woman in her mid thirties with beautiful raven hair and a friendly face but she was under no delusion as to who was the beauty of the family.

"I'm Theresa Napolitano--Tessa--Jo's sister. Say hello to your future sister-in-law."

"Jo! I'm so excited to be here and to meet you--both. I can now see why Frank fell for you like a ton of bricks. Thank you for letting me be a part of your wedding."

"Of course we want you to be part if the wedding but I'm not sure that I see you as best man. We've got to come up with a better plan than that."

"Come on you two. Frank may be another half hour. Let's take one case each and find a cafe where we can rest our feet. We can have the whole wedding mapped out before Frank gets his breath back. You know that men just get in the way when really important matters are to be decided."

The two younger girls picked up their assigned suitcases and they trailed out of the Customs shed. They grinned at each other, friends already, acknowledging that when Theresa Napolitano was in charge, it was best not to resist. Some twenty minutes later the three were deeply engaged in animated discussion concerning the myriad decisions that would be needed before Jo could be married in a manner worthy of the Lucca and Kelly families. Theresa had made a generous suggestion to resolve the knotty problem of having Kate appear as Frank's best man.

"Jo, I know that you have asked me to be your matron of honor but I would be happy to let Kate fill that role and you could have one of our male relatives act as Frank's best man."

"Oh Tess! That's a brilliant idea. Are you sure you don't mind? What do you think, Kate? I'd be thrilled to have you as my maid of honor and it would be a shame to have such a good looking girl as you disguised as man."

"I'd love to be your Maid of Honor," Kate gasped. Things certainly did move fast in the United States.

"That's settled then," Tessa chimed in." Who do think would make the best man for Frank?"

"I know just the man: my cousin, Marco. He's always been my favorite cousin and he's one of very few of my relatives who wouldn't be intimidated standing next to you. You'll love him, Kate, and he'll think he's gone to heaven when he sees you. He's six feet six and weighs 230 lbs. He used to play football when he was at Boston College. It only needed for Frank to show up and be informed as to who his best man was to be. Frank, as it turned out, had exciting news of his own. After giving his bride-to-be a resounding kiss and his future sister-in-law a rather more temperate embrace, he could scarcely contain his excitement.

"You'll never believe what just happened," he said. "I've just been given a wedding present. The crew had a whip round and we've got two hundred and forty dollars"-- (a small fortune in 1928). "Would you believe it? Even the Captain chipped in a fiver. Kate, I'll finally be able to reimburse you for the cost of your trip."

To Frank's surprise, his sister burst into tears and threw her arms around him. Then regaining her composure she deadpanned to Jo, "Forget what I said about him before. He really is very sweet. I hope you don't mind him spending some of your first wedding present on his sister but at least now I'll be able to buy a new gown worthy of adorning your Maid of Honor. By the way, Frank, your new best man is Marco Tessla and he's six feet six."

"There you are, little sister, didn't I tell you that they grow their boys tall on this side of the Atlantic. Of course, I'll look like a midget standing next to him but what the heck, every one will be looking at Jo."

They then took a cab to Jo's apartment where it had been planned that Kate should stay with Jo until the wedding and Frank was to be housed, for the last time he hoped, at the Seamen's Hostel.

****

The wedding was to be held in exactly one week's time; one week in which to make all the preparations that, in most marriages, require months. The most pressing need was to introduce the groom to his bride's family and to ensure that all the formalities, both civil and ecclesiastic, had been met. Birth certificates were produced and a marriage license obtained without difficulty. A visit to Brockton was a much more important event. Jo still had her hospital duties to attend to as she had requested the week off for a honeymoon and would be working up until two days before the wedding.

The wedding party, to include Theresa and Kate, arranged to meet at the Lucca family home. Jo's parents were, naturally eager to meet this mysterious Englishman who had so suddenly appeared in their daughter's life. They had been taken a little aback by the news that their prospective son-in-law was not only not Italian but also not even American. They had been somewhat re-assured by the fact that he had met the approval of their eldest daughter. Theresa was generally acknowledged within the family as having her head screwed on. They had resolved to welcome the Kellys with true Italian hospitality and so the evening of the wedding party's visit to Brockton was set aside for a family dinner. The evening would also give Frank an opportunity to meet his best man.

Marco Tessla was Jo's cousin by virtue of her mother's side of the family. Signora Lucca had been christened Carmela Tessla. Marco was a Brockton boy who had helped to pay his way through Boston College by playing football, which is to say 'American football' (to distinguish it from real football). He was now just starting the fourth and final year of his Ll.B. at Suffolk University's Law School. Kate was a little intimidated by this information. She was still thrilled by the prospect of being paired during the wedding celebrations with her 'giant' but was worried that a budding attorney might be too cerebral to find her worthy of his attention. In that she had little to fear. Not even Oliver Wendell Holmes would have been able to ignore Kate Kelly, nor wished to, once he got a look at her, particularly in her bridesmaid's gown which she and Jo had purchased on a pre-nuptial excursion to Lord and Taylor's.

The happy couple paid a visit to the rectory at St Anthony's and Father Baldini was re-assured that Frank was a Catholic in good standing. He had remembered to bring his baptismal certificate from home on his last trip. Jo did not need one. Fr. Baldini had baptized her himself twenty-four years earlier.

"It'll be a Nuptial Mass of course and so you will both be receiving the Sacrament. Would you like me to arrange to hear your confessions?" Father Baldini had been a priest for a long time and had, long since, discovered that he could not count on even the most innocent looking of couples to be approaching their wedding in the 'state of grace' that the church deemed was appropriate for the reception of the Holy Communion.

"Thank you Father." It was Frank who answered first and Jo was a little surprised. She knew that Frank was Catholic. Almost all the Irish that she had met were but she did not realize that he would conform so readily to the requirements of the faith. She was, surprisingly, reassured by this. She had not been particularly devout (to put it mildly) but when she had dreamed of raising a family she had always envisaged that it would be in the context of a Catholic home. They both took the wise priest up on his offer, made their peace with God, and promised to avoid 'occasions of sin.' This would mean curtailing their lovemaking but they thought that they could probably forgo that for the few remaining days of the engagement. It would make the honeymoon even sweeter.

Jo's parent's natural anxiety at first meeting with their daughter's fiancé was rapidly removed. Like many mainstream Americans, they had a very stereotypical idea of the English; mostly obtained from the cinema. Intellectually, they knew of course, that in a population of thirty million, there must be a full range of personalities and occupations; from coal miners to professors of physics but somehow they feared that Jo's Englishman might have a pencil thin mustache and address Gaetano as 'old chap.' It was therefore very reassuring when Frank Kelly turned out to be clean shaven and addressed them respectfully. He was, of course, one short in the eye department but even that was evidence that, when called upon, he had 'done his bit.'

"Mr. and Mrs. Lucca, I am so pleased to meet you. Thank you for welcoming me into your home. I love your daughter and promise to make her a good husband."

Frank had worked hard on this speech and it had been worth the effort. The Luccas were charmed. Gaetano was now a respectable, albeit illegal, tavern owner but in his youth he had been a pretty tough customer and he still placed a high value on a man's ability to look after himself in a brawl. Frank's war torn face was incontrovertible evidence that he had earned his scars in an honorable manner. To Gaetano, a man's scars were his badges of honour. He could now rest assured that his daughter was getting a real man. Carmela had only to look at her daughter's face to know that she was head over heels in love. She would have preferred her son-in-law to be Italian but, at least, he was Catholic. As for his sister, she could hardly wait to see the effect she would have on her nephew, her brother's eldest. The matchmaking urge that was so near the surface in most women was already going into overdrive at the thought of the juxtaposition of Kate Kelly and Marco Tessla.

Marco Tessla was, truth to tell, not looking forward to the family meal or to his involvement in Jo's wedding. He was fond of his cousin and he was only two years older than she but their paths had deviated years ago when he had gone off to college while she was still in high school. They were not close friends. He was now just starting his final year of law school and he had a very heavy workload. Consequently his social life was compressed into his weekends and he prized those hours away from the books. As a formidable physical presence and with some residual status as a former member of the B.C. football team, he had no difficulty in attracting young women. Weekends never found him without an attractive female on his arm and, occasionally, in his bed. He therefore had given only grudging acceptance to the invitation to give up not one but two of his prized weekends to act as best man to his cousin's mysterious husband to be. Still, family is family and there was the promise of meeting the even more intriguing Kate who, it was hinted, was quite something to behold. He had driven down from Boston on his motorbike: a Springfield Indian, and was taking off his greatcoat, helmet and goggles in the kitchen when he was met by his cousin and introduced to Frank. Mrs. Lucca was busy preparing the first of the five courses that she had planned for dinner.

"Thank you for agreeing to be my Best Man," Frank said. "I'm going to need some moral support," he added shyly. "Even my sister has abandoned me to be Jo's Maid of Honor."

He looked slightly overwhelmed and Tony felt a little sympathetic towards him. The Luccas and Tesslas *en masse* could be a formidable proposition. Still, he thought, he's got one member of the family firmly won over. Jo had linked her arm through Frank's and was gazing at him adoringly.

"Come and meet my Maid of Honor. She's in the front parlour talking to Papa."

At first glance Kate appeared unremarkable. True, she had a pleasant face, flawless, lightly freckled skin and a rather wild looking mop of auburn hair. She was seated in an overstuffed chair and was deep in conversation with Mr. Lucca who appeared to be enjoying the attention.

"Kate," Jo said, "come and meet my cousin Marco-- Frank's Best Man. Marco, this is Kate; Frank's sister."

As Kate stood up from the depths of the armchair, Marco felt that all the eyes in the room were on him. Even Mrs. Lucca had followed him into the room to witness the encounter. All of a sudden, Marco Tessla felt like he had been stunned as for the first time in his life he found himself gazing almost eye to eye into the face of a tall, slim and very attractive woman. His first glance had misled him. This magnificent creature, smiling an unashamedly delighted greeting, was the most beautiful girl he had ever seen. Carmela had watched the encounter. She did not need to hear the conversation. Seeing them had been like watching a match set to a bonfire. All that was needed was a little fuel. She could supply that.

"Dinner's ready. Everybody sit down," she cried and the family gathered around the table to eat the first of the five courses that she had prepared, to drink a little wine and to talk about the great upcoming event.

"We really must find a place to live after our honeymoon. The lease on my apartment runs out at the end of September and I don't think we can afford to keep it up," Jo admitted as the family finished the antipasto and started in on the *Pollo con Funghi e Pomodoro* enhanced by an amusing *Pinot Grigio*.

"Do you know whether there are any cheap apartments coming open in the North End, Tess?"

"Fredo and I have been thinking about just that," her sister replied. "You know when we first opened the deli, we lived above the shop. It has a tiny apartment; just two rooms, a kitchen and a bathroom but it might do. It would certainly be big enough, at least until you start a family and you can't beat the price. You can have it free; our present to you. Maybe you can babysit for us once in a while."

"Oh Tess! That would be wonderful. Thank you," Jo said and gave her a sisterly buss. "We'd be happy to babysit. Wouldn't we Frank? We'd even help out in the shop on weekends if you'd want us to."

"If you do that, you'd better teach Frank to make change in Italian. Some of the locals go through life in the North End and never learn to speak English."

"Speaking of honeymoons," said Carmela as she served the *Melone e Prosciutto* along with a *Trebbiano di Romangio*, (a light, dry unobtrusive wine with hints of flowers and fruit.)

"Gaetano and I would like to offer you our cottage on the Cape. It's not very palatial, Frank, but it's right on the beach and it's very quiet at this time of year." She smiled warmly at Frank. She was now so happy at Jo's impending wedding that she was willing to overlook that he was not Italian.

"Oh Mama. That would be wonderful. Wait till you see it Frank. The whole family used to go there every summer until we all grew up. It has four bedrooms and you can hear the surf beating on the shore when you're in bed."

"How about you, Kate? Where are you staying after the wedding?" her father chipped in. Kate had worked her magic on him as effortlessly as, in earlier circumstances, she had charmed Captain Iskandar.

"Tessa has offered to let me stay at her home while Frank and Jo are on their honeymoon. I can get around and see Boston while they're gone. Frank has told me about your MTA. It sounds just like our Liverpool trams so, I'm sure that I'll do just fine."

"Hey! I can do better than the MTA," Marco jumped in with the quickness off the mark that had once terrorized opposing quarterbacks. "If you don't mind riding on a motorbike, I'll take you to see everything that's worth seeing in Boston. We could even hit the Cape on the weekend if Jo and Frank don't mind lending us a couple of bedrooms. We could take the car, then stay overnight and bring them back with us."

"That would be great, Marco. I'm sure that Frank will be happy to see Kate after a week seeing nobody but me," Jo said disingenuously.

"I know I'll never be tired of seeing you, Sweetheart." Frank was not a smooth talker but he could recognize a cue when he heard one. "I don't think that even having Kate around is going to ruin our honeymoon. I'm just teasing Kate," he relented. "You know that we'd love to see you and Marco."

After that exchange, it required the company only to do justice to Carmela's *Stinco di Vitella Arrosto*, which despite its unappetizing title, turned out to be a deliciously aromatic roasted veal shank accompanied by a hearty *Sangiovese di Romangia*. They were amused by its presumption. Not even Tony, whose appetite was legendary, could manage the *dolci* but the men did manage a postprandial Sambuca and a memorable evening came to an end. The wedding was celebrated two days later on Saturday.

Catholic weddings, in 1928, took place in the morning. The wedding party, and indeed anyone who chose to, would be receiving the Eucharist. This required the communicants to be fasting. The wedding breakfast, which traditionally followed the ceremony, would be held in the Knights of Columbus Hall and it therefore, literally, broke the fast. The Nuptial Mass was at eleven o'clock.

The wedding was to be a small one gauged by most standards. The bride was attended only by her maid of honor and, similarly, only Marco Tessla was standing up for the groom, but the church was full. The Luccas were a well-liked family of long standing in the parish and the Club Genovese played a large part in the social life of many of the parishioners. Gaetano was a former Grand Knight of the St.

Anthony's Council of the Knights of Columbus and its Honor Guard of portly gentlemen in plumed hats and sashes provided a little dramatic flair to the proceedings. The best man towered above the groom but Frank with his eye patch and dark rented suit looked almost distinguished and provoked most of the interested speculation among the congregation as they awaited the arrival of the bride.

However, the bride is the cynosure of all eyes at a wedding. She had followed the tradition of wearing *something old; something new; something borrowed and something blue*. Her gown was simple and elegant. She and Kate had made a joint excursion to Brockton's leading couturier and they had enjoyed a few hilarious moments in debating how she could meet the requirement for *something blue* before settling on an ornamental garter decorated with a gathering of lace and blue ribbon. Her mother's wedding veil met the 'old' requirement and Theresa had loaned her sister her treasured pearl earrings to round out the ensemble. Josefina Lucca walked down the aisle on her father's arm. Gaetano lifted her veil and kissed her before leading her to her place at her groom's side. She was breathtakingly lovely and Frank felt that his heart would burst with joy. They recited their vows and exchanged rings and became man and wife in the eyes of God and the Commonwealth of Massachusetts. Mass followed and they received the Eucharist and the ceremony concluded with the traditional Nuptial Blessing.

The wedding breakfast was served to two hundred and then the wedding party moved on to the Club Genovese where Gaetano presided, the wine began to flow and the real party commenced. Mandolin music filled the air and all the traditional dances were performed. The 'Dons' of both of the nearby big cities put in their ceremonial appearance, danced with the bride and added their envelopes to the basket that was discretely placed near the head table. The wedding donations totaled, it was discovered that night, a staggering two thousand six hundred and seventy dollars.

Chapter Twenty-Three

Boston and Cape Cod, September, 1928

Jo had been thrilled to accept her parents' offer of the use of their cottage for her honeymoon but it was on Popponesset Bay on the ocean side of Cape Cod. It was not easily accessible by public transportation after nightfall. East Falmouth was the nearest town of any size. They had, therefore, decided to spend the first night of their marriage at Jo's apartment in Boston. It would be theirs for only one more week. Marco had received his father's permission to borrow the family car for the weekend and had offered to drive them to Boston. He would return with Kate the next morning and they would all drive to the Lucca family cottage. Marco's attitude towards the wedding had altered considerably since he had discovered that Kate was a part of it. Now he was anxious to find reasons to be in her company and he was eager to see her in a bathing suit at the beach.

Jo was still in her wedding gown when they arrived in Boston and had required help in getting into it as it had a row of pearl buttons down the middle of the back from her neck to below her shapely rump. Frank was tantalizingly slow in unbuttoning them. They hadn't made love in almost a month and she was eager for him to take her to bed. He had shed his trousers and when she finally stepped out of her gown she felt his erection against her back. He slid his hands around her and cupped her breasts. She was already excited and wanted to consummate their union but Frank appeared strangely reluctant.

"Take me Frank. I know you want me. I'm your wife now. Make love to me," and she pulled him after her under the covers.

"Are you sure I won't hurt you or hurt the baby?"

So that's what was bothering him, she mused.

"Trust me Frank I'm a nurse. I need you and now. I promise you that little Julia can take care of herself."

He entered her gently and they moved together slowly but with gradually increasing intensity. Julia did not seem to mind and Jo abandoned herself in an orgasm of pure physical ecstasy. They climaxed together and Jo felt the gush of Frank's semen and was satisfied as never before. They had had a long and emotion-filled day. They fell asleep in each other's arms and slept till dawn. When Frank awoke he found that Jo was already up, showered and dressed. He was momentarily disconcerted. In the minutes before he was fully awake he had had thoughts of taking up where they had left off the night before but Jo had other ideas.

"Frank! It felt so good to receive Communion yesterday after so long. I'd like to go to early Mass; sort of bless our marriage. I want to thank God for my sexy husband. How about we can pick up some bagels and lox for breakfast at the Jewish deli on the way home? Marco and Kate will be calling for us before noon and I thought we could use the time in boxing up some of my stuff. We have to be out of here almost as soon as we get back from the Cape."

This was not exactly how Frank had hoped that they would be spending the morning but he reconciled himself to the inevitable with the thought that he would have Jo to take to bed for the rest of his life. He resolved to do just that in about twelve hours but realized that Jo would not be a silent partner in any forthcoming family decisions. The thought made him grin. He liked a girl with moxie. And where did that 'little Julia' come from? He had planned on naming the baby 'Francis Xavier the Third.' I bet that little Julia will have plenty of moxie too, he thought. She had certainly taken her parents' uninhibited lovemaking in her stride without apparent ill effects.

Kate and Mark showed up with the transportation shortly after eleven to find the apartment, a hive of activity. Jo was wearing the slightly smug proprietorial smile of a new bride whose aspirations for wedding night bliss had been thoroughly satisfied and Frank was meekly following all her directions as they finished stacking her boxes for next weeks relocation. It was obvious to Kate that the marriage had gotten off to a good start. Kate, too, had had a marvelous evening. With her fair Celtic complexion, statuesque figure and luxuriant auburn hair, she had been quite a sensation at the reception where most of the women were dark haired, rather more olive skinned and markedly shorter. Tony had exercised his prerogative as Best Man to claim her as his 'date' for the evening and their obvious infatuation with each other had set tongues wagging.

Marco Tessla, football hero and aspiring attorney, was considered a prize catch in the parish and it looked like the young British girl was well on the way to catching him. They danced together all evening. Marco had proved to be a surprisingly good dancer for such a big man and Kate, with seven years of Atlantic House behind her, could hold her own on any dance floor. They made a spectacularly handsome couple. The attraction that they had felt when they first met could not but flourish in such a festive atmosphere; there was music, wine and laughter. Love was in the air and they felt its strong pull. Marco had discovered that not only was Kate a perfect fit when they danced the slower dances but she possessed a lively intelligence and an irresistible sense of humor. He was truly smitten. Only the proximity of a dozen of his closest relatives had prevented him from making more obvious overtures to her but he did hold her ever closer on the dance floor as the evening progressed.

His parents--the bride's aunt and uncle--were of course, in attendance. He had introduced them to Kate and the elder male Tessla, who was only a few inches shorter than his son, and who had an equally keen eye for a fine looking woman, and had taken advantage of the opportunity to take her for a spin around the floor. This left Marco alone with his mother and she had used the opportunity to see how serious he was about this exotic stranger. The Tesslas had not failed to notice the obvious infatuation of the couple as they had danced or snuggled together in one of Club Genovese's booths oblivious to all the other guests.

"How serious are you about this girl, Marco? You've hardly been able to keep your hands off her all evening."

"We only met two days ago and she'll only be here for a week or so. She's an English girl. I don't suppose that we're going to get very far as a couple but, tell you the truth Mom, I wish we could. I've never felt this way about any girl before."

"Well don't go getting into any trouble. She seems to be a very nice girl. I know you Tessla men," she added with a wry glance towards her husband who was obviously thoroughly enjoying his turn around the floor with Miss Kelly. Kate had worked her magic on yet another middle-aged male.

"Don't forget, Marco, you have a whole year of school left before you can even start to think about getting serious with a young woman."

"I know, Ma," he admitted sadly.

It would be at least a year until he could think of supporting a wife and he had the feeling that Kate was not a girl who would welcome the idea of a casual fling. However, 'nothing ventured, nothing gained,' and he had the next eight days to see how far he could get. They finally left the wedding party and climbed into his car and sat for a while and then, without prompting, Kate initiated a lingering kiss which made his pulse race. He attempted to maneuver into position for a more comprehensive embrace but two far above average sized young adults in a small Chevy with a manual transmission was not conducive to greater intimacy.

"We've got the car for the weekend, Kate. Let's go to Boston right now instead of tomorrow morning. We could stay at my place," he urged throatily.

"Marco, you know that I've fallen for you. I've dreamed of meeting you since I was fifteen years old but when I go to bed with you I'll be wearing your ring."

"You know that I can't afford to get married until I finish law school and get a job."

"I know that, sweetheart, but we still have a week together. Ask me to marry you next year and I'll come running. In the meantime, this gearshift is sticking into my solar plexus. Let's get into the back seat for five minutes where I can kiss you without impaling myself. Then you can take me to the Lucca's house. I'm sleeping in Jo's old room tonight.

They arrived at Jo's apartment for the trip to Cape Cod next day, brimming with excitement at the prospect of a whole day together. Kate had met her 'dream giant,' won his heart and laid down the 'rules of engagement' and Marco had a week to look forward to in which he could try to break those rules. Even if they only became bent, he would enjoy trying. He suspected that his efforts would be appreciated even if they were doomed to failure. Their five-minute goodnight embrace had left them both in a state of high excitement and gave promise of a memorable week ahead.

"What did you do to Dad while you were dancing last night," Marco asked, as they were en route to Jo's place next day. "He couldn't stop talking about '*La Bella Katerina*' at breakfast."

"Oh! I told him that he was almost as good looking as his son," she said with a flirtatious grin.

"What did he say to that?" Marco asked. He could almost guess. He knew his father well.

"Oh! he said. What do you mean-almost?"

Marco had guessed correctly. She did not mention that, as they left the dance floor, he had pinched her bottom.

If what a newly married couple desired for their first extended period of time together was beautiful beaches, warm sunny days, cool nights and solitude, it is hard to imagine a place more perfect than Cape Cod in late September. Jo and her cousin were familiar with the family cottage on Popponesset Beach from childhood visits. Cape Cod was only two hours away from Brockton. They opened up the cottage and aired out the rooms. It was like visiting an old friend. The Kelly siblings were most amazed by how few people were in evidence. In Britain, perfect weather like this would have resulted in throngs of people and crowded beaches. They had not previously experienced the phenomenon that, in the United States, summer ends on Labor Day as though someone had thrown a switch. Here on Cape Cod in late September, they had miles of beautiful beaches, sand dunes and temperature in the 80's and not a soul in sight.

While they had access to a car, they all rode into East Falmouth, the nearest town with shops open on a Sunday afternoon, and laid in the basic supplies that they would need for the upcoming week's meals. Until Marco and Kate returned next Friday afternoon with the Tessla's Chevy, they would be dependent for transportation on the two rather ramshackle bikes which came with the cottage along with beach chairs, towels and assorted seaside paraphernalia.

"I think that we should have a picnic on the beach tonight" said Jo in her role as host. "We'll need some fire lighters but I saw enough fire wood out back to keep us warm all week."

"You know a bonfire on the beach is always best as it gets dark. I don't think I can wait to eat till seven-thirty," chimed in her cousin. "Let's grill hamburgers in the cottage and then we can toast marshmallows on the beach for dessert. We could even make s'mores if we had some graham crackers and some chocolate bars."

"S'mores! Great idea Marc," his cousin agreed.

"Are s'mores another of your American delicacies like BLTs?" said Frank getting into the spirit. "Kate! You haven't lived until you've tasted one of Jo's BLTs."

"Come along you lot. Let's round up everything we need. We've just got time for a dip in the ocean before Marco dies of hunger."

"I'm afraid that I'm going to have to limit myself to paddling," confessed Kate. "I never thought to bring a swimsuit from England."

"Perhaps you could borrow one from Jo," suggested Marco disingenuously.

"If Kate wore one of my suits, she'd have to cut it in half and wear one half on each end or the police would lock her up."

"Cut it out you two. You're making my brother blush. I promise I'll have a suit of my own when we come down next Friday." *Who'd have thought to bring a swimsuit to a wedding?* Kate couldn't help thinking--not that she was complaining. She knew how she looked in a bathing suit.

The water was still nearly 80 degrees and the beach shelved steeply enough so that they could swim within fifty feet of the shore. Kate had to content herself with wading in the shallows but consoled herself by surreptitiously admiring Marco's body that was still a thing of beauty even after two years away from the gymnasium. The horseplay of the honeymoon couple began to get rather more romantic. Marco left them to it and waded back towards the shore, swept Kate up in his arms and pretended to dunk her in the water. Nobody had ever even attempted to pick her up since she had been twelve but Marco did it effortlessly and she squealed delightedly in mock horror. She felt positively girlish. If she had had any doubts that Marco was the man for her, this dispelled them. *I really must find a swimsuit that will knock his eyes out*, she resolved. *I hope I can remember how to find Lord and Taylors when I get back to Boston.*

They dined on hamburgers and drank Coca-Cola. To Frank's relief the store had been out of Moxie. Then, as dusk arrived, they built a fire on the beach and ate s'mores. These, it turned out, were marshmallows toasted over the fire and served as a sandwich between layers of chocolate and graham crackers. Marco had discovered an old ukulele in the cottage and, to everyone's surprise, they found he could play it. Jo regaled them with the hit songs from her days at St. Anne's School of Nursing. They were easy to pick up and soon the strains of 'Matches' were to be heard from one end of Popponesset Beach to the other. The tune was *Jada*.

> Matches! Matches! M-A-T-C HES
> Matches! Matches! M-A-T-C HES
> You can strike 'em on wood. You can strike 'em on glass.
> I know a girl who can strike 'em on her (clap) (clap)
> Matches! Matches! M-A-T-C-HES

Oh! They were wicked, those St Anne's girls!

All in all, it had been a very enjoyable day but Kate and Marco still had a two-hour drive back to Boston and so they left with the promise to return in five days. On the drive north, Kate snuggled up to Marco as far as the gearshift would permit. She has something important to say to him.

"Marco! I know that you have offered to spend all next week showing me round Boston but I don't think you should. You know I love being with you but how are you going to marry me if you flunk out of school." She hoped that he realized that she was only half kidding with the reference to matrimony.

"You've got the wrong idea about Suffolk Law," he laughed. "It was established for working stiffs like me. I go to school in the evening and that leaves me with all day to earn my tuition. I've been going there for three years. I've only got one more to go. So, you see I wouldn't have to skip classes. We could drive up into the country and see the leaves changing color. It's what tourists are supposed to do."

"Law school at night and work during the day to help pay for it. What a great idea. I might even try that myself one day but if you are going to give up a day's pay I don't really want to go off into the woods. I'm a city girl. Tell you the truth; I'm not that big on leaves. What I'd really like to see is Boston College and the place where you used to play football and what are the chances of me sneaking in and watching one of your classes at the Law School?"

"I don't think we can manage that," he admitted. "At Suffolk, we have to show tickets to a monitor when we go in to make sure that we've paid our tuition and that's how they know that we're showing up for class. As for my daytime job, I work in construction for my Uncle Tom's building firm; Mom's brother. I'm his best worker. I'm sure he'll give me a couple of days off without docking my pay. He was at the wedding and I noticed him giving you a long look. I am fairly sure he approved. I'll bring you in to see him and you can flirt with him like you did with my old man."

"I did not flirt with him," she said indignantly. "Well only a little," she admitted with a grin.

As he kissed her goodnight at Tessa's front door, he reflected, *if we weren't picking up the honeymooners, I could have taken her to see the Eagles play next Saturday. A girl who looks like she does and likes sports too; I think that I've found the girl for me.*

****

The young couple awoke on Monday morning to find themselves the only occupants of the cottage and virtually the only residents of Popponesset Beach. There were a handful of hardy souls who lived there year round. An elderly couple that lived two hundred yards down the beach walked slowly by, hand-in-hand, collecting shells and, in the afternoon the female partner set up an easel on the beach and painted. They found that they had a whole week with nothing to do but be in the sun and make love. Jo found that being both married and pregnant was a curiously liberating experience. With no concerns about conception (it would be a little late for that) and with the blessing of the church, they were free to make love whenever their desires took them, which was often.

She was already finding that, even though he was passionate and eager, he seemed more anxious to please her than to achieve his own satisfaction. He was deeply in love with her. His delight in her body was almost palpable and she gave herself to him unreservedly, reveling in his caresses. She was a happy young woman. She was married to a man who adored her and she was carrying his child. God had forgiven her for her wild youth and she wanted only to be a loving wife and mother. Their days were lazy and unplanned. They resurrected the ancient bicycles and made a daily visit to the General Store in East Falmouth where they bought the ingredients for their evening meal.

On the second morning of their stay they purchased some sun tan lotion. Frank's Anglo- Irish skin had not taken kindly to the brilliant New England sunshine but he enjoyed the administrations of his nurse. Jo gently anointed his sunburned areas with the lotion and then applied the medicine, prophylactically to the rest of his body. She, with her Mediterranean heritage, reveled in the sunshine and became visibly more tanned with each passing day but, having seen how her massage had affected Frank, she insisted that she receive the same attention and the outcome was very satisfactory for both nurse and patient.

Most of the time they stayed close to the cottage but they did manage to put in two minor expeditions. They took a day trip to Martha's Vineyard where they lunched on delicious, freshly caught flounder. On Thursday they bicycled to Sandy Neck Beach for a picnic. It was on the north side of the Cape and about five miles from Popponesset. The water temperature on the south side was moderated by the Gulf Stream and was still in the high 70s. The waters of Cape Cod Bay, although only a few miles away, were controlled by the Labrador Current coming down from Canada with temperatures in the bone chilling 50s. Frank had plunged gaily into the water at Sandy Neck only to emerge seconds later.

"God! That water's colder than New Brighton," he gasped.

New Brighton was where Liverpudlians traditionally dipped their toes into the notoriously frigid Irish Sea. Jo was, of course, very familiar with the waters of Cape Cod Bay and had been watching Frank's arctic plunge with amused anticipation. She was ready to wrap him up in a large beach towel.

Most afternoons they swam in the balmy Atlantic waters. Later, Frank could savor the salty taste on his tongue as he gently teased his bride's nipples. He knew that she took pleasure in this and to his surprise, when she reciprocated, he, too, found the sensation very stimulating. Each day they found new delights in each other's body and, before falling asleep in each other's arms, they thanked God.

Chapter Twenty-Four
Boston and Cape Cod, 1928

Boston's North End was, in 1928, overwhelmingly an Italian enclave and most of those Italians had come from Southern Italy or from Sicily in the two decades surrounding the centenary. It had, however, been the most important section of the colony in its earliest days and was home to some of the most famous landmarks from the Revolutionary era. Although he was unaware of it, Marco was re-tracing some of the paths that Jo and Frank had traveled on the Fourth of July, but Marco was a much better informed guide.

"I know that I promised to give you a ride on my motor bike," he said when he picked Kate up at his cousin's home on Harris Street, "but Paul Revere's House is within walking distance and the 'Old North Church' is only one block away."

"I hope you've boned up on your facts. I've heard of Paul Revere. Wasn't that the name of a horse? They didn't place too much emphasis on American History at Everton Valley."

They strolled amicably through the streets that were both crowded and noisy. The street vendors cries were as often in Italian as in English and pushcarts vied for space with horse drawn wagons and motor vehicles. At the historic landmarks Marco enjoyed his role as history teacher and Kate listened dutifully. However it was during his account of the 'Great Molasses Flood' that she first gave him her undivided attention. As they approached the harbor they passed beneath the tracks of the Atlantic Avenue Elevated Railway.

"See how this segment of the overhead is much newer than the rest? The original tracks were demolished by a wave of molasses that was fifteen feet high and traveling at thirty-five miles an hour. This took place only nine years ago. I was already seventeen years old. I remember all about it. The 'Globe' was full of it. Tessa and Fredo were already living in Harris Street when it happened. That's only a couple of hundred yards away."

"Was any one hurt? Where on earth could that much molasses have come from? It must have taken thousands of gallons to have made a wave like that."

"Two point three million gallons to be exact," Marco said bitterly. The memories of the event and the legal battles that had followed for five years were still deeply etched into the consciousness of the Italian community and had contributed to Marco's decision to study law. His face became almost angry and Kate thought that she would not want to be cross examined by him if she had a guilty secret to conceal.

"Right over there," he pointed. A big firm--the US Industrial Alcohol Company--built a storage tank 50 feet tall in which to store molasses, pumped directly off the ships that had brought it up from the Caribbean. They kept it there and then pumped it, as needed, to their distillery in East Cambridge, just across the river there. The tank was shoddily built, not up to safety standards and the company ignored signs of leakage for years. The local kids would fill cans with molasses as it leaked through the seams. In January 1919, the walls of the tank simply gave way and millions of gallons of molasses destroyed everything in their path. Twenty people were killed; some drowned. Can you imagine anything more horrible than being drowned in molasses? Others were swept into the harbor and others killed in collapsing buildings. The company tried to blame it on Italian anarchists. There was a lot of anti-immigrant bigotry back then but, this time, the poor won the battle in the courts. Thank God things have gotten a little better since then. Business has been booming for the past ten years. That has helped a lot."

Marco had spoken with passion and Kate was intrigued to see this other side of his personality. She had been impressed by his imposing physical presence and entertained by his playboy charm but when he had spoken about the tragedy with such feeling and eloquence she could see that he had the makings of a fine attorney.

"This man I could love. I think I already do. Lord please make him the man for me," she prayed.

"What were the anarchists up to?" she asked. "Anarchists were never a major problem in Britain. We've had plenty of labor unrest though. You can hardly blame the men though; out of work and starving, particularly the boys who have come home from the war. But I never understood what anarchists hoped to achieve by throwing bombs."

"Don't get me started on politics," Marco said allowing his face to shed the intensity that his account of the tragedy had engendered. "I don't want to waste my chance of winning the heart of a beautiful maiden by getting too serious."

"Don't stop getting serious with me," she thought ambiguously.

"I'm not just a pretty face," she added to lighten the conversation. She did not want to come on too strong. After all she had a full week to convince him that she was a woman he couldn't live without.

"Not just a pretty face, eh! Do you think I hadn't noticed the rest of you?" he replied with a lecherous leer, reverting to his Don Juan persona and preening his non-existent mustaches. "Let's go over to Fredo Napolitano's deli and get a bite to eat."

He had only had ham, two fried eggs, toast and three cups of coffee for breakfast and he was feeling peckish.

"It's on Salutation Street near the North End police station. You're wondering about anarchists. They exploded a bomb, eighteen sticks of dynamite, in the basement of the precinct house back in 1916 and blew a hole in a three foot thick brick wall; blew out every window in Tessa's store. Luckily, that was before they took it over."

Kate recognized Alfredo, Theresa's husband, who was serving an elderly Italian lady who was clad entirely in black. The transaction was in Italian. This was the shop were Frank and Jo would set up house at the conclusion of their honeymoon. It certainly smelled delicious. The tantalizing odors of salami, cheese and recently baked bread filled the air. They exchanged pleasantries. After dealing with his customer, Alfredo smiled a warm welcome to Kate who had been an overnight guest in his home. They had breakfasted together a few hours earlier and he was eager to show off his establishment. He and Tessa had taken it over ten years ago, a couple of years after the bombing, and they were now an integral part of the neighborhood. They had an ice cream to prevent Marco from starving and Fredo showed off his most recent acquisition of which he was inordinately proud. It was a G.E. Monitor refrigerator; so called because the cooling element sat on top of the refrigerator box like the gun turret that had crowned the *USS Monitor* during the Civil War.

"Tessa and I lived upstairs until we had our first *bambina*. It will be nice having Jo and Francesco so close."

The week passed pleasantly and all too quickly. Because of Marco's odd schedule with law school classes in the evening, their time together was topsy-turvy: sightseeing during the day and work at night, but they adjusted their courtship to accommodate this. They managed to terminate their inspection of the sights of Greater Boston by early afternoon and retired to Marco's apartment to pass the time.

The French say *"l'amour fait passer le temps"* – 'love helps to pass the time'--but, at least in their case the cynical second half of the aphorism, *"Le temps fait passer l'amour,"* didn't hold up. By Friday, they were still as besotted as a couple could be with the reservation that they had not taken their lovemaking to its physiological conclusion. Kate Kelly was still adamant that her first true love affair would reach its climax on her wedding night and Marco accepted her decision with good grace if without enthusiasm. Saturday was to be their last full day together. Kate was due to sail back to England on Monday morning and they could anticipate that Sunday would be frantic. They would be driving the newlyweds back to Boston and helping them with the transfer of their household goods from Jo's apartment to their new address on Salutation Street. They were both resolved to end their last hours together on a high note. They arrived at the Cape at 10:00 a.m. to find the honeymooners finishing a late breakfast with a leisurely cup of coffee. They appeared ready to sit around in the sun all day until they could summon up enough energy to have a nap. Marco was not about to tolerate such inertia.

"Come on you slackers. Kate and I haven't driven a hundred miles to watch you two gazing at each other all day. We've got the use of the car today. Jo, let's show these two Brits that there's more to the Cape than Popponesset Bay. Let's drive out to Provincetown and have lunch there. On the way back we can show them the Atlantic beaches. Wait till you see those, Kate; forty miles of unspoiled sand. I believe that there's a move to make them into a National Park. At this time of year we will hardly see a soul. We can go skinny dipping if you like," he ventured optimistically.

"Down boy," his cousin replied. "I'm a respectable married woman now."

"We haven't been exactly jostled by teeming throngs here," observed Frank, "but I'm up for a change of scenery. Anything that doesn't involve seeing Kate in the buff."

"I'm game for anything," Kate chipped in, "just as long as we get back here in time for a swim. I've come prepared this time. Lord and Taylor's have assured me that mine is the very latest thing in women's swimwear and I want to get the chance to wear it."

"Well we could always swim at the Atlantic beaches but I must say it's much more comfortable getting changed in the cottage than in the back seat of a car and I don't fancy driving back fifty miles in a wet swimsuit," said Jo, acknowledging that she was not going to be allowed to lounge around on the beach all day soaking up the sun. Perhaps it was just as well. Despite her application of sun tan lotion, Frank's skin was notably pink and his nose was beginning to peel.

Provincetown was well worth the trip. It was only sixty miles away and the roads were virtually empty. They were there by noon and had time for a walk around the town to soak up the atmosphere and to work up an appetite. It had been one of the earliest North American settlements and was situated at the tip of the fishhook that was Cape Cod at the point where it curled back west and then south into the Bay. It looked and felt like an old fishing village and, indeed, had been just that for most of the 19th Century. During that period, Portuguese sailors from the Azores had established a thriving whaling and fishing industry and settled there. Portuguese heritage was still claimed by much of the population. In 1898, a gale of historic proportions had destroyed the fishing infrastructure and the fishing industry had declined. Artists and writers had moved into the abandoned buildings and, by now, there existed a thriving colony of artists.

Most of the summer visitors were long gone but there was still plenty of evidence of artistic activity and everything from scrimshaw to sophisticated seascapes and portraiture was on display. It would have been almost sacrilegious to have eaten meat in such a setting and so they lunched elegantly on Grilled Scrod--young cod fish. Marco refrained, with heroic self-control, from regaling the party with the old chestnut 'Where Can You Get Scrod in Boston?' for which Jo was grateful. She was quite familiar with the old joke and didn't want to scandalize their English companions. In that regard she need not have worried. Liverpudlian humour was every bit as raucous as anything prevailing in New England. Indeed, Frank, with four years in the British Army behind him, could have sung ten rather racy verses of 'Mademoiselle from Armentières' without repeating himself. Happily, he too refrained and they enjoyed their lunch with blushes spared.

When they reached the small town of Barnstable on their way home they got off the main road and headed east to see the fabled Atlantic Seashore Beaches. The surf was more pronounced there as the Atlantic breakers met the shore after an uninterrupted 3,000-mile journey from Europe. The beach seemed to go on forever and the honeymoon couple rested at the edge of the dunes while Marco and Kate went for a stroll. They walked hand-in-hand and appeared to be very much at ease in each other's company.

"I think that cousin Marco is quite taken with your sister, Frank," Jo observed.

"Do you really think so?" he replied.

Brothers are notoriously unobservant where their sisters are concerned. He hadn't registered that a man might consider Kate attractive. In his mind she was still his kid sister.

"Oh Frank! You really are hopeless. Maybe you haven't noticed but your sister is a grown woman. In fact she and I are almost the same age and, believe me, I've seen the way Marco looks at her. Just wait till he sees her in that new swimsuit she bought. She showed it to me before we left this morning. Poor Marco doesn't stand a chance."

"You really think they're serious? They've only known each other for a week."

"Frank. Didn't I fall for you in twenty-four hours?"

"That's just because I had appendicitis. I took advantage of your soft heart. I think that Kate had her appendix out when she was ten so I hope she's not counting on that to capture his sympathy."

"I don't think that it's her appendix that he's interested in," she acknowledged. "But while they're away down the beach, let me take care of your poor sunburned skin. I've brought along the suntan oil."

"Darling, you know what that can lead to," he said guilelessly.

"I know, sweetheart. I'm counting on it," she said shamelessly.

Her confidence was well founded.

****

Olympic swimmers, both male and female, have, arguably, the most beautiful bodies in the world. It is a beauty that transcends the merely sexual. The image of a cheetah at full stretch or of a thoroughbred horse at the gallop delights the eye without exciting the libido, unless of course you are another cheetah or stallion. Kate, when she emerged from the cottage for their late afternoon swim, had that effect on all who saw her. The swimsuit that she had invested a fortune in was a simple leotard in deep emerald green that beautifully set off her auburn locks. Lord and Taylor had justified the price by marketing it as a *maillot de bain* and claiming that it was the latest Parisian fashion. It clung to her figure like a second skin and although modest--it covered her from her breastbone to her thighs--it clearly outlined her figure from her small perfect breasts to the gentle swell of her hips. Her shoulders were wide and her legs shapely and long. Marco Tessla was lost, as his cousin had forecast. He was spellbound and could not take his eyes off her. He was almost overwhelmed by the urge to sweep her up into his arms. Instead he sought refuge in the ocean to cool his ardor and the girls grinned at each other knowingly before joining him. Another proud male had been laid low. Score one more for womankind. It was early twilight when they finished their frolicking in the water. It had been five hours since lunch and they were hungry. Marco, in particular, who had a large stomach to fill, was feeling the pangs most cruelly despite having eaten three of the half dozen doughnuts that they had bought at a store in Hyannis on the way home.

"I'll volunteer to make omelets for us all," Kate offered. We can use up everything that we've got left since we're leaving in the morning."

"You see Marco; she cooks too. You better grab this girl while you can," laughed Jo.

"I know that, smarty. She's been making supper for us both all week before I go to class," Marco admitted.

"So that's what you've been getting up to. I thought you were supposed to be showing her the sights of Boston."

"Ah well! You know; the way to a man's heart," Kate grinned, "and that's some stomach," she added with a playful pat.

Kate managed to empty the larder for her omelet. It contained cheese, bacon, onions, tomatoes and the remains of a roast chicken and was proclaimed a culinary masterpiece. It's amazing what six hours of 'near starvation' can do to healthy young appetites. They again built a fire at the edge of the dunes and reclined in the soft sand; the couples on each side of the fire gazing out at the ocean as daylight faded. They were tired and content but their happiness was tinged with a certain melancholy. This marked the end of Jo and Frank's honeymoon. Never again would they have the opportunity to devote whole days to simply loving and being loved and as for Marc and Kate, in thirty-six hours she would be on board ship and sailing back to Britain. Perhaps they would never be together again. With these sobering thoughts they huddled together, each couple lost in their own thoughts and conversation died away.

"Let's go in Frank. It's getting a little chilly and it's been six hours since you told me how much you love me."

"Ah, let me count the ways," Frank declaimed. "Besides, actions speak louder than words," he whispered in her ear as he carried her off into the cabin. They were both laughing by the time they reached the front door.

Marco and Kate were left alone for what would probably their last time before she sailed. They had put terrycloth robes on over their swimsuits as it had grown cooler but these were soon shed as they clung together. Marc kissed her and her lips opened softly to invite his tongue. His hands ran over her body and she gasped as she felt herself moisten. She rolled onto her back. Marco was struggling to get out of his swimming trunks and she could see that he was prodigiously erect. Her thoughts were in turmoil and she felt tears coursing down her face.

"Don't you want me, darling? I love you and I think that you want me too," Marco said, alarmed at her agitation.

"Oh! I do. I do. I want so much to feel you inside me but I'm scared. I've never made love before. I'm still a virgin and I always wanted to give myself to my husband on our wedding night. I want to marry you and have your children," she sobbed and started to peel down the top of her leotard.

"I can wait.," he groaned. "I promise you we'll be married next summer. I want you to be sure that you really want me to when we make love for the first time. Let me kiss you and then cover up while I am still able to keep control of myself."

She lay still and he gently kissed her breasts as she sobbed quietly. After a minute he retrieved his trunks and walked down the beach and into the ocean to enable him to regain his composure. When he returned to the fireside ten minutes later she had retired to her bedroom. The cottage was quiet and he followed her example and laid tossing and turning restlessly. He was glad that he had not forced the issue. He was still desperate to possess her but he wanted her to give herself to him without reservation. If that meant waiting till they were married then so be it. Half an hour passed and he was just settling down when his bedroom door quietly opened. Kate was standing by his bedside. She was wearing her robe.

"Shhh! Be quiet! Come with me. Don't waken the others," she whispered beckoning him to follow her. He was sleeping naked and he reached for his robe.

"You wont need that, darling," she smiled and let her robe fall to the ground. She led him back to the fireside and reclined on the sand. She reached up to him and guided him down between her thighs. "Are you sure darling? A year will go by quickly. I can wait," he gasped throatily.

"I can't, Marco. I want you now. Even if you never love me again, I want this night to remember. I love you and I'll always love you."

She drew up her legs and raised her hips to receive him. She was, indeed, a virgin and there was a brief moment of pain as he entered but he was gentle and filled her physically and emotionally. When, finally, he was spent they remained entwined in each other's arms.

"Kate! I pledge to you that we will be married. I don't need to wait till next year to know my mind. We will be married as soon as I graduate."

He removed his college ring and gave it to her. It was a little smaller than a golf ball but not by much.

"Wear it on a chain round your neck until I can buy a proper engagement ring. I don't think that this one will stay on your finger. Your big toe maybe."

"Oh, Marco! I love you. You have made me so happy," she laughed and then burst into tears. This time they were tears of joy.

As the girls were cooking breakfast next morning, Jo noticed the ring.

"What was all that whispering last night?" she asked innocently.

Kate's face turned almost as red as her hair.

"You did, didn't you? You little devil," Jo prodded.

She had been an interested and amused witness of the rapid progress of the romance between her new sister-in-law and her cousin.

"You tell Frank and I'll kill you," Kate admitted and the two dissolved into delighted laughter. The North Atlantic alliance was strengthening by the minute.

CHAPTER TWENTY-FIVE
Liverpool, December, 1928

By mid December, Jacques had been working for three months on his campaign to get Isabel into his bed and he hoped that she was about ready to respond to his urgings. They had fallen into a pattern of spending the evenings together when she had been working at the Consulate. He drove her home and she would change and they would go out to dine or pay a visit to the theatre or cinema. They invariably ended their evenings at her cottage where Jacques was able to bring her to the brink of acquiescing to his urgent demands but she resisted. They both enjoyed the kissing and fondling but the failure to consummate their relationship was becoming increasingly more frustrating-- for Isabel almost as much as her lover.

"Let's spend the whole day together this weekend," he suggested.

He had decided on an all-out assault and, to improve his chances, he threw in a hint that he might be interested in a more formal relationship.

"I'd love to meet your parents. We could visit them on Saturday afternoon if you think that they would be amenable and then we can have a night out on the town; dinner and a show--maybe the Philharmonic if they're performing."

"Would you really like to meet them? I know that they would be delighted to meet you." *Could he really be contemplating marriage?* she asked herself. *Surely wanting to get to know my parents is a good sign.*

Isabel asked her parents if they could come to visit and they, in turn, were quite intrigued to meet the man who had brought the colour back into their daughter's cheeks. They agreed to invite the couple for lunch on the next Saturday.

The lunch was quite successful. Jacques was his urbane self and Adlai was quite impressed. This was the sort of polished man of the world that he had always hoped for his daughter. The Frenchman soon realized that he had Isabel's father in his corner and turned his attentions to Marie.

"You have the most accomplished daughter, Mrs. Iskandar. We at the consulate are quite in awe at her linguistic talents but, now that I've met her parents, I am no longer surprised."

Marie was the perfect hostess and had arranged to serve her guest with an elegant lunch but she was not entirely overwhelmed by his charms. There was something calculating in his manner, she felt, and then she was struck by the difference in their ages (despite her previous protestations to the contrary). Isabel looked so young and excited while the Frenchman was self-contained; his compliments practiced and, she thought, insincere. He had the predatory look of a big cat sizing up his prey and she was worried.

"Rumour has it in the city that Monsieur le Comte will be retiring next summer. Does that mean that you will take over as Consul General?" Adlai asked.

"That would be almost unprecedented. I suppose that there is a chance that I will be promoted but if that happens they will almost certainly move me somewhere else; perhaps somewhere my Arabic might be a plus. But you know the way governments work. They'll probably send me to Minsk or Iceland."

That evening Isabel and Jacques dined in style at Sampson and Barlow's restaurant on London Road and then stayed on to dance for a while. The atmosphere was romantic and they decided to pass up on the Philharmonic that was featuring Wagner. The theatres were all presenting their Christmas pantomimes and Isabel's memories of *Aladdin* were still too poignant.

"Why don't we get a drink at the Jolly Miller and you can take me home early. Maybe we can amuse ourselves in front of a nice warm fire for a while," she added a little unwisely.

She was not usually so forthright but she felt that the visit to her parents had marked a positive step forward in their relationship with Jacques and she was eager to build on her success. They were, by now, sufficiently comfortable with each other that they embraced as soon as they arrived at Isabel's cottage. They subsided onto the sofa and were soon intimately interlocked. He kissed her passionately and leaned backwards on the sofa pulling Isabel on top of his body. His arms were around her waist and Isabel took his hands and guided them into unclasping her bra that she shrugged out of to permit access to his mouth. She gasped as he suckled and threw back her head almost overwhelmed by the intensity of her reaction. He had pulled her skirt up to her hips and she realized that she was rapidly losing control of the situation. Jacques was clawing at his belt to unleash his erection and she was almost ready to give way to their mutual desire. She had to stop. This was not how she wanted the evening to end. She grasped his hands and pressed them against her breasts.

"Stop Jacques. We must stop this. You can feel how much I want you but not this way. It is not right."

She held his wrists tight and gradually he realized that she was in earnest. He was furious; not only frustrated sexually but he felt he had been led on and humiliated. He rose, adjusted his clothes and prepared to leave.

"Mademoiselle Iskandar, you led me to believe that you were in love with me. I hope you enjoyed making me look a fool. Goodnight. I will see myself out."

His fury subsided as he drove home. He was still determined to have her; perhaps now even more than before.

Perhaps tonight's debacle could serve as a lever. Isabel had been on the verge of submission. Her body's reaction had not been faked. She wanted him almost as much as he wanted her. *Let's see what guilt and a little cooling off can get me,* he mused.

He set about to treat her coldly. In his dealings with her within the consulate he reverted to the formality of his behaviour during her first weeks of employment. He had always been reserved in his public dealings with her. Even though it was general knowledge throughout the office that they had a romantic relationship, they had both maintained a strictly professional demeanour in public. Now, however, he treated her with a cold politeness even within the confines of his office. The change in his behaviour was both cruel and abrupt. On the first day of work following his furious departure from her cottage she took the first opportunity afforded her to reconcile with him and attempted to explain why she had been unwilling to consummate their relationship. She had spent most of the preceding forty-eight hours reliving the events that had led up to her refusal to surrender her virginity. She had hoped that he could be made to understand her reluctance; that she believed that sexual intercourse was to be reserved for the marriage bed and that she accepted that she had done him an injustice in permitting him liberties; that she was as eager as he and as aroused as he by their lovemaking. As soon as they were alone in his office and assured of privacy she reached out, took hold of his arm and smiled in a conciliatory manner.

"Please, Jacques! I hope you have forgiven me for our last evening together. I should never have let us get so heavily involved with each other. You know that I am as much in love with you as you are with me."

"You have made your feelings perfectly clear, Mademoiselle. There is no more to be said." He was stone-faced and chillingly remote.

"Leave my correspondence on my desk. I will call if I need you."

"But Jacques! Surely you can see that what I want is best for both of us. If you love me then we will marry and you know that I will make you happy."

"That will be all. You may go," he said, and shrugged off her hand, sat down behind his desk and ostentatiously busied himself with the morning mail.

Isabel was taken aback by his behaviour. She knew that she had been partly to blame for his anger. She should never have allowed such a degree of intimacy between them and she could understand that he had left her house in a state of intense sexual frustration but she had hoped that when she took her share of the blame and admitted that she too had been filled with longing, that he would cool down and they could resume their courtship; only now with rather more physical restraint. Now she was faced with a dilemma: how to deal with Jacques in the routine business of the consulate. She had very little option. She was his administrative assistant and, consequently, in almost constant contact with him during office hours. He was, therefore, the arbiter of their relationship and he had chosen to treat her with a cold formality bordering on incivility. This was the strategy that he had decided upon quite cold bloodedly.

He had set out to make her fall in love with him. He had courted her aggressively and considered that he had swept her off her feet with his wealth, his charm and, most of all, his ardour. He knew that at least one of her parents was somewhat starry-eyed at the thought that his daughter had attracted a wealthy and sophisticated man of the world as a suitor. Now, with the door apparently slammed on her aspirations, she would moderate her attitudes, he thought. She could live for a few weeks with the constant reminders that, entirely because of her ridiculous scruples, she had forgone the delights of his company. A month of his overt disapproval would, he was sure, render her much more pliant when he re-admitted her, as he planned, to his favour.

If his behaviour was designed to render Mme. Iskandar more amenable to his demands he could hardly have chosen a worse victim. Isabel was a young woman with a vigorous sex drive but she had had a strong religious upbringing and a healthy self-esteem. She was introspective and now aware that she had misread the character of Jacques Martin. She had perhaps led him to believe that she was promiscuous but his subsequent behaviour was that of a petulant child. She was coming to the realization that M. Martin, despite his wealth, looks and sophistication compared unfavourably with her only other serious admirer. Frank Kelly had wanted to marry her and had accepted unquestioningly the limitations that she had placed on their lovemaking. She had, of course, been bitterly disappointed when he had fathered a child with an American nurse but, at least, he had done the honourable thing and married the girl. Jacques Martin was revealing himself as a self-centered adolescent. Isabel admitted to herself, wryly, that she had not always had such a charitable opinion of Frank's behaviour but time had taken the hard edge off her feelings of ill use and her recent *affaire* had reminded her how potent are the human urges that explode when circumstances permit. Maybe she could forgive Frank--say in a decade or two. In the meantime, she continued to work in the consulate in the uncomfortable atmosphere generated by her superior's icy demeanour. Fortunately, the rest of the consular staff chose to ignore Martin's nastiness and went out of their way to be pleasant. Even M. le Comte, the Consul General himself, seemed to be trying to make up for his deputy's behaviour. Isabel became reconciled to, once more, traveling back and forth to work on the tram.

Christmas came and went without significant development but early in the New Year an incident occurred which completely altered the dynamic of Isabel's situation vis-à-vis M. Martin. The deputy consul was absent in the mid afternoon. He was attending a business session with the

Chamber of Commerce. Isabel, in her capacity as his Administrative Assistant, fielded an emergency request to speak to M. Martin. An agitated voice came through the wire speaking lightly accented French.

"*Il faut que je parle avec Monsieur Jacques Martin,*" said a woman's voice.

"*Avec qui ai'je l'honneur de parler,*" responded Isabel in the elegant, if rather stilted manner in which the consular staff were taught to respond to unidentified French speaking callers.

"*Je vous en supplie Mademoiselle! Permettez -moi de parler avec Jacques. Il y a une situation critique.*" (I beseech you Mademoiselle. Let me speak to Jacques. It is an emergency.)

"*Il ne se trouve pas dans le consulat a ce moment. Je suis son secretaire. Je lui donnerai un message de bon coeur.*" (He is not here at the moment. I will gladly give him a message.)

"*Je vous en supplie dites-lui que Jean-Claude est très malade. Il a de diphthérie. Il faut qu'il y vienne immediatement.*" (Please tell him that Jean-Claude is very sick. He must come right away.)

"*Je lui ferai de répondre dès que possible. S'il vous plait, Madame, comment vous appelez vous? A quel numéro peux t'on vous parvient.*" (I will have him call back as soon as possible. Please Madame! What is your name and how can we reach you?)

"*Dites-lui que c'est Yvette qui lui appele.*"

In the background Isabel heard a child's voice speaking. The language was Arabic and the child was addressing her mother.

"Be quiet, Anni. Mummy's on the telephone," she heard Yvette say, still in Arabic.

"*Je vous en supplie. Dépêchez-vous. Le numéro est 197-97492. Il se trouve en Algérie Francais. Il faut qu'on se remette en route a Paris Central. Jacques est bien place pour le savoir.*" (The number is in Algeria. You must go through the Paris exchange. Jacques knows how to do it.)

When the connection was broken, Isabel sat down at Martin's desk to gather her wits. Who was this Yvette and why was she calling the Deputy Consul from Algeria for an emergency concerning a sick child? The most obvious answer was that Jacques was married, that Yvette was his wife and that he had at least two children: Jean-Claude and the other Arabic speaker, Anni. I suppose that there are other possibilities, she decided, but, in her heart, she knew she was on the right track. Jacques Martin, wealthy, handsome and in his mid-thirties was too smooth and experienced a ladies' man to have been un-attached when he met her, she now realized with a sinking feeling in her stomach. She now assumed that Yvette was complacently tucked away in the family home in North Africa and, presumably, innocent of his philandering while her husband was fulfilling his diplomatic assignments around the world. Isabel now had half an hour to decide how to deal with the situation before Jacques would return. For the first few minutes she sat almost trancelike, overwhelmed by the significance of the call. She had been seriously in love with a married man and had been very close to surrendering her virginity to him in expectation that they would marry. She had had a narrow escape and she was suddenly glad that she had seen him for a self centered Lothario even before the panicked call from his wife. She had enough time before his return to consider how she would relay the message. She decided that she would deliver it as if she were telling him about his next appointment.

"You received a telephone call from your wife in Algeria. She was very agitated and she did not give me her family name. She said that you would know how to reach her. There is an emergency. Your son has diphtheria and is very ill."

"I am not married, Isabel," he said turning very pale and slumping down into a seat behind his desk. He had not addressed her by her first name in over a month.

"I apologize Monsieur Martin. I assumed that the caller was the mother of your son. She gave her name as Yvette."

"Yvette is the mother of my son but we are not married. She is an Arab."

He apparently assumed that this was an adequate reason. He was sweating profusely and looked imploringly at Isabel.

"My career will be over if it came to light that I had married an Arab and a Muslim at that. You can understand that can't you?"

He sounded almost tearful and Isabel was overcome by a feeling of disgust that she had ever considered him a possible husband. He had just learned that his son was dangerously ill and he was concerned about his wretched career.

"Monsieur Martin, I have no desire to hurt your wife and family. You forget, perhaps, that I was born in Egypt and that I, too, am half Arab by blood. I suggest that you make plans to travel home to your sick child and that you promptly request reassignment. I don't care where; anywhere that isn't Liverpool. Do this and I will not reveal the existence of your family to M. le Comte nor tell him of your attempts to seduce me. I thank God that you were unsuccessful. I hope never to see you again. She turned on her heel and informed the receptionist--Miss Longbottom's replacement--that she was leaving for the day. She then waylaid Kate in her nearby office and the two girls made their way home together on the tram as they had so often in her early days at the consulate.

"I'm so glad to see you. I've got big news to tell you," said Kate when they were settled in on the top deck and were trundling down Byrom Street towards Everton Brow. The tram was packed, as was always the case during the evening exodus from the city.

"Go ahead; you first. I have some new developments in my life too but, by the look of you, your news is more cheerful than mine," replied her friend.

"You know that I met this chap in America when I was in Boston for Frank's wedding. Well we fell for each other in a big way and talked about getting married but he still has a year to go before he finishes Law School, so we decided to keep it quiet and not get officially engaged. At Christmas he sent me this. Now it's official we're getting married this summer."

She was scarcely able to contain her excitement as she showed off her engagement ring and the two girls hugged each other with squeals of delight as the passengers in the surrounding seats pretended not to notice this unseemly display of emotion. A few suppressed smiles, however, revealed that some, at least, were enjoying the news.

"That's wonderful, Kate. Will the wedding be in summer? If your husband is going to be a lawyer, then that means you'll be living in the States. Will the wedding be in Boston?"

"We haven't definitely decided on the location. Marco's family is from Brockton, which is about thirty miles south of Boston. That would be the same church that Frank was married in. In fact, Marco is the first cousin of Frank's wife." Kate stopped suddenly and looked a little embarrassed that she was gushing a little too enthusiastically about events that might still be sensitive for her friend.

"Don't worry about mentioning Frank. I've got over him. My most recent boyfriend turned out to be a far bigger stinker than Frank. Frank, at least, didn't have a wife and children."

"Do you mean to tell me that that Frenchman you've been seeing has a wife? I've sometimes wondered why a good-looking fellow like him wasn't married at his age."

"Well, I don't know for sure that he has a wife. I took a panicky call from a woman in Algeria who said that his son has diphtheria. I heard another child in the background refer to her as 'Mummy.' She was speaking Arabic and the woman replied the same way calling her Anni and saying, "Hush sweetheart, Mummy's on the telephone." Jacques admitted that they were his children but denied that he had married their mother. If that was supposed to make me think better of him, he was deluded."

"What did you say?" Kate said. "It must have been a terrible shock to you. I had the impression that you were pretty keen on him."

"I admit I was for a while but about a month ago he started to treat me as though I had wronged him after I wouldn't go to bed with him; gave me the cold shoulder. He was barely civil in the office. I got the feeling that he was trying to manipulate me and I had just about written him off when I happened to get this call. Papa will be very disappointed when I tell him the news. He rather fancied me married to a French diplomat but *Maman* has always had some qualms about Jacques. It seems that she was right."

"You had a narrow escape, if you ask me," said Kate. "You're well rid of him. What did you tell him?

"I told him to go home and take care of his sick son."

"Well now! Look on the bright side," Kate said.

"Now that your social calendar has opened up again and now that I'm engaged maybe we can get together again like we used to. I'll scout up some likely prospects for you and you can chaperone me and make sure I don't get into any mischief."

"I don't think that your fiancé need worry about you, Kate. I've never seen you so excited or so happy since I've known you. He must be quite a chap to have sent Miss Hard-to-Please into such a state."

"Oh Izzy! He's wonderful," and she spent the rest of the journey describing Marco's amazing qualities in glowing terms that would have caused the subject, blessed though he was with a healthy self regard, to blush at their extravagance had he overheard them. She suddenly stopped the flow of her raptures as a thought struck her. "Izzy! Why don't you come to the wedding? It's to be in the summer. You'll be on holiday. I would love you to be my Maid of Honour. I know that it would be very expensive but, I bet if we both work on him, your dad would help finance the trip. Say you will. It will be such an adventure and you're my oldest and best friend.

"Oh Kate! That sounds just wonderful. Thank you. It would certainly give me something to look forward to and to take my mind off what a fool I nearly made of myself. Let's see what Papa has to say. I'll bring you along when I ask him. You could always get your way with him."

"You're not worried about running into Frank?" asked his sister. "He's sure to be part of the wedding. Marco was his best man and I understand that Frank and his wife see quite a lot of him."

"I think I can handle that. I'm sure we've both moved on. He'll have a baby by then. I believe that his wife is due around Easter. Look out! Here's your stop. I'm off to my folk's home to bring them all my news. Why don't you come over for supper after you've checked in at home and we'll hit them with your invitation and see how they react to the idea of me coming to your wedding?"

Kate stopped at home and told her Mam that she had been invited for dinner at the Iskandar's and then made the ten-minute hike to Stanley Park. By the time of her arrival, Isabel had related all the details of the break up of her affair with Jacques Martin and most particularly of the dramatic telephone call that had, once and for all, rendered it irrevocable. Her father, who had held out the highest hopes for the relationship, was the more shocked and indignant. Marie Iskandar was saddened. She realized that this was now the second time that her daughter's romantic attachments had come to such a disastrous end. She was sympathetic for the unhappiness that her daughter must be experiencing but she could not help feeling a little relieved. She had never been quite so convinced that the glib Frenchman was the right man for her daughter.

With Kate's arrival the conversation took on a happier tone. Kate broke the news of her engagement to the Iskandars and her ring was duly displayed and extravagantly admired.

"Tell us about Marco," they asked, and were left in no doubt that Kate had been swept off her feet by the young American law student.

"When will the wedding be? Is it going to be in Boston?" they asked.

"When he graduates this coming June and then, I believe he has to take the Bar Exams. The wedding will probably be in early July and in Brockton. In fact, that's one of the reasons I weaseled an invitation to dinner out of Izzy. I want her to come to the wedding and be my Maid of Honour. I know that it will be an awful lot of money for the fare but once she's arrived it won't cost her a thing. These Italian people are the most hospitable people in the world. I couldn't spend a penny once I got there for Frank's wedding."

"How's Frank doing?" Marie asked.

"I believe he's very happy. They're expecting a baby in a few months and as well as their regular jobs they work in Jo's sister's grocery on the weekend. Its what they call a 'deli.' I've never seen one in Liverpool. It means delicatessen. I think that it's a German word and it means that as well as selling the normal stuff, they sell all sorts of cheeses and meats. You can eat sandwiches and buy soft drinks there so it's like a miniature cafe. Frank's learning Italian. Can you imagine our Frank speaking *Italiano*?

"I've always thought that boy had more to him that meets the eye," said Marie.

"I suppose that you'll be living in America. With both of you gone, your mother may have to make some changes in her life. I don't want to poke my nose into your family affairs but I worry about her. We chat for a few minutes every Sunday after Mass. I know she misses Frank and now you'll be leaving."

"That's been keeping me awake at night too ever since Marco proposed. With Frank and me gone, how will she be able to keep up the rent on Garnet Avenue? We'd like to bring her over with us but there's still Brendan and the two girls to consider. Brendan's got at least four more years at St. Ed's and two more if he goes on into the sixth form and then maybe even University."

Adlai cleared his throat. He had made up his mind.

"Isabel, ma chère, I think you should definitely go to Kate's wedding. It'll be a great adventure and you've always been the best of friends. Don't worry about the cost. You can consider it your Christmas present," he announced and then added with a grin, "for the next fifty years."

"Oh *Papa, Maman*! Thank you both," and she hugged them with delight and the two girls left the kitchen where most of their meals were eaten and adjourned to the front parlour to discuss their plans for the great adventure.

With their departure, Marie took the opportunity to bring up with her husband another matter to which she had been giving a lot of thought for over six months.

"You must recall, Adlai, your worries about the economy and we discussed re-investing our money in retail shops. I have been thinking about it a lot and I have been keeping my eyes open for suitable locations. I believe that there is a grocer's in Westminster Road that is coming on the market. It's within a mile of here and the area it serves is respectable and heavily populated. I think that it would be a good place to make our start into the retail grocery business. When Kate was talking about how her mother might have to move out of her house, it made me think that she might be a suitable tenant. She's a decent respectable woman and she's worked in retail, I believe; in a poultry stall in the market. She's also well known in the neighbourhood; a life long member of St John's Parish. She might be willing to take on the management and as it comes with living quarters it might suit her if the Kellys have to give up their place in Garnet Avenue."

"*Chérie!* As always, I think that your instincts are spot on. I have been a bit remiss in not following up on my ideas and,

I agree with you, the spot you've found sounds like a good place to start. I'd also like to find another tobacco shop or two. They've served as sound investments for a long time. Lets see what the estate agents have to say. If the shop on Westminster Road is available and not too pricey we can sound out Mrs. Kelly. I think it might be a good deal all round."

"How about if I invite Kate and her mother for dinner sometime next week and, in the meantime, I can follow up with the estate agent and get all the details about the business and the possible terms? We can see whether the Kellys might be interested. If everything goes well we could have the business up and running with Mrs. Kelly installed in her new home by the time Kate goes to America. Oh Adlai. I feel really good about this."

CHAPTER TWENTY-SIX
Boston, July, 1928

Boston's North End was recognized by the general population of the city as the 'Italian Section' but the description did little justice to the reality. The massive wave of Italian immigration that had occurred around the turn of the century had been overwhelmingly from the southern half of the peninsula or from Sicily. They were the least literate, even in their native tongue, and they were considered by the northern Italians to be virtually of a separate and inferior race. Even in their native land there was little sense of nationhood. They regarded themselves as Sicilians or Neapolitans. With the passage of time there had been some blurring of these distinctions. Just as America was working to make Americans out of its Irish, Polish, German and Scandinavian immigrants so also, at the local level, those same influences--universal education, intermarriage and the pervasiveness of spoken English--were making Italians out of its Genovese, its Avellini and its Calabrese. The North End still had its ethnic divisions but, by 1928, they were becoming blurred. Theresa Tessla, whose forebears came from Tuscany and had married Alfredo Napolitano and become Tessa Napolitano, was just one example and the Napolitano grocery and delicatessen was an accepted part of two districts straddling as it did the line between the Genoan and the Neapolitan enclaves.

Still the arrival in their midst of Josefina Lucca and her Anglo husband, Francis Xavier Kelly, caused a level of curiosity if not outright hostility. For not only were the young couple to be residents in the district but they were to be participants in its life. First of all, they were noted to be regular attendees at Mass. This phenomenon was almost as much of a surprise to Jo as it was to the women of the parish of Saint Agrippina di Mineo who comprised most of the communicants. Despite her epiphany at the time of the wedding, she would probably not have remained very conscientious in the practice of her faith had if it had not soon become apparent that Frank took their joint attendance at Mass as a matter of course. The initial surprise of the parishioners at the presence of the young Englishman at Mass was explained in short order when it was noted that Kelly was an Irish name.

"Ah! That accounts for it" was the consensus. The Irish were a well-known commodity in Greater Boston. Indeed one of their enclaves, Charlestown, was separated from the North End only by the width of the Mystic River. It was, of course, soon well known that the young couple was related to the owners of Napolitano's Deli and had moved into the apartment above the shop and that they were expecting. By Christmas Jo was six months along and was obviously pregnant.

She and her husband had started to help out in the shop. Jo had learned her Italian in the cradle and very rapidly regained her fluency. Frank, of course, spoke no Italian but spent the hours between returning home from work and the shop closure observing the transactions and trying not to get in the way. The Napolitanos were very happy with the arrangement. They were happy to have reliable occupants living above the store and Jo and Frank were doing everything they could to ingratiate themselves with the community. Frank had spent nearly ten years dealing with the public on board ship and he had the God-given gift of being likable. Most of the regular customers were housewives and Tessa made a point of introducing them to 'Francesco,' her English brother in law and he, in turn, charmed the good ladies with his smile and diffident and courtly response in his halting Italian.

They were a very happy couple. They worked very hard but they had the sense that things were going well and they were very much in love. Both started work early. With her relocation to the North End, Jo had to leave for work at 6:00 a.m. and did not return home till 6.30 in the evening. They could both take the Atlantic Avenue Railway together on their way to work. Frank was home by 5:30 and helped the Napolitanos to close up the store and he then made a start on preparing dinner by the time Jo arrived home. At weekends they both worked in the shop and it was then that Frank made his greatest progress with his Italian. The store was open all day Saturday till 6:00 p.m. and on Sunday afternoon.

By Christmas time, Frank was able to handle the business as long as one of the three Italian speakers was there as a backup and the Napolitanos were delighted to have an occasional day off without the responsibility of the business. Frank was, by no means, able to hold a wide-ranging conversation in Italian but he had picked up enough to handle the routine transactions of the business and the customers seemed pleased that the native English speaker was making an effort to speak their language.

Julia was expected on the eighth of April--(Frank had reconciled himself to Jo's certainty that she was carrying a girl)--and Jo hoped to be able to work until the end of March. With both of them earning respectable salaries and with no rent to pay they were doing quite well financially but they wanted to save as much as possible to pay their medical expenses and to allow Jo to stay home after the baby was born. Their only concern was the decline in the transatlantic steamer business. Frank's job would be imperiled if Cunard were to cut out Boston from its ports of call.

With this threat in mind, Frank set about regularizing his status as a non-U.S. citizen living in the United States. If the Cunard Company were to close down his position in Boston he would need to find other employment or else be willing to relocate and this he would not do. This was where he had asked Jo to marry him. This was where they would live. He set about applying for immigrant status. It was a tediously bureaucratic process but it was not likely to be too controversial. He had a ten-year history of visits to the United States. He was gainfully employed in Boston and he had married a native US citizen in the Commonwealth of Massachusetts. All that was required was the production of innumerable documents, the filling of mind numbing forms and the passage of time. By February of 1929, Frank was the possessor of a card attesting to his status as a 'resident alien.' This term gave him a momentary start. As an Englishman he had been raised with the conviction that the world was divided into British and 'foreigners.' Non-British English speakers--Aussies, Canadians, Kiwis and Yanks--occupied some vague halfway status. It was a tribute to his devotion to Jo that he accepted his status as an 'alien' with barely a moment's hesitation.

"Que sera, sera," he said to himself flexing his new linguistic muscles. He enjoyed his new language. *Why even a commonplace expression sounds like music in Italian,* he mused; *Que sera, sera;'doh ti lah ti lah' would have just the right lilt for a catchy tune,* he thought fleetingly, for he had a good ear, but he was distracted by a customer's request for a quarter of a pound of *Parmagiano reggiano* and 'Ti re doh lah so doh so' did not see the light of day for another twenty-five years. Serendipity is a two edged sword.

Marco Tessla remained a major part of their life. True to his word to Kate he had curtailed his pursuit of other females. He had promised her that they would marry upon his graduation and he applied himself to his studies with dedication and this helped him to keep out of temptation's way. With dalliance with the opposite sex ruled out, his social life was drastically reduced. He found that he was counting on the young married couple for company. They had all hit it off during their visit to Cape Cod and, as a bonus, Frank served as a link with his sister and as a two-way conduit of information between them.

Not only could Marco assure Kate of his undying love and faithfulness but Frank could reassure her that her American admirer was spending all of his scant leisure time with her brother and her old friend Jo. In her turn Kate could pass on to her anxious swain the depths of her longing and the eagerness with which she looked forward to their re-union. Somehow these considerations, delightful to the subject, were somehow more convincing when coming through the medium of a third party.

Marco fell into the pattern of visiting the North End every weekend on either Saturday or Sunday. He arrived on his motorbike as the shop was closing and they would have dinner, play cards and exchange their views on the events of the preceding week. About once a month they would be invited to the Napolitano's for a larger family gathering. Marco made a practice of bringing his bike into the store for safekeeping. Family cars were virtually unknown in the North End and parking on the street was a sure fire way of becoming bike-less. Violent street crime was, somewhat surprisingly, less of a problem in the North End than in the other poor sections of Boston. This circumstance was due to the remarkable degree to which the district was divided up into 'Paesos,' in which the population still owed allegiance to the town or area of their Italian origin. There was a great reluctance for the residents to seek redress from the police for crimes of property or of violence.

Prohibition was now entering its second decade and with prohibition had come the iron grip of organized crime on the Italian communities in the major cities across the United States. Southern Italy and Sicily had provided most of the immigrants to the United States and by 1929 the Sicilian *Cosa Nostra* were the *de facto* rulers of the North End of Boston. The power structure was almost feudal with the neighborhood enclaves of Genoese, Neapolitans and Calabrians functioning like feudal baronies; unchallenged within their domains but, in turn, owing loyalty and paying tribute to the monarch, the Sicilian, Don Filippo, 'Phil' Buacola, whose word was law. Random violence was uncommon and brought to transgressors prompt and violent retribution.

As long as weekly tribute was paid for 'insurance,' small businesses were not importuned and the natives walked the streets unmolested. Random violence was uncommon but not unknown and to Guido and Vinny Capello, the recurring presence of Mario Tessla's motorbike was becoming a serious temptation. At seventeen and nineteen they were first generation Americans, their parents having been born in Palermo. They had lived their whole lives in the family home; a second floor apartment in a wooden three decker situated just north of the spot where the Atlantic Avenue Railway made its sharp left hand turn before arriving at the North Station. They were large, brutish and stupid. They were employed intermittently as laborers on the docks but it was their goal in life to be fully-fledged members of Don Filippo's inner circle.

"We can take them easy when they come back from Harris Street and are wheeling that bike out of the shop. It'll be dark and the big guy will have his hands full with the bike. A knife to the other guy's throat and we can clean out the shop and take the bike too," Vinny suggested when they noticed that the Sunday night socializing of the Kellys was falling into a predictable pattern.

"What about the broad? If she screams it could wake up the whole street. The Don won't be happy if we start a war with the Genovese and the Neapolitans," his older and marginally less stupid brother worried.

"We can bring Bruno Cavelli along to keep her trap shut. Don't be a chicken, Guido. We'll be in and out in five minutes. It's outside the Don's home turf. A nice clean job like this is just what we need to bring us to his attention."

This evaluation of Buocola's reaction could hardly have been more wrong. As long as the other ethnic subdivisions of his domain remained tranquil he was content with the steady flow of income that came into his Salem Street headquarters. The last thing he wanted was a potentially murderous attack on the Napolitano's deli, which represented in its two owners both the Genoese and the Neapolitan populations of his realm but insight into the complex political power structure of the Italian community was not a gift that had been given to the Capello brothers; brawn yes; brains, considerably less so. Bruno Cavelli was recruited.

"All you gotta do is grab the broad and keep her quiet. She's pregnant. So grab her from the back and hold a cloth over her mouth. We don't want to jump them until the big guy has got his bike out onto the pavement but before he has kick started it. If he comes out by himself its three of us to his one. The other guy shouldn't give us any trouble. We'll keep our knives handy in case anyone acts up."

The intended victims had enjoyed a pleasant evening with the Napolitanos. Frank was, by now, a fully accepted uncle by the Napolitano children and they reveled in the boisterous humor that prevailed and which the two uncles brought with them to the normally decorous Sunday family gatherings. They loved to tease their new uncle about his attempts to speak Italian and thoroughly enjoyed the reversal of the adult to child relationship that this brought about. Frank took their teasing in good part and indeed reveled in it. He was making great progress and the badinage with his new nephews and nieces was a very useful tool that expanded his vocabulary far beyond the routine dealings in the shop. They had dined well and sung a few songs. Alfredo was a decent mandolin player. After the children were sent to bed they played cards for an hour and then made the short walk back to Salutation Street in a mellow mood. Jo's pregnancy was going quite well after her early bouts with morning sickness. She was now in her third trimester and was obviously, albeit not grotesquely, rotund. As she walked home, arms linked with her husband on one side and her giant cousin on the other, she was filled with a sense of serene satisfaction. How much more truly gratifying was her present married state than her early years of promiscuity and self indulgence. The streets were almost empty. It was ten o'clock and the February temperature in Boston was not conducive to recreational walking. Close to home they did pass three darkly clad youths who were standing aimlessly at the entrance to an alley and she called a genial *'buona sera'* which, however, received no response.

Marco made a habit of buying some of his staples for the upcoming week and taking them back to his apartment on his bike. He straddled the bike that was parked, nose in, in the open public space in front of the counter on which, during the workday the redolent cheeses and meats would be arrayed on display. He backed out onto the pavement as Frank held the door open and Jo followed him out with his groceries parceled and bagged for transfer to his saddlebags. The door swung closed behind his wife as he stepped back to the counter to bring the salami that had not fit into the bag. He had paid rather more attention to the three loafers whom they had passed in the street. He was still new in the neighbourhood and rather more aware of phenomena that seemed not to fit. What were three idlers doing in the deserted streets when the temperature was in the low 20's? He therefore passed an appraising glance in the direction in which they had passed them and caught a glimpse of furtive movement.

The three assailants had the advantage of surprise. The shortest one caught Jo from the rear and, with his left arm around her, forced a leather glove over her mouth while with his right arm he pinioned her right arm to her side, pulling her back off balance. Marco was hampered by the fact that he was astride his motorbike and the Capello brothers attacked from the rear, one from each side. They had not reckoned on Frank. He was not an imposing physical specimen like Marco but he was solidly built and, more significantly, was a veteran of four years in the trenches of Flanders. Unlike the Capello brothers who saw their knives as weapons of intimidation, Frank's reaction to the attack on his wife revealed him as a killing machine.

Quietly opening the door he unleashed a blow to the back of Bruno's skull. He fell poleaxed to the ground. The blow would have fractured his skull if it had been made with a policeman's truncheon but it was delivered by a five-pound, two-foot-long salami and merely laid him out. He then swung his 'club' backhand across the nose and upper teeth of the nearer Capello brother who instantly lost interest in the encounter as blood poured from his nose and he spat out teeth from his wrecked mouth. The shock from this unexpected riposte had left the remaining Capello suddenly immobile and Marco was able, with the removal of his left side assailant to swing his left leg back over the seat and, his feet now planted firmly on the ground, he smashed his right elbow backwards into Vinny's throat leaving him choking desperately as his bruised larynx closed down. The entire encounter took less than a minute and the three victors stood like heavy weight boxers in the ring after successful knockouts with their would be assailants laying on the ground; one out cold, the second crawling on hands and knees with blood pouring from his wrecked face and the third turning blue as he attempted to force enough air through his vocal cords to sustain life.

They spent an anxious few minutes but they, apparently, had not killed any of their three attackers although it would be a long time before they would again be threatening the citizenry. The Cavelli who Frank had clubbed with the Salami was beginning to stir and although Vinny was still bleeding profusely, his life was obviously not in danger while the frantic attempts to breathe of the elder Capello were apparently becoming more effective.

"Shouldn't we call the police? I'm surprised that they haven't shown up yet," said Frank. "The precinct house is just a hundred yards down the street."

"That's not the way things are done around here. The cops are all Irish. They like to keep disagreements within the family down here. Who are these bozos anyway?" Marco asked of the small crowd who were gradually emerging from the surrounding tenements to see what the row was all about.

"They're the Capello brothers. They're hangers on with the Sicilians. If they pulled this caper off with Buacola's blessing things are going to get very nasty round here."

"Somebody get the word to the Don to send some people over to clear up the mess or we'll have a war going," urged Marco. "Signor La Guardia," Jo requested, recognizing her next-door neighbor. "Please hurry round to Harris Street and tell Signor Napolitano what has happened."

Alfredo arrived on the scene within minutes and pushed his way through the crowd that now numbered close to a hundred. They were growing angry as the Neapolitan and Genoese populations circulated ever more inflammatory interpretations of what had transpired. It would only have required a match to set off a riot. Marco stepped into the breech. He hauled the three stunned Sicilians over to the wall and propped them so that they were sitting with their backs to it and their feet straight out in front of them. He then took the salami that Frank was still holding in his hand and bound it into Vinny's hands with twine taken from the shop. He then stuck the short end into the front of his assailant's trousers. He stood on the step of the shop and waved the crowd to silence. He was a dominating physical presence.

"Calm down everybody. There's no reason to be upset. Young Vinny here was out for a stroll and needed to pee. He tripped over his own dick and knocked his *paesanos* into my bike. Don Buacola is sending a cart over to haul them off to hospital."

This unexpected and ribald explanation for the mayhem changed the mood of the crowd and they filed past the thoroughly subdued thugs with derisive but mainly good-humored comments. In a surprisingly short time, Nicolo Calabrese, one of Buacola's lieutenants arrived with a truck and four hefty minions. The truck normally was used for the transport of contraband liquor. The three bodies were dumped unceremoniously into the back. The capo sought out the owner of the deli.

"Signor Napolitano," he said quietly but in a voice loud enough to be heard by most of the crowd, "Don Buacola sends his regrets and apologies for the behaviour of these three vermin. Rest assured that their actions were taken without the knowledge or the blessing of the Don. The Sicilian people wish only to live in peace and harmony with their Neapolitan and Genoese neighbors."

He the tipped his hat with elaborate courtesy and prepared to get into his car that had accompanied the truck.

"One moment, Signor," the voice of Jo Lucca piped up. "You have forgotten to pay."

He looked back blankly, one foot on the running board.

"The salami, signor. Five dollars and thirty-five cents, please!"

He peeled off a ten-dollar bill and handed it to her.

"Keep the change and I'll be sure to tell the Don how well the Napolitanos handled this matter."

"Remind him that I'm Jo Lucca, Gaetano's daughter from Brockton. He danced with me at my wedding."

"I will certainly pass that onto the Don and Signora, allow me to apologize for the behavior of these 'Salami brothers.' It will be a long time before they live this evening down."

Chapter Twenty-Seven

Boston, March, 1929

"How did your visit to the doctor go today?" asked Frank when his wife came home on a rainy evening late in March.

"Any day now. My due date is the eighth of next month but you know that that could mean any day from now till mid-April. He says that everything is fine. I haven't gained too much weight and my blood pressure is okay. The only thing that is a little out of line is that the baby's head is not engaged."

"What does that mean? I didn't even know that it was going steady."

"Okay, Smarty," his wife smiled tolerantly at his mild quip. "It just means that the baby's head has not got itself settled into the pelvis. With first babies that normally happens towards the end of pregnancy but its not unusual for it not to happen and there's nothing to worry about."

"How are we going to get you to the hospital when you go into labor?" Frank worried.

"Don't worry about that. The problem with first babies is that they take too long not that they come too quickly. We can take the overhead and we'll still be there with hours to spare. It's the women having number two or three or four who sometimes have to call an ambulance to get there in time. Besides! Boston has one of the best ambulance services in the country and one of the first. If we did need it, the local police station is just a block away."

Three days later the drama commenced; on the first of April as it happened. The opening scene was innocuous but dramatic enough to send Frank into a frenzy of preparation.

"I think that my water has just broken," said Jo. "It looks like we're going to have an April Fool's baby."

"Just as long as she's as beautiful as her mother. Come on sweetheart. Get your coat on," he said and went into the bedroom to start gathering up her nightclothes. When he emerged a few minutes later Jo was sitting on a kitchen chair looking frightened and holding a bloodstained towel.

"It's not my waters Frank. I'm bleeding."

"How serious is that, Jo? Come into the bedroom and lie down. I'll see if I can reach your OB doctor. Do you have his number handy?"

"Get the ambulance, Frank. I remember from nurses training that if you start to bleed towards the end of pregnancy, you need to get to the hospital as soon as possible."

She was starting to look pale and her breathing was becoming shallow and rapid. It was early evening and the Napolitanos had closed up and left for home. Frank was terrified. Jo, to this point in her pregnancy, had taken everything in her stride and had minimized its dangers and discomforts. He had no experience with delivering babies and very little knowledge of medicine. He had always looked to Jo as the oracle; the last word in the arcane world of medical knowledge. If Jo was saying that there was a desperate emergency he accepted it totally and he was terrified. He tore out of the shop and sprinted the two blocks to Harris Street.

"Get over to the house quick, Tess. Jo is bleeding. I'm off to the police station to call an ambulance."

By the time he returned, Tessa had arrived at Salutation Street and was getting her sister ready for transportation. The bleeding was now very obvious; there was a bloodstained towel on the floor as well as her soaked underwear. Jo was conscious but pale and clammy. The ambulance with its Emergency attendants arrived in the remarkable time of ten minutes from the time of dispatch and the medics loaded her into the ambulance on a stretcher. Frank was permitted to ride in the back of the ambulance and Theresa promised to tidy up the mess and follow on to the hospital as soon as possible. The ambulance made its way with flashing lights and blaring sirens but there was still a lot of evening traffic on the roads and it was a full fifteen minutes before it made its screeching halt at the Emergency Room.

The Emergency Room staff at Boston General was well trained and vastly experienced. Every day brought dozens of patients through their doors with a full array of life threatening conditions as well as hundreds of others who had no other access to medical care but the arrival of one of their own--a popular nurse of some stature--brought on an intensity of reaction and a heightened awareness even beyond the normal. The intern who was serving as the triage officer--sorting the sheep from the goats; the critical cases from the walking wounded--was pre-empted. The Head Nurse of the Emergency Department, immediately recognizing who Jo was and that she was seriously ill, wheeled her into a critical care bay and bypassed the normal hierarchical structure. She summoned directly the Chief Obstetrical Resident, Bob Dwyer, as well as his junior, Dr. Castellano. Castellano was Jo's one time suitor, and now a third year resident.

He arrived first, ahead of his seniors and asked her the critical question: "Did you have any pain with the bleeding, Jo?"

He had been horrified to see the ashen appearance of the girl he had once been crazy about but he kept a grip on his emotions and allowed his training to take over. Jo was bleeding heavily and was obviously in shock. Regardless of the underlying cause of her hemorrhage, she obviously desperately needed blood transfusion. He promptly drew a sample of Jo's blood for typing and cross matching and established an intravenous lifeline. Jo's whispered response that she was in no pain made the next decision unavoidable. Before any further step was to be taken to make a diagnosis, she had to be prepared for immediate Caesarian Section; the overwhelming probability in a pregnant patient with profuse painless bleeding in the last weeks of pregnancy is a condition known as Placenta Previa. In this condition the placenta, the organ that develops as the interface between the mother's and the baby's circulation, is attached to the lower segment of the uterine wall. It is about the size of a bread plate and is about one and a half inches thick and is connected to the baby by the umbilical cord. Normally it is attached to the inside of the upper end of the womb--the Fundus--and thusly doesn't interfere with the progress of the baby out of the pelvis. When, however, it is attached to the lower segment it prevents the descent of the baby's head and its passage through the birth canal becomes an impossibility. The diagnosis is made by the obstetrician feeling for the placenta with his finger inserted through the cervical opening. The examination runs the risk of producing calamitous hemorrhage and when this occurs, immediate Caesarian Section is the only option.

Dwyer and Castellano were caught on the horns of a dilemma. Should they wait upon the availability and the transfusion of cross-matched blood or go ahead with the procedure with the patient already in shock. Their hands were forced. Jo was bleeding so profusely that, with any further delay, she would exsanguinate.

"We have to operate, Mr. Kelly. She's bleeding to death and the only way we can stop it is to do a Caesarian Section, deliver the baby and get the afterbirth out. That's where the bleeding is coming from," Dwyer told the distraught husband.

"Do what you must do," he replied.

"We'll do our best. We'll be taking her in right away. Every minute delay is critical."

The Napolitanos arrived thirty minutes later. Theresa had cleaned up the apartment and she and Alfredo had called a taxicab for the trip from the North End. They found Frank sitting on a bench in the waiting room, his head resting on his clenched fists and supported by his knees. He was praying; his rosary beads between his fingers. He told them that Jo was in the operating room and that the lives of Jo and the baby were in peril. In a surprisingly short time, little more than half an hour after his disappearance, Dr. Dwyer returned with a grim look on his face. So much of obstetrical practice is joyful; healthy babies and delighted parents. The occasions like the present one are the downside of the obstetrician's lot.

"Your wife has come through the operation, Mr. Kelly," he said, sitting next to Frank and putting his hand on his shoulder. "She's alive still but barely. She's still unconscious and not out of the woods. The anesthetist wasn't able to get any blood pressure for most of the operation. The baby appears to be all right, thank God. You have a daughter, Mr. Kelly. We must just pray that her momma makes it through. We've taken her to Recovery and we're still getting blood into her as fast as it is available."

"Thank you Doctor. I know you've done your best. I'll always be grateful to you and your staff," he stammered.

"Can we see the little girl, Doctor?" Theresa asked.

"She's had a pretty rough go of it too. Why don't you go home and come back first thing in the morning. I'm sure that she'll be in better shape to meet the family and maybe we'll have a better idea of your wife's condition, Mr. Kelly."

"I can't go home with my wife's life hanging in the balance. I'll just stay in the Waiting Room if the hospital doesn't mind."

"I'll stay with Frank," Theresa told her husband. "You go home and take care of the shop and the kids. Close up and come back in the morning and we'll decide what needs to be done then. You'll need to let Mama and Papa know what's happening with Jo and stop in at St. Agrippina's and get Father Anselmo to have prayers said."

Even when under severe emotional distress, and she was devastated at her baby sister's plight, Tessa was a tower of strength and practicality. In the Recovery Room, the battle for Jo's life continued. The uterus, despite the removal of the Placenta remained flaccid and continued to bleed. At 2:00 a.m. the infant's condition was sufficiently stable to be able to be brought to Jo's bed. Jo was not fully conscious but when the baby was placed in her arms she reacted, perhaps reflexively, and brought the child to her breast. This was the best and last hope of stopping the blood loss. Suckling produces a powerful reflex that helps the uterus to contract.

Sadly, the prolonged shock had done too much damage and even that last resort was taken in vain. Shortly after 4:00 a.m., Josefina Kelly died and Frank Kelly's world fell apart.

Fredo returned the next morning, having completed his various missions, to learn of Jo's death. He found his wife red eyed from tears and lack of sleep but she was alert, and her mind was wrestling with all that needed doing and all the questions that needed answering: who needed to be told, how long would Frank's employers allow him to be off work and give him time to re-organize his life. How could Frank look after the baby when he returned to work? Frank had fallen into an almost trance-like state of total passivity. His face showed no emotion even when he and Theresa were admitted into the Newborn Nursery and he had his first look at the little human for whom Jo had given up her life to bring into the world.

"What will you name your little girl, Frank?" Tessa asked.

"Jo wanted her named Julia. I suppose that's what it will be," he monotone; his face an expressionless mask. The bassinet in which the baby was swaddled in pink blankets had a card in a holder that read 'Baby Kelly--born 1 April

1929--birth weight 6lbs 12oz.' She had the helpless vulnerability of the newborn and Tess felt a surge of maternal affection for her little niece and a desperate sadness that she would never get to know her mother. Frank would have to be both father and mother to the little tyke but, at least for the moment, he appeared to be in shock. They were directed to the Registrar's office, the baby's name was duly recorded as Julia Marie Kelly and they were assured that they could take the babe home on the 4th barring complications.

"Let's go Frank. We're both dog-tired. We need sleep. I'll have Fredo contact the Danieli Brothers Funeral Home in Brockton if that's all right with you. I think that that's the best idea, don't you? I know that Mama and Papa would like that and Father Baldini married you. We also have to arrange to have Julia baptized. I don't think you'll want to make that into a big affair with Jo's death on everyone's mind."

"Whatever you think best, Tess and thank you for helping me to hold together last night."

"Once we've caught up on our sleep there'll be so much to do. You need to let your family in England know and also the people at work. I expect they'll give you some time off to see to the funeral and get your life organized."

"Oh Tess! I'll never get over this. How can I go on without Jo? We were so happy," and he burst into tears. Tess held him as they sat in the empty waiting room and he sobbed brokenheartedly. After about three minutes she pulled away and braced him by the shoulders.

"Let's go Frank. You've got a little girl whose counting on you. Right now you need about twelve hours sleep."

****

In due course, life returned into a semblance of normality. Frank returned to work after a week during which his wife had been returned to her hometown and buried by Fr. Baldini out of St. Anthony's. He managed to get through his work and his social obligations but the *joie de vivre* that had so characterized his affect was completely extinguished. The Napolitanos had undertaken to look after the baby during the day while Frank was at work. Tessa simply brought the bassinet into the shop and parked it on the counter where the baby was cooed over by the housewives who comprised the bulk of their regular customers. Julia was a good baby and Tess was required to make only infrequent stops for feeding and the changing of diapers.

Fortunately, the availability of baby formula was by now an established fact. Henri Nestlé, a Swiss chemist had, in 1869 introduced a highly popular product marketed, rather grandly, as *'Farine Lactée. Henri Nestlé,'* while 'Mellin's Food for Infants' manufactured in Boston according to the precepts of the German, Baron von Lustig was widely accepted. Gerber's Baby food, released only the previous year had also its passionate adherents among the ladies of the area and Tessa, whose store sold all three products, declined to offend by naming a preference while surreptitiously feeding the baby Horlick's; a concoction which featured malted milk and which baby Julia consumed with apparent gusto.

Frank took over the responsibility for his daughter's care once he got home. The profound depression that had overtaken him on Jo's death had reduced him to an almost zombie-like state but when Julia was placed in his arms at the time of her discharge and he was brought to face with reality. This beautiful and innocent creature was his responsibility and his alone. He examined his daughter's hands and she caught his index finger in her tiny grip and he felt an overwhelming wave of tenderness sweep over him. He consciously pulled himself together and resolved to devote his life to her wellbeing. Apathy and inertia were simply self-indulgence. He simply had to buck up. He now realized how fortunate he was to have such a supportive family as Theresa and Alfredo but, even as he thanked God for them, he realized that he could not expect them to look after Julia indefinitely. They had a large and boisterous family of their own to look after but he was deeply grateful that, for the short term, Theresa had undertaken to take on the daytime responsibility for Julia's care. He wrote to Kate and to his mother and received their condolences, which were heartfelt, particularly those of his sister who had taken a great liking to the feisty American girl at the time of the wedding. She had offered to move up the date of her arrival in Boston for her wedding, now only three months distant, and undertook to pitch in with the looking after of the baby but Frank, worried about the effects on their mother of their joint relocation, thanked her for her offer but turned it down.

"We still have to figure what to do about Mam but we can put that off until we get together for your wedding." He added the postscript that, although Julia's hair represented only a faint dusting on her head, he thought that she might have inherited her (Kate's) and Da's red hair.

As April ended, another troubling rumor started circulating through the Boston offices of the Cunard Shipping Company. Regular transatlantic service between Liverpool and Boston had already been discontinued and for several months only cruise stopovers had occurred. The *Carmania* was scheduled for the scrapyards in 1931 after a distinguished career and it appeared very probable that the shore based Cunard staff would be drastically cut back if not eliminated completely. This possibility raised a lot of conflicting questions in Frank's mind. If the Boston office and bonded warehouse were to be relocated, would he be offered employment elsewhere. If so, would it be in the USA or back in Britain? If in Britain would it be in the corporate headquarters in Liverpool.

Jo's death had precipitated a complete re-thinking of his situation. With his marriage to Jo he had undertaken to sever his formal ties with Britain if the only alternative was to leave the United States. On the strength of that commitment, he had initiated the process of applying for US citizenship. He would be eligible for that step in 1934 after five years of residency. Now, Jo's ties with home and family were no longer germane and other factors had come into play. He had ten years of service invested in the Cunard Company and he felt pride in and a degree of loyalty to the Company not to mention financial considerations such as potential pension benefits. Then there was the situation of his mother and brothers and sisters to be considered. With Kate's impending wedding and her plans to settle in Boston with her husband-to-be, he, Frank, would undoubtedly enjoy her proximity but Mam might be faced with financial difficulties if he, too, were to remain in the United States. If his position in Boston were to be closed out he could, at least, hope for a job with the company in England.

CHAPTER TWENTY-EIGHT
Liverpool, April, 1929

The news of the death of Frank's wife produced a curious mix of reactions in Isabel when it reached Britain. She had long since put aside brooding over her lost love and had set about getting on with her life. Her affair with Jacques Martin had demonstrated to her own satisfaction that she was capable of falling in love and that she was a desirable young woman. Jacques had turned out to be a louse but there was no doubt that he had wanted her. It was therefore an unpleasant shock to her to observe that her first reaction to the tragic news was that now Frank was unattached and therefore, presumably, available. That this thought had crossed her mind not only shocked her but infuriated her too. *How dare that Frank Kelly come back into my life?* she fumed. *The gall of that arrogant blighter thinking that he can jilt me, marry some American floozy and then expect me to come running after him when he has disposed of her. Who does he think he is?*

The extreme unlikeliness of these sentiments passing through Frank's mind finally dawned on her for she was, at heart, a rational creature and not normally given to paranoid imaginings. She had months ago accepted the fact that Frank had met a beautiful girl when he was in a vulnerable state from illness and had fallen head over heels in love with her. Isabel had forgiven him and moved on. She had simply been taken by surprise by the news and her initial reaction had been an antic thought that in no way reflected her true feelings. On a more practical note, she wondered, should she or should she not continue with her plans to go to Boston to take part in Kate's wedding. How would this appear to her friends and family? She was well aware that she had made her plans and agreed to Kate's invitation at a time when Frank and Jo were a happily married couple with a baby on the way but would people think that she was pursuing her lost love in the ghoulish hope of regaining his favour? *Would Frank have the nerve to think that I'd come chasing him with his wife still fresh in the grave, the conceited rat?* She noticed that she was getting herself worked up into a frenzy with no rational basis and she cooled herself down with the wry recollection that, of the two of them, Frank had been the more committed to their relationship and that, if he had a fault, (*He does,* her brain chipped in), it was an excess, rather than a lack of humility.

Despite these valid arguments in favour of going ahead with her plans to attend the wedding, she was still a little uncomfortable with the possibility that her motives in making the trip might be considered suspect. The following Sunday she made her weekly pilgrimage back to St. John's from the wilds of rural West Derby and waylaid Kate after the eleven o'clock mass.

"Come home with me. We can have lunch with my folks. There are some things that I want to discuss with you all."

"This is the first time we've seen you, Kate, since the awful news from America. Please tell your mother how sad we are to hear it," said Adlai.

"What a tragedy. I believe that there is a little girl."

"Yes. Julia Marie is her name and thank you for your prayers."

"I asked you for lunch particularly because I wanted to see whether you are still happy to have me in your wedding and to give you a chance to change your mind if you think that I might be an embarrassment," Isabel said anxious to get to the matter that had been bothering her.

"Well of course, I still want you, Izzy. Why ever not?" Kate replied taken completely by surprise.

"I'm afraid that people might think I'm chasing Frank now that he's single again," Isabel admitted.

"Izzy! No one who knows you would ever think that. We've had our plans for months. Frank knew you were coming. Jo knew you were coming. They were both as pleased as punch that you were coming. I think that Frank took it as a sign that you had forgiven him."

Isabel digested this reassurance and then Kate was struck by another thought.

"I've just had a fantastic idea which might make the idea of the trip more acceptable. Why don't you bring your mum and dad too? I would be honoured to have you at my wedding. How about it Captain Iskandar? And how about you Mrs. Iskandar; coming to America to see me launched. Wouldn't you like to see the United States?"

"I'll say this for you Kate. You're full of surprises. Thank you for your invitation," Adlai said. "I know that I'll not be able to take you up on it, much as I would like to. I have two potential business opportunities coming up at just about the exact time that your wedding is due to take place. It's a pity. I would love to come and see you launched. However, there is no reason why Marie couldn't go and keep Isabel company. What do you think, Marie? Are you ready to brave the North Atlantic and see what's on the other side? You haven't had a really good holiday in ages."

"Adlai, you really wouldn't mind me going without you?" Marie replied.

"You know, Kate, I would love to be at your wedding and while I'm there I can see what's new. America always seems to be about ten years ahead of us in all sorts of ways. If we're going to go into the grocery business perhaps I can catch up with any new ideas that they may have dreamed up in America. Maybe I can even write off my trip as a business expense," she added with a conspiratorial grin.

"One thing I can tell you right off," Kate interjected, "America is miles ahead of us in keeping food from spoiling.

Of course its much more critical over there where the summers are so hot but even in the poorest homes, they keep an ice box in the kitchen and the food shops are beginning to have electrically powered refrigerators; even some private homes have them. There's a popular model that I saw in Frank's father-in-law's tavern. It's called a 'Frigidaire.' Just think what a difference it would make if you could do your food shopping a week at a time without worrying about everything spoiling," said Kate.

"That would probably be the end of the local shops. I don't think we need to worry about that though. Our customers over here are set in their ways. The daily shopping trip is part of their social life. Besides, how are they going to carry a week's worth of groceries home at one time. Now, if every household came with a car. Well! Maybe in another hundred years," Adlai pontificated.

"But you do see don't you Adlai," his wife argued, "how important it can be to be out in front of new ideas? Here, I haven't even arrived in America and Kate has got me planning to revolutionize the grocery business. Oh, I'm really going to love my visit to America."

"You're right as always, *ma chérie*," said Adlai indulgently. "But don't spend so much time researching the grocery business that you forget to have a good time at Kate's wedding."

"You can count on that Papa. Mama and I are going to find ourselves a couple of oil millionaires while we are over there."

Adlai did not appear too alarmed at this dire threat.

"Don't worry, Captain Iskandar," Kate reassured him anyway. "I promise to keep a close eye on them."

****

Mrs. Iskandar and the two girls made the voyage to America on board the *Mauretania* that, at the time, was considered to be finest liner in the world, and certainly was the flagship of the Cunard Line. They sailed into New York Harbor and passed Ellis Island on which emigrants had first set foot on the 'promised land' in their tens of thousands. The deserted buildings had been abandoned decades before but the passengers as they sailed by could not but reflect on the fact that they were part of an episode in human affairs of historic importance.

The ladies traveled together in First Class; a consequence of the Iskandars undertaking the cost of Kate's trip as their wedding present to her; a truly princely gift considering that the first class fare would have paid a laboring man's annual wage several times over. Kate's earlier experience as a passenger in Third Class on the *Carmania* had been, to her, the epitome of elegance but traveling First Class on the *Mauretania* was an experience beyond her imagination. She made her majestic way past the Battery at the tip of Manhattan and was shepherded by the accompanying tugs up the Hudson into her berth at the West Side Passenger Terminal where she took her place between the French *Ile de France* and the Hamburg Amerika line's *SS Bremen*, which had just that very day completed its maiden voyage in the new transatlantic record time of four days sixteen hours.

Kate readily picked out her fiancé from the throng waiting to greet the passengers when they emerged from customs. He stood head and shoulders above the rest of the crowd. They were meeting after an interval of nine months following a courtship of barely two weeks and so Kate had anticipated their reunion with a slight trepidation; had she allowed the romantic circumstances of their first acquaintance to see Marco in an unrealistic light? Would the reality of his physical presence live up to her idealized expectations? Would Marco still find her as desirable as he had done last September in Cape Cod? Marco extinguished her apprehensions in about ten seconds when he kissed her enthusiastically and folded her into an embrace that threatened to squeeze the air from her lungs. Then recovering his equilibrium and his sense of decorum he broke off the embrace and bowed ceremoniously to the Iskandars who were observing the spectacle with amused indulgence and not a little awe.

"You must be the Signora and the Signorina Iskandar," he said with a dazzling smile. "Welcome to the United States. I am so delighted to meet you. I know how much it must delight Kate to have you to be a part of our wedding. Kate has told me in her letters so much about you that I feel I know you." After his speech of welcome he appeared eager to go on but not sure whether he should. After a few more seconds he could restrain himself no longer.

"You must excuse my excitement but I am bursting to tell Kate. Yesterday I received the results from the Bar exam. Ladies! You are looking at the newest member of he Bar of the Commonwealth of Massachusetts."

"Oh Darling! What wonderful news," screamed Kate who, by virtue of Marco's letters, was aware of the importance of the announcement. "I'm so proud of you," and rewarded him with another ecstatic kiss.

"Congratulations, Marco," Mrs. Iskandar chimed in. "Obviously, that's good news but what exactly does it mean?"

"It means that he's doesn't now just have a law degree but that he's now an honest to God lawyer, qualified and authorized to practice in Massachusetts. He can now get a job and support his new English wife. I've got to warn you, darling. After five days on the *Mauretania* I've developed some really expensive tastes," Kate said with a grin. "How do you go about getting a job? How difficult is it to break in?"

"Well, I don't expect to be hearing from J.P. Morgan or any of those big Wall Street firms; they tend to focus on Harvard grads but don't worry, we'll get by. Right now, let's see about collecting your luggage and getting it to Grand

Central. That'll give us just about enough time for lunch before the 2:15 to Boston."

"I'm glad to see your appetite hasn't dwindled away since I last saw you, sweetheart," his fiancée teased.

"I understand that you and Isabel will be staying at the Parker House, Mrs. Iskandar. It's, arguably, the finest hotel in the city and the oldest in the country. You'll be following in the footsteps of your Charles Dickens. He stayed there during his second visit to America," Marco said politely including them into the conversation.

"Well, I can't really claim Dickens as a countryman although I have lived in England for thirteen years. I was born in Lebanon but I read in the literature that the hotel sent me that Khalil Gibran, who is also Lebanese, used to hold court there while he was writing *The Prophet*. He was born in Lebanon but came to America as a youngster."

"He was all the rage when I was studying Arabic at the University. He actually went back to Beirut as a young man to re-learn the language," Isabel added.

They took the short cab ride to Grand Central and deposited their bags in the Left Luggage lockers before having lunch at the surprisingly elegant restaurant on the Grand Concourse. The meal was noteworthy for the excellence and abundance of the ham in the sandwiches and for the appalling tea.

"I should have warned you to stick to coffee in American restaurants," Marco observed. "Kate used to tell me that American tea is as bad as English coffee."

"Restaurants think that you make tea by pouring water from the hot tap over a tea bag," Kate added.

"Mon Dieu!" responded Marie who still tended to relapse into French in moments of intense emotion.

They reclaimed their bags and were comfortably on time for the 2:15 train. The journey was pleasant in the late summer afternoon sunshine. It made only two stops; in New Haven and Providence and afforded tantalizing glimpses of

Long Island Sound as it chugged through Connecticut and Rhode Island before pulling into South Station in the early evening. They made the short journey to their hotel by cab and Marco proudly pointed out his legal 'Alma Mater', the Suffolk Law School, which was located on Tremont Street within a stones throw of the Palmer House which was just around the corner in School Street. The Palmer House proved to be as elegant as advertised and Marie conceded that the furnishings compared favorably with any of the hotels that she and Adlai had stayed in in London or Paris.

"To be honest, Mrs. Iskandar, I passed by the building every evening for four years but I've never been inside before; too rich for my blood but I'm glad to have the opportunity to look around. Did you know that John Wilkes Booth stayed here the week before he assassinated President Lincoln? The hotel doesn't emphasize that too much. Well, I'll leave you to settle in. I'll take Kate to my cousin's house in the North End. She's staying with them till the wedding. They're old friends. Kate got to know them when she was here for Frank's wedding. They're the Napolitanos and they own the deli where Frank lives with his daughter. They have invited us all for dinner tomorrow evening. I'll be back to pick you up tomorrow at 6:30. Do you think that you can amuse yourselves till then?"

"With the whole of Boston to explore I don't think that we'll have any trouble amusing ourselves," Marie responded, "and thank you for meeting us and making us feel so welcome."

"If you're having dessert with your dinner, don't forget the Boston Cream Pie. They invented it at the Palmer House," he added as they set out for the North End.

"Do you think we could stop in at your apartment for a little while before we head on up there?" Kate said innocently as they descended in the elevator. "Once we get to the North End we wont have a minute to ourselves. We've got so much to talk about and you still haven't told me now much you've missed me."

It had been a long time since their first and only love making on the beach at Cape Cod. On arriving at Marco's apartment, their future home, they expended the nine months of pent up passion in a joyful and exuberant coming together which left them exhausted and delighted with each other.

"I adore you, *ma bella Katerina*," he murmured as they lay amid the wreckage of the bedclothes.

"Oh Marco! I know that we should have waited until the wedding was over but ever since we made love on the beach I have dreamed of giving myself to you. I just didn't want to wait any longer. Just think, in three days this will be our first home."

Only with the eyes of the star struck could Marco's bachelor apartment be considered an ideal 'love nest' and Marco hastened to reassure her that their tenure there would be brief.

"We'll only be living here for a short while: until I'm sure of a job. Then we can look for our first real home together."

"Where do you think we should be looking? I don't suppose that you'll be making too much money at first and how do you go about getting a job as a lawyer anyway?"

"You know, I first thought of becoming a lawyer to help give my people, my *paesanos*, a fair shake; not just to practice law but to make sure that every body has equal access to it. For centuries, the WASPS ruled New England; you know, the White Anglo Saxon Protestants. They were here first, if you discount the natives and, by and large, they did a pretty good job but they claimed all the land and built all the factories. When the immigrants started to pour in they were left with pretty slim pickings and were used as cheap labor, even if they could get work at all. The Irish were the first to arrive in large numbers and the Brahmins--the Boston establishment--treated them as if they were sub-human. I've heard that there were signs posted at job sites saying 'No Irish Need Apply.' Sometimes it just read 'NINA.' Well then the Irish caught on to the fact that they were here in sufficient numbers to have political power. James Michael Curley became Mayor of Boston and then Governor of Massachusetts. With power comes patronage. The public sector jobs have been owned by the Irish for twenty years: the police force, the fire brigades and even the legal profession. This could affect me. All the Public Defenders and the County Attorney's office people are Irish…Irish Americans I mean."

"Is that what you'd like to do, Marco; go into politics? Maybe you'd better change your name to Kelly."

"I'm not sure that I'm quite ready to do that but if I do run for office in this town it won't hurt for me to have a wife whose a gorgeous red-haired colleen and my having played football at Boston College will help. The Italians are just beginning to realize that they have political muscle if we choose to use it. There are thirty thousand of us in the North End alone. Those Irish 'pols' aren't stupid. They are realizing that we cannot be ignored and they'd be better off including us rather than fighting us. I'm planning to apply for a place in the Suffolk County Attorney's office. It would be a great place to learn my trade. As soon as you start out, you are thrown into the deep end. You get worked to death but, if you survive, you become a pretty darn good lawyer with a lot of experience. It's also the recognized way to get your foot into the door politically."

"I never realized that getting a job as a lawyer was such a political matter," said Kate. "I thought that you just put up your sign and waited till the customers came pouring in for you to make out their wills."

"My sweet Kate. In Boston every thing is political."

"What do you think our chances are that you'll be taken on by the County Attorney?" she asked.

"I think that I've got a fair chance. My best friend is one of Curley's men. His name is Paddy Donovan. You'll meet him soon. He's going to be my Best Man. He was our quarterback in my last year at BC. I think you'll like him. Maybe he'll fall for Izzy like I did for you. He's a handsome dog."

As they were talking, they had been lazing under the top sheet propped up against the pillows with Marco's long right arm draped around her shoulder and his hand absent-mindedly caressing her breast. He suddenly noticed that Kate was beginning to breathe more deeply and that her nipple was hardening beneath his fingers. He squeezed gently and she made a soft moan deep in her throat and reached towards his groin to see what was going on down there. She felt him becoming erect and she threw her right leg over his thigh and straddled him and gazed admiringly at what she had wrought.

"Oh no you don't, my little tigress," he murmured, then reversed their positions and entered her. He was a very big man and hugely muscled. He would have flattened a smaller girl but Kate was almost six feet tall and had unusually long legs. She wrapped them around him and as he climaxed she dug her heels into his back and rose to meet his final thrusts. At this point the bed, completely overmatched, collapsed and they were pitched unceremoniously on the floor.

"We needed a bigger bed anyway," Marco grinned when they had regained their composure.

"Perhaps it's just as well. The bed's had it. We'll have to make do with our memories of tonight for the next few nights once we've cleared our souls with Father Baldini. Come on Marco, you better get me to Theresa's or she'll be wondering what we've been up to."

"If you don't straighten your hair up, she'll have a pretty good idea."

"Oh, but you're a wicked lad," Kate cried --"but you're *my* wicked lad," and she rewarded him with a kiss and went off in search of a comb.

They deposited most of Kate's luggage in Marco's apartment and thus were able to able to make the trip to the North End on his motorbike. Kate recalled that, though she had been very welcome at the Napolitano's, storage space had been at a premium with a lively growing family crammed into three bedrooms. Much of what she had brought with her from England was destined for life in her new married home and could therefore be left where it would be needed after the honeymoon. Arriving at Harris Street, they were made welcome and Kate was re-acquainted with her future nieces-in-law and was appropriately amazed at how much they had grown in the past nine months. In the occasional gaps in the general frenzy of their arrival Kate reflected on what a huge change there was going to be in her life. This vibrant Italian speaking community was to be her new home and the complex ethnic jungle of Boston politics the world in which her husband wanted to make their living.

Still, it's not that different, she thought. *The tenements lining the narrow streets, the screech of the passing streetcars and the teeming vitality of the area were not too different from the working class neighborhoods in Liverpool. There was even a Catholic church every quarter mile; just like on Scotland Road.*

"Where's Frank? I'm dying to see my new niece," she asked once the clamor had died down.

"He'll be here any minute. He's been coming across every thirty minutes for the last two hours to see whether you've arrived," Tessa assured her.

Sure enough, Frank arrived ten minutes later carrying the baby. Theresa's preferred infant formula had obviously been doing the trick and Julia appeared to be thriving. Kate felt her heart melt at the sight of her young niece who had apparently inherited the Kelly red hair; it having skipped Frank. It was still scant, at three months age, but promised to be the same dark red that was her crowning glory. In addition, young Julia had dark brown eyes and long black lashes that would provide a dramatic contrast in another twenty years. Frank was very happy to see his sister and greeted her warmly but Kate sensed that he had lost some of the zest for life that had been so much of his charm. He had obviously not got over the loss of Jo and was also finding the uncertainties of his current life weighing heavily on his shoulders. They enjoyed a pleasant hour and even Frank seemed to shed some of his worries in the playful give and take that the uncles indulged in with their three Napolitano nieces. Kate noticed, with considerable amazement, the confident and, to her ears, perfect Italian with which her brother dealt with his American family. Shortly after nine o'clock, the young Napolitanos were bundled off to bed and Kate took the opportunity to have a few private moments with Frank.

"Marco, I'm just going back to Salutation Street to tuck the baby into bed and to have a few minutes with Frank. Would you call for me in about half an hour?"

"I'll send him over, Kate," said Theresa, "but you don't need to worry. None of the neighborhood 'hard cases' would dare to mess with the fiancée of Marco Tessla or the sister of Francesco Kelly. Your brother and future husband are living legends in this part of town."

"There's got be a story there that I've just got to hear but right now I want to see Frank's home and bring him up to date on the family doings back in Liverpool."

She took his free arm as they strolled the short distance between the two homes.

"She's a lovely baby, Frank. I know you've had a heartbreaking loss but you'll always have Julia to remind you of Jo. Part of her will be there forever in her."

"Every time I look at her eyes I see Jo and it breaks my heart."

"Well, just concentrate on her hair and you'll be reminded of me and have a good laugh," she said and nudged him in the ribs. He smiled. Kate could always cheer him up. They unlocked the front door and entered the shop. Frank pointed out the space allotted to the three tables that stood, crowned by their accompanying chairs, for their patrons who chose to eat their sandwiches in the shop.

"You know Frank, the Iskandars are planning to invest some of their money in neighborhood grocery stores and Mrs. Iskandar is eager to see whether there are any American innovations that they could incorporate into their new businesses. Not only that but she has approached Mam to see whether she might be interested in running the old 'Whitely Grocery.' You remember. It's the one just down from the baths on Westminster Road. Adlai was putting in a bid to buy it just about the time we set sail. By now, he's probably the owner and Mam's interested. With us both over here, she doesn't see how she can afford the rent on Garnet Avenue and if she takes Adlai up on his offer the shop comes with quite nice living quarters; certainly big enough for her and Brendan. You know that she's always enjoyed dealing with people down at the Market. With a grocers in her home neighbourhood she'll be seeing her old friends every day."

"That's amazingly good news, Kate. I've been worrying about Mam for months; in fact, ever since I learned of your engagement. I've had news about my situation too. I have a big decision to make and your news will have a definite impact on it. The Cunard Company is really cutting back on its Boston operation and if I want to keep my job I have to relocate back to Liverpool or Southampton. If I were to come back home there wouldn't be enough room for me and the baby in Garnet Avenue what with Mam, Brendan and the two girls. But if Mam moves out with Brendan, we could just about afford to stay in the old home and keep it in the family and Brendan could still walk to school. I never would have considered leaving America if Jo were still alive. Julia is American and the Lucca family is very much a part of our lives. I'd already resigned myself to staying here forever and then she died and everything has changed."

"When do you have to make your decision and when do they want you to move back?" asked Kate.

"I have to let them know by next Wednesday and I'd be due to leave at the beginning of September," he replied.

"What do you think you'll decide Frank? I'd certainly love to have my favorite little brother living nearby but you must do what you think best."

"I think I must go, Kate. I won't even have a job over here after September and I've got a baby to bring up. I suppose that I'm the head of the family now."

"Oh, Great White Father," she said with an exaggerated bow. "You know best," but then she relented as she realized from his expression that he was making a decision that was not just difficult but painful. He truly loved this Italian-American family that had so warmly embraced him. Frank would always do what his conscience told him was the right thing.

"I know that you'll make the right choice and I'll support you no matter what it is." She realized that Marco would be arriving at any minute and that her opportunities for a heart-to-heart talk with her brother would be very limited but she had to know how he felt about Isabel and her presence in Boston.

"You'll certainly be running into Isabel over the next few days. How do you feel about her? I was responsible for your meeting her in the first place and I hope that her being here won't be painful for either of you."

"I don't think so. I'm sure that it will be a little tense for a few moments when we first meet but I imagine we've both got over it. I was in love with Isabel and I think that we could have been happily married to each other but then I met Jo and for a year I was the happiest man on the planet. Now she's dead and I simply feel numb. Izzy is a beautiful woman and I was crazy about her. I think that I loved her more than she loved me. I know that I never felt that I was good enough for her. After letting her down so badly, I know that she deserves better than me now."

"Don't be too hard on yourself, Frank or on her. We're all only human. Izzy's had some pretty rough times since you left. Be nice to her."

"I've left it a little late for that. You don't get that many chances in life and I've already had two."

"Well, third time's a charm," she said as Marco knocked on the door and brought their *tête-à-tête* to a close.

Frank did not fall asleep readily that night. His mind had too much to easily digest. He tossed and turned and Julia, possibly disturbed by his restlessness, awoke and voiced her displeasure. After three months of fatherhood he had pretty much mastered the routine and, indeed, Julia had shown recent promise of 'sleeping through' but tonight she needed a clean diaper--(He would have to re-learn to call it a nappy if he went home)--and a bottle of Horlick's Patent formula. When she finally finished the bottle, he performed the mandatory 'burping' ritual and gazed adoringly on the innocent face of his daughter. At that moment the decision was made. He would hold onto his job and return to England. Having made his decision he considered some of its implications. Julia was an American citizen. She would always be able to make that claim but she would be growing up in Britain. He was still British but he was uncertain what would be his daughter's status. He had a full day's work ahead of him but he knew he could get to the British Consulate during his lunch hour. Next day he discovered that it was situated at No. One Broadway in Cambridge and he barely made it in time but he was told that, to guarantee his daughter's claim on British citizenship, he should register Julia's birth with the Consulate. He resolved to take care of that before his departure.

While Frank was taking care of his family's temporal needs, Marco and Kate were attending to the spiritual. They took the thirty-mile motorbike trip to Brockton where they had an appointment with Fr. Baldini. Kate loved riding pillion with Marco. She loved wrapping her arms around him and snuggling against his back, trying, unsuccessfully, to prevent her hair from blowing all over the place. She had remembered to bring her baptismal certificate with her and the formalities were rapidly completed. Like Frank and Jo before them, they were afforded an opportunity to confess their sins. They were not totally sure that they were truly sorry for their most recent ones but they gave it their best shot and received absolution. They recited their ten 'Hail Marys' and ten 'Our Fathers' and promised God never to 'do it' again. In actuality, they planned to 'do it' again and frequently but not until Saturday night when 'it' would have not only the blessing but also the encouragement of Holy Mother Church.

Kate then had a re-union with the Lucca family who had made her so welcome during Jo's wedding. They were offered a delightful lunch and received heartfelt good wishes but Kate was saddened to observe that Jo's death seemed to have aged them ten years. One more call had to be made before their return to Boston. Kate was re-introduced to the senior Tesslas, Marco's parents, and, as before, she won them over effortlessly; the male Tessla making no bones about his approval of his statuesque daughter in law; his wife withholding judgment but willing to wait and see. *I must remember to ask Mother Tessla how to 'cook Italian,'* Kate thought to herself.

The Tesslas would be hosting a family gathering on the eve of the wedding and Kate suspected that the repast would out do the Lucullan feast that her sister had provided before Jo's wedding or Mrs. Tessla would die in the attempt. She made a mental note to pace herself tomorrow evening.

That evening Isabel and Marie Iskandar had their first introduction into Kate's future family and to the pervasive Italian-ness of the North End. They had had a pleasant day; their Mediterranean skin reveling in the scorching July sun. They had taken a city tour on an open roofed motor coach and had indeed passed briefly through the Italian district for the required viewing of the Old North Church and Paul Revere's home but that had been just two of the stops on a three-hour trip which took in the *USS Constitution, the famous*

Old Ironsides, Bunker Hill, Boston Common, the site of the 'Boston Massacre,' Chinatown and the Harvard Yard. Now, with Marco picking them up at their hotel in a cab, they were able to drive more slowly through the town with Marco pointing out the salient features as they drove.

"This is where I think that Kate and I will look for our first home," he told them as they passed through the Fort Hill section. "You'll note that there's no hill. The area is as flat as a fluke. They carted the hill away to use for fill dirt when they were filling up Back Bay. Boston's area is more than twice what it was in 1800 and the North End was the original downtown of Boston."

The North End was teeming with activity but the ambience was a far cry from the restrained elegance of Beacon Hill with its Georgian houses and London-like squares that they had admired earlier in the day. The streets were narrow, the tenements too close together and the general impression was depressing. It reminded Marie very forcibly of the stretch that filled the north side of Liverpool between Scotland Road and the docks with its squalid slums.

There was nothing depressing about the welcome they received. The Napolitano's home on Harris Street was, indeed, a couple of steps up from the worst of the decrepit wooden dwellings. As the owners of a popular local business they were considered among the more prosperous members of the community and they occupied the entire bottom two floors of a brick three-decker apartment building. In addition to Isabel and Marie, the party consisted of the entire Napolitano family, Kate, Marco, Frank and the baby. Everybody went out of his way to make the Iskandars feel welcome. The food was abundant and delicious and the wine, prohibition not withstanding, flowed plentifully. The children could hardly believe their good fortune. They had their two uncles to tease for two nights in a row and they were allowed to stay up till nine o'clock.

Isabel--no mean linguist herself--was as amazed as Kate had been the previous evening at the fluency with which Frank conversed with the girls in Italian. She had always liked Frank but she had to admit, she had always thought that she was significantly smarter. Maybe she had mistaken lack of opportunity for lack of intelligence. The party got quite festive and the normally reticent Alfredo broke out his mandolin and regaled the party with a ballad currently popular in the country:

Italiano! Italiano!
Women and wine. Oh they're divine.
New York's dry. The girls are shy.
So back to Napoli, I'll go happily, by and by.
Americano is good but ah! No. Give me the lights of old Milano.
Under the moon so bright, Drinking the wine so light,
Making da love and da fight Italiano.

This offering was greeted with wild applause and Marie, to her daughter's astonishment was prevailed upon to sing *Come Back to Sorrento*, which she did--in French. The party was a huge success.

"Signor Napolitano," Marie said as they were leaving. I understand that you own and operate a grocery shop nearby."

""Indeed, Frank and the baby live there. It's just a couple of blocks away from here," he replied.

"My husband and I have just purchased a grocery business at home. I would deem it a great favor if you would permit Frank to show me around and perhaps to give me some insight into the business," she said.

"I would be honored, *bella Signora*, and let me tell you that your fellow countryman is the biggest asset that my business has ever had. All the old ladies want to mother him and the young ones want to marry him," he said with a chuckle. "Frank doesn't get home from work till 5:30 but I would be delighted to give you the grand tour at any time during the day."

"Thank you, Alfredo, and thank you for such a wonderful evening. I will certainly take you up on your kind offer."

Marie arranged to visit Alfredo's store the following day. Frank offered to meet her after lunch as he had managed to get the afternoon off; the workload at the warehouse had already dwindled down to a trickle and consisted mainly in arranging the transfer of the inventory from Boston to the New York premises of the company.

Having the wedding and accompanying festivities in Brockton did pose some complex logistical problems. There would be large family gatherings on both Friday and Saturday evenings and the major players would have to stay in Brockton. The Lucca and Tessla families were both large in number and interrelated so accommodations were tight. Gaetano and Carmela Lucca had offered their home to Kate and her bridesmaid while Marco and Paddy Donovan, his best man, would be overnighting at the Tessla home. Theresa and Alfredo were to split the parties between them with Fredo attending the dinner at the Tessla's while Theresa would represent the family at the wedding itself.

They had generously undertaken to not only free Frank up to attend both events but to keep the deli open for business. Tessa would look after the baby on Friday evening until his return and it was agreed that Julia could be brought to the wedding on Saturday when there would be plenty of doting females who would attend to her needs. The three Napolitano girls were all destined to be bridesmaids and were eagerly looking forward to sleepovers on two consecutive nights and sharing the room with their cousin Cecilia (Cissy), Marco's younger sister.

Marco had prevailed on his father's generosity and had been given access to the family Chevy for the weekend. He delivered Isabel and her mother shortly after 11:00 a.m. The two girls had spent the morning inspecting their wedding clothes for damage brought about by the Atlantic crossing and had been relieved to find that only a brief session with the iron was required to put them into the required condition of pristine perfection. Now Marco was charged to take them, along with Alfredo and the three youngsters, to Brockton leaving Marie to follow on by train with Frank after her visit to the deli. The Brockton-bound group crammed themselves into the Chevy with great hilarity. Marco, fortunately, given his size, had the driver's seat all to himself. Fredo sat in relative comfort next to him with only his youngest daughter on his lap while Isabel and Kate had to cope with the remaining two Napolitanos--both of them substantial teenagers bouncing with energy and excitement.

"If only we had Frank along, it would be like coming home from *Aladdin*," Isabel reminded Kate and smiled sadly. "Will we ever be as happy and carefree again?"

"Of course you will, Iz. We're both only twenty-four. Our lives are just getting started."

"Wait till Paddy Donovan and my other BC pals get a good look at you, Isabel. You won't get a moment to yourself," Marco chipped in from the front seat. His groomsmen, who would be functioning as ushers, had all been football players and were enthusiastic partygoers and ladies' men.

Kate introduced Isabel to their hosts who made a great fuss over them and Isabel was again struck by the warm-heartedness of the Italian-Americans whom she had met. Here were the Luccas who were opening their homes and their hearts to a couple of girls with whom they had had only a very brief acquaintance and whose presence could only stir up memories of the tragic end of their daughter's life. Gaetano did note that Kate had chosen for her bridesmaid a girl who made a dramatic contrast to herself.

"Why! Signorina Isabella could easily pass for an Italian girl and a *bellissima* one at that."

Carmela Tessla welcomed her nieces and parceled them off to their cousins' bedroom leaving her to continue her preparations for the stupendous meal that she confidently expected would go down in the annals of family history and remove from the collective memory the feed that her sister had presented on the eve of her daughter's wedding.

Meanwhile, Marie Iskandar was making her scheduled visit to the Napolitano's delicatessen and grocery. The tour only took ten minutes--the shop's frontage was only twenty feet and the depth thirty--but the cheeses, freshly baked bread and sliced meats filled the air with enticing aromas. There were three elderly ladies finishing their lunch and a couple having a *gelato*. Batons of salami, salsiccia Bolognese and mortadella were suspended with twine from a metal bar that ran the length of the counter along with smoked hams. An array of pasta was displayed in open bins and open-cabinet lined walls behind the counter were filled with dry goods, sugar, flour and rice. On display were items that would never be seen in a British grocer's--they being within the province of the 'greengrocer'; an entirely different personage--onions, fruits and vegetables, tomatoes, mushrooms and even such exotic fare as aubergines. With the exception of fresh meat and fish, the Napolitano's deli appeared to sell every foodstuff known to man. Even milk and butter were available; these being kept in Alfredo's 'pride and joy:' the GE Monitor fridge. Notably absent were potatoes and cabbage. For these staples of Liverpudlian cuisine, Marie mused, you would probably have to find yourself a grocer in Charlestown where, she had been informed, the ethnicity was markedly more Hibernian.

"What do you think, Frank?" Marie asked as they sat at a table, savoring a gelato while Theresa attended to a customer who was buying a quarter pound of prosciutto, a pound of butter and half a dozen eggs. "You know Liverpool and you've worked here for almost a year. Your mother has agreed to manage a grocery store for us and it's our plan--Adlai's and mine--to buy other similar places around town; rather like we did with our little chain of tobacconists. Do you think that there is anything that you do here that we could incorporate into our businesses?"

"I've given that some thought, as a matter of fact, Mrs. Iskandar, because in so many ways this place is so unlike shops back home. I think British housewives are very set in their ways. As you know, within a couple of hundred yards of most Liverpudlians there is a little row of the same kinds of shops, individually owned and operated by some local resident who is part of the neighborhood. There'll be a grocer, a green grocer, a tobacco shop, a sweet shop, a chemist and a butcher; maybe even a chandler. Except for fish and chip shops there's hardly any place to eat out unless you go downtown and you know how often working class people do that; about every Preston Guild. (A Preston Guild is a fair held every thirty years.) Working class folks eat all their meals at home; it's cheaper. I don't think that a typical Liverpool grocery like Whitely's, for example, would be big enough to put in an eating area and I don't think it would attract any customers. I think that, if you want to try something as new as what you are talking about, you and the Captain should consider building from scratch. Liverpool's growing outwards and the new areas that are opening up are better off. The middle classes will be settling in places that, right now, are farms. They'll be teachers and bank managers, doctors and lawyers. They'll have more money and they'll tend to be a bit more adventurous."

"You really have given this a lot of thought, Frank. You know, I think this stay in America has brought out qualities that you never knew you had. Look at the way you picked up Italian."

"Having a wife and a child on the way was a greater motivator, Mrs. Iskandar. You know, if I were going to open a retail business, I'd try to find a spot where there are a lot of people concentrated in one area who want what you are selling and can afford to buy it. Look at my sister, Bridget. She opened a hairdressers shop outside the main gate of

Walton Hospital; hundreds of nurses who want their 'shampoos and sets.' She's doing really well. She's thinking of opening a second shop outside Alder Hey Hospital. She just wrote to me. It's the biggest Children's Hospital in Europe and yet there's nothing outside the main gate except farmland. Think of the number of nurses who work there taking care of fifteen hundred beds; at a shilling per shampoo and set and ten bob for a perm she'll be coining it. You can bet those fields are going to be filled with nice semi-detacheds in the next few years. That's where you should build your deli. I'll bet those doctors get fed up with eating hospital food at lunchtime. They're also the sort of people who are more likely to try something new. Those suburbs are the first place you'll see private cars too; even refrigerators in their own homes.

"Frank, you're a real visionary. You're wasted at Cunard."

"Right now, I'm just happy to have a steady paycheck and, by the way, thank you for offering my mam the chance at your new grocery. It will really make a difference in her life--mine too if I decide to go home."

"Are you thinking seriously about that?" Marie enquired. This question loomed large in her mind. She still hadn't quite given up the idea that Frank and Isabel would make a good match.

"Well Cunard wants me to go and I've got a baby to support. I need the job."

"I'm sure that Izzy would be happy if you came home."

"I doubt that Mrs. Iskandar. I let her down. I had my chance with Izzy and I threw it away. I don't think she'll ever give me a second chance. She deserves a better bloke than me anyway. Maybe she'll meet one of those pals of Marco. They're all college men; more her style."

Don't sell yourself short, Frank. Marie thought to herself.

Between them they changed Julia's nappy and prepared a bottle before their departure for Brockton. Frank, by this time, had a fairly comprehensive knowledge of the railway connections in Greater Boston and had been appointed Marie's designated escort to the evening's festivities.

"Let me feed her, Frank. I haven't fed an infant since Izzy was a baby. Its high time she gave me a granddaughter. You go up and change and I'll talk with Theresa while I'm giving Julia her bottle."

The two matrons chatted amicably between the occasional demands of the customers and, once again, Marie was struck by the degree to which Frank had endeared himself to his extended family. In her turn, Theresa shrewdly concluded that Marie Iskandar had not yet given up hope that her daughter and Frank might, one day, reconcile. For her own part she knew that Frank had adored her sister and had been a devoted husband. He was still feeling devastated by her death but she had always been the realist in the family and knew that time would heal the wounds of Frank's loss and that he would eventually want another wife and a new mother for his child.

"I see you haven't lost your touch, Mrs. Iskandar," Frank said as he re-entered the room wearing his best suit. "She's sleeping like an angel."

"It's like riding a bicycle, Frank. You never forget how to feed a baby."

"Well we're off, Tess! I'll be back before eleven to take over and thank you again for looking after Julia for me."

The feast presented to the wedding party by Carmela Tessla was as gargantuan and delicious as expected by those who knew her. Comparisons are odious, it is said, and so none of those who had been present at the corresponding event the previous year would have ventured a preference. Suffice it to say that no one left the table hungry and Kate had a fleeting fear that she wouldn't be able to fit into her wedding dress for the ceremony. Paddy Donovan proved to be a strapping and self-confident young man who had the coloring and complexion of the 'black Irish.' He had raven black hair, heavy brows and a pale complexion. He had the 'gift of the gab' and the easy affability of the professional politician and made no bones about staking his claim, as best man, to the attentions of the maid of honour.

Kate was, of course, the girl of the evening and the center of attention. She was the picture of love's young dream. She couldn't help casting frequent covert glances across the table at Marco as if to reassure herself that he was still there but she did notice, incidentally, that as Isabel seemed to blossom with the flirtatious attentions of Paddy Donovan, Frank seemed to retreat further and further into his shell. Isabel had not been the object of such uninhibited admiration since the end of her disastrous affair with Jacques Martin and she was thoroughly enjoying the attentions of the charming Donovan and gave as good as she got in the exchange of lighthearted chaff but she was fully aware that neither she nor Paddy were likely to become seriously enamored. They would enjoy each other's company for the brief hours of the wedding festivities but would then get on with their real lives.

She was twenty-five, still in the prime of young womanhood but seeing Frank's baby had stirred up maternal feelings that she had never previously experienced. She was realizing that she was ready for a man to love, to marry, and with whom to raise a family. The image of little Julia inevitably brought with it thoughts of Julia's father. Could it be that, after all, Frank was destined to become her fate? She had always found him physically attractive although she couldn't have explained why if asked. It would have created the same dilemma that was asked in the song, *Bill*, which had been introduced with enormous success the preceding year in the play *Showboat*.

She found herself humming, "I love him because he's--I don't know--because he's just my Bill."

But was she, in fact, in love with Frank? She had been ready to marry him a year ago and, to her surprise, she felt more attracted to him now than she had been then. He seemed to have grown in maturity and stature. He still wasn't glib or facile. Indeed he was almost the anti-Jacques Martin. *Perhaps that's what I like about him but does he even still like me?* she wondered. He had been no more than cordial to her since they had arrived in America but even in that she could not be too upset. She would have thought the less of him if he had thrown off his grief with a mere shrug as if Jo had meant little to him. Her instincts told her that he still liked her. *I think that he's even a bit jealous that Paddy Donovan is making such a fuss of me. The only person he seems to be talking to is Maman. I wonder what she's up to.* She was unable to interrogate her mother as Marie had to make a relatively early departure along with Alfredo and Frank to catch the last train back to Boston to relieve Theresa of her babysitting chores--Alfredo to escort her home and Marie to make her way back to the Palmer House.

Frank retraced his tracks the next day; this time accompanied by Theresa and carrying the baby who, it had been decided, could make her public debut at the wedding. There were the customary moments of panic before the ceremony; where had the best man put the ring?; a small tear in the bride's train was repaired and, the prenuptial feast notwithstanding, Kate was able to fit comfortably into her dress. In most ways the wedding ceremony and the wedding breakfast were almost a replica of Jo's wedding. The ancient rituals of the Nuptial Mass, do not change much over the centuries and, with the sad exception of the missing Jo, the principal participants were again present. The focus of attention however was, of course, on Marco and Kate and rarely can the Church of St. Anthony of Padua have witnessed the vision of such a strikingly handsome couple. Patrick Donovan and Isabel Iskandar, who followed them down the aisle in the 'Grand Procession,' made a nice picture but, on this day, all eyes were on the towering groom and his statuesque bride; all eyes except one and that one belonged to the bride's brother who was gloomily observing how well suited the best man and the maid if honour seemed to be.

The wedding breakfast was, again, held in the K of C Hall. It was a substantial meal and it was well after 4:00 p.m. when the best man claimed the floor to toast the happy couple. This was not, at that time, a traditional part of Italian wedding celebrations but, in deference to the bride's British heritage, it was included and Mr. Donovan was never one to miss a chance to give a speech. He had been informed that his toast should consist of wittily insulting references to the groom and reminiscences of the most embarrassing moments in his life. His oratory was applauded; mainly in gratitude for its brevity and he was followed by the groom's traditional toast to the bridesmaids that Marco did very gracefully; the bridesmaids blushed winsomely at the enthusiasm with which Marco's footballing pals seconded his remarks.

There then followed a brief hiatus as the hall was cleared and set up for the evening's festivities while the guests retired to their quarters to get their second wind. A band had been hired for the evening and by 7:00 p.m. the party was ready to resume. The alcohol was not quite so abundant as it had been at Jo's wedding celebration and which had been held at the Club Genovese but the Knights of Columbus were not conspicuously vigilant in enforcing Prohibition. The punch was generously spiked and flasks were produced from many a pocket. In short order the party was in high gear. With the exception of Isabel, the bridesmaids were all in their early teens and Marco's ex-footballers had to look elsewhere for suitable targets. One exception was the eldest Napolitano girl, a somewhat precocious fifteen year old, who found herself hotly pursued by an ardent twenty four year old, much to her gratification, until her mother, the ever-vigilant Theresa, put an end to that particular romance with some well chosen words in emphatic Italian. There were plenty of other more suitable unattached females and the floor was soon filled with dancing couples.

Isabel, who was, with the exception of the bride, by far the most striking woman in the hall, was in great demand and was rarely off her feet for most of the evening. She harkened back to those earlier evenings when she would be danced off her feet by the sailors at Atlantic House. There, at least, we had a ladies' lounge where we could rest our weary limbs but this thought only brought Frank to mind. Wasn't he ever going to ask her to dance? Surely those clamoring ex-football players hadn't frightened him off? Kate, too, had noticed that her brother was not joining in the dancing but was sitting, looking rather subdued, talking politely with two elderly ladies. He was still apparently concerned that Isabel would not favor his inclusion in the swirl of her admirers. She decided that he needed a push.

"Marco! I need you," she said drawing her new husband into her arms.

"I'm yours to command, my little chickadee," he replied with a passable impression of W.C. Fields.

"I want you to ask Izzy to dance. I'm going to get Frank to dance with me and then we'll work the old switcheroo."

"What chance does poor Frank have with such a scheming sister?" he grinned. "But I'll be surprised if he can keep Isabel away from my old BC buddies. She's quite a looker."

"Watch it, boyo, you're only getting her on loan for a couple of minutes. You're mine now."

I'm counting on it. Now go and round up Frank and I'll exercise my *'droit de seigneur'* with Izzy"

"I hope that that's not as nasty as it sounds," she ventured.

"It's worse, I believe, but don't worry. I don't speak French."

Frank had indeed been feeling sorry for himself and had resigned to not dancing but he could hardly refuse his sister on her wedding day and he followed her onto the dance floor. After one revolution around the room he suddenly found that he had Isabel in his arms and Marco was whirling away with Kate to the other side of the room. Isabel appeared to be as startled as he and for the moment they were both tongue-tied.

A memory came from his past and he blurted out "You're still gorgeous, I see."

He blushed as though this was their first meeting and he had made an awful *faux pas* but then it felt so right to be holding Isabel in his arms. The memory of their hundreds of hours of dancing together in happier times kicked in and they circled the dance floor with all the polish of Fred and Adele Astaire.

"No one could ever dance like a Liverpool lad," she murmured, and Frank felt his senses come alive for the first time since Jo's death. His heart gave a lurch but, next minute, before he could respond to Isabel's encouragement, he felt a tap on his shoulder and turned to find Paddy Donovan demanding to 'cut in.' His first instinctive reaction was to tell this importunate blighter to get lost but he was unsure of the protocol. Perhaps 'cutting in' was an accepted part of American dancing etiquette. He didn't want to start a brawl at his sister's wedding so he accepted the intrusion with as much grace as he could muster and watched meekly as his old flame was whisked away. He caught a glimpse of her stricken face over her partner's shoulder. She didn't look any happier than he felt at the new pairing and he thought, *could it be that there was still a chance for us?* and he cursed himself for his timorousness. He shouldn't have given up on Isabel quite so readily. He set off to reclaim her but the crowd had started to swirl around the exit from the hall.

The evening was still young but the bride and groom had changed out of the formal clothes and were preparing to depart on their honeymoon. Marco's father was driving them to Boston where they would be taking the night train for Niagara Falls. Kate tossed the ceremonial bouquet to the single bridesmaids and, to nobody's surprise it fell into the unsuspecting hands of her maid of honor who was now destined to become the next bride according to tradition. As the next oldest bridesmaid was ten years her junior this promised Isabel very little consolation but she received the subsequent teasing with good grace. She could no longer see Frank and so she wandered into an anteroom where Tess was preparing to give Julia a bottle.

"Let me look after the little girl, please Tess. My feet are killing me and no one will ask me to dance while I'm feeding a baby."

Theresa smiled to herself and passed the baby over to the pretty English girl. *I think I know what's on her mind but 'good luck to her.' She seems to be a nice girl and Frank needs someone like her to get him out of the doldrums. I'm sure that Jo would approve. She wouldn't want Frank to stay single for the rest of his life and that little girl is going to need a mother.*

Isabel made herself comfortable in an armchair and the baby nuzzled into her chest until she was able to find the bottle. It was the first time that Isabel had ever fed an infant. She had no brothers or sisters. The baby finished the bottle in short order and, after a burp, promptly fell asleep with a look of innocence and serenity on her face. Isabel felt a great peace descend on her. *Somehow,* she thought, *everything is going to turn out all right.* Frank, who had been looking for her for some time, finally found her and, coming to the door of the anteroom was astonished to find her almost asleep and holding his daughter in her embrace with a look of contentment on her face.

He coughed gently and said, "You'd make a fine mother, Izzy."

"I believe I would Frank and, you know, I think I'd make you a fine wife."

Theresa returned to the room a little later to relieve Isabel of the baby to find Frank with his arm around Isabel who was holding the baby against her breast.

She smiled knowingly and said, "I'll look after Julia now. Go back in and enjoy yourselves."

They reentered the hall and were promptly approached by Mr. Donovan again wanting Izzy to dance. *Not this time,* Frank thought to himself.

"Go and find your own girl, Paddy. This one's mine."

Epilogue

In September of 1929, Frank returned to Liverpool with his daughter and took up residence in the family home in Garnet Avenue, which they shared with Bridget and Mary. Isabel became a full time French teacher at Broughton Hall Convent and, shortly thereafter she and Frank announced their engagement and their plans to marry early in 1930. At Christmas time, the Cunard Company announced their decision to move the Corporate Headquarters from Liverpool to Southampton and Frank was offered two options; move to Southampton or lose his job. He opted to stay in Liverpool and set about finding employment.

The Iskandars continued the expansion of their commercial 'empire' by the acquisition of two more established grocery businesses but also, in a more speculative venture, they opened Liverpool's first mini-Supermarket and Delicatessen on Eaton Rd. opposite the main gates of Alder Hey Hospital. They asked Frank to assume the managerial responsibility for the grocer shops and the delicatessen and, on the strength of their new found affluence, the newly married Kellys contracted to buy one of the new houses which were being built on Honeysgreen Lane, exactly halfway between Broughton Hall and Eaton Road and less than half a mile from either.

In July 1929, Bridget met a teacher from the local parochial school while at a dance at Wavertree Town Hall and, while attending Frank and Isabel's wedding, they announced their engagement. With their accumulated savings they undertook to build Bridget's second hairdressing salon just two doors away from the Iskandar Supermarket. In the Summer of 1930, they opened for business and, in the

September of that year, they married and moved into the living quarters behind the shop.

Mary Kelly gave up her dead end job at Hartley's and entered nurses training at the Liverpool Royal Infirmary. This decision drastically curtailed her leisure time but she and her devoted admirer, P.C. Illingworth, continued to see each other regularly and three years later, in 1934, and at the third attempt, he passed the examination for sergeant. That year, Mary also completed her schooling and earned her prized nursing certificate and became eligible to add the letters S.R.N. after her name (State Registered Nurse). They married in the summer of 1935 and set up house near the 'Old Roan' within earshot of the Aintree Race Course.

In 1935, Brendan Kelly passed the Higher School Certificate with Distinction and won a Liverpool Senior City Scholarship to study Medicine at the University.

On the 29th of April 1933, Alexander Francis Kelly was born to Isabel and Frank and, on that same day, Everton won the F.A. Cup beating Manchester City 3-0.

Author's Note

The process of preparing Blue Shirts Red Sox for publication has been, very much, a family affair. My children have given their critical input and my sons have been particularly deeply involved; Joe produced the first version to look like a real book and Dan was a very painstaking editor as well as being responsible for the illustrations on the front cover. My son-in-law, a professor at Austin College in Texas, steered me through the labyrinth of the cyber world. My wife was unfailingly encouraging and her cousin, John Ossolinski, introduced me to Lulu--the company that produced the finished volume.

As the story takes place on both sides of the Atlantic, as did my acquisition of the English language, I have elected to try to write using British English for the English chapters and American English for those taking place on west side of the Atlantic. After fifty years in America I frequently have trouble remembering which is which.

The historical facts in the story are valid to the best of my knowledge with a few minor exceptions: the Apostleship of the Sea did not move to Atlantic House until the late 1930s and my SS Osiris is a figment of my imagination but I have learned since writing that there was a real SS Osiris which, happily, was not sunk in the Atlantic during the First World War.

I wish to thank Ursula Esteves and Ann Gadsby of California--(the Wharton sisters)--for their insights into life at Mount Pleasant Convent and at the Apostleship of the Sea; both of which institutions they are alumnae. Dr. Ben Myatt, my oldest American friend, brought to my attention the tragedy of the Great Molasses Flood and to Stephen Puleo's book, Dark Tide: The Great Boston Molasses Flood, which proved to be an invaluable source of information about the event and about the ethnical and political circumstances of the period.

Finally, I wish to give credit to Joseph Keating, my father, a marvelously talented musician and a man of great wit. While teaching Mathematics at the Cardinal Allen Grammar School in Liverpool, he and the Rev. Fr. John Higham wrote, produced and directed six original musical comedies. The songs in the pantomime chapter of the book first appeared in those productions.